I0810125

POSTCARD HISTORY SERIES

Canton

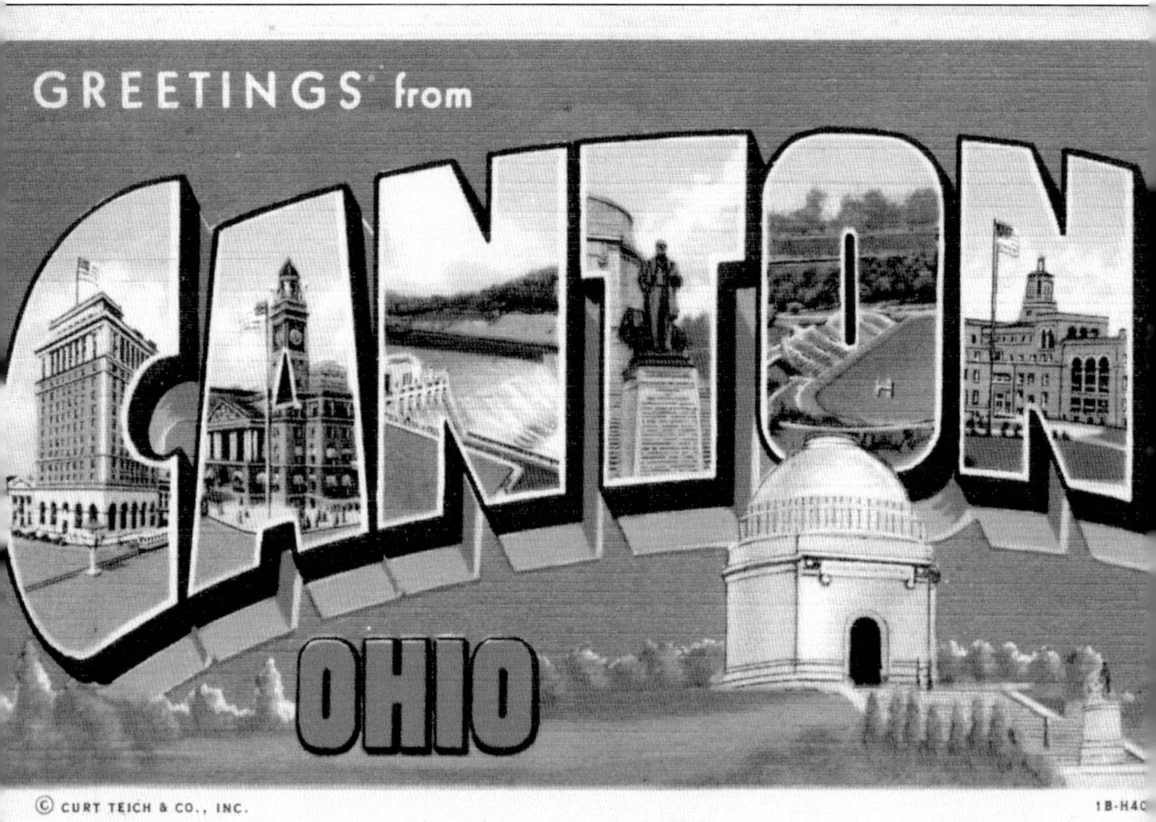

In the 1940s, Canton had a number of outstanding public structures. They include the First National Bank building, the courthouse, Dover Dam, William McKinley's statue in front of his monument, Fawcett Stadium, Molly Stark Sanatorium, and the McKinley Monument. (Author's collection.)

On the front cover: This 1917 view shows the west side of the public square. The electric streetlights, shown here, had been in use in Canton since 1883. Canton was an early adopter of electric street lighting. Thomas Edison's company completed the project in Canton only 15 months after installing the first central light station in New York City. Edison's wife, Mina Miller, was the daughter of Lewis Miller, a partner of Canton industrialist Cornelius Aultman. (Author's collection.)

On the back cover: In 1903, Meyers Lake was described as "a picturesque resort two miles from Canton, conveniently reached by trolley and steam trains. Hotels, private cottages, bowling alleys, tennis grounds, sail boats, fishing, toboggan slides, and pavilions make it a popular place for the people of Canton." This 1909 postcard shows an early bathhouse. There was little beach area, so swimmers jumped into the spring-fed lake directly from the bathhouse. (Author's collection.)

POSTCARD HISTORY SERIES

Canton

Gay Morgan Moore

ARCADIA
PUBLISHING

Copyright © 2009 by Gay Morgan Moore
ISBN 978-0-7385-6029-8

Published by Arcadia Publishing
Charleston, South Carolina

Printed in the United States of America

Library of Congress Control Number: 2008942694

For all general information contact Arcadia Publishing at:
Telephone 843-853-2070
Fax 843-853-0044
E-mail sales@arcadiapublishing.com
For customer service and orders:
Toll-Free 1-888-313-2665

Visit us on the Internet at www.arcadiapublishing.com

To my aunt Mary Esther Myers, who taught me to love reading and gave me an appreciation for preserving history. To my husband, Sandy, whose love and support make good things possible.

CONTENTS

ACKNOWLEDGMENTS

Acknowledgments are rather like Academy Award acceptance speeches; they could go on and on, for the assistance and encouragement of many people are essential to any book. However, there are some special people without whom this book would not have been completed.

First is my aunt Mary Esther Myers, to whom this book is dedicated. A retiree from both the Hoover Company and the Canton Preservation Society, she has shared her love of reading and history with me throughout my life. Canton's biggest booster, the materials she collected over the years made this book much easier to write. I am indebted to her in many ways.

My husband, Sandy, spent many hours leafing through postcards in antique shops and hunting for them on eBay. More importantly, his loving support of my interests and writing is a gift I appreciate more than I can express.

I would also like to thank my sons and daughters-in-law, Bryan, Melanie, Matt, and Carrie, as well as my sister, Linda Cleveland, and mother-in-law, Kathryn Moore, all of whom have supported my efforts throughout the years. In addition, I would like to thank my friends and colleagues, who if they were surprised that I actually had a contract for this book were gracious enough not to mention it.

Thank you also to the fine staff of the reference department of the Stark County District Library for their unfailingly professional and courteous assistance. The citizens of Stark County should be very proud of their excellent library and its staff. Lastly, thank you to all the people, including the staff of the Canton Regional Chamber of Commerce, who returned my telephone calls and patiently answered my many questions.

The *Canton Landmarks Calendar* published by the Canton Preservation Society, 1982–1996 and 2008, was a valuable resource. All the postcards featured in this book come from the personal collection of the author.

INTRODUCTION

In the five decades following the end of the Civil War, Canton grew from a small farming community to a city of international political and economic importance. By the 1920s, Canton had not only produced a president of the United States, but was also shipping manufactured products from its plants around the world.

Founded in 1805 by Bezaleel Wells, Canton was located on what Canton historian Edward Heald states was "perhaps the most inaccessible point of Ohio then open to settlement." A Baltimore surveyor and land developer, Wells apparently chose the site because it was on a plain relatively free of trees and mosquitoes. Wells's plan for the new village he named Canton is essentially the same as the present-day city.

He designated a two-block-long public square on the major north–south street, Market, running on either side of the major east–west street that he named Tuakarrawas. He also gave three lots to the village, one for a school, one for a house of worship, and one for a cemetery. The school lot is now the site of Timken Vocational High School, the second parcel is occupied by the Christ United Presbyterian Church, and the cemetery became McKinley Park in the late 1800s. Having founded Steubenville several years earlier with long blocks and narrow streets, Wells decided to make the streets and even the alleys wider. He made the public square area 160 feet wide and Market Street 100 feet, tapering to 80 feet. Other north–south streets were also 80 feet. The east–west streets were 60 feet. Thus Canton has a large public square mall and wide thoroughfares.

Canton grew slowly at first. Indeed, Massillon had a larger population in 1850 due to its proximity to the Ohio-Erie Canal. Canton, whose primary business was the support of agriculture, did not become a city until 1854 when the population reached the required 3,500. The advent of the railroad construction in the 1850s diminished the importance of the canal but effectively increased Canton's importance as an industrial center.

William McKinley, former Union army major and newly minted lawyer, arrived in town in 1867. By 1871, he had married the most eligible young woman in Canton, Ida Saxton, and launched a successful political career. Losing only one election in his career, by 1876 he had advanced from county prosecutor to the U.S. Congress. After serving 14 years in Congress, he was elected governor of Ohio in 1891 and president of the United States in 1896 and 1900. His assassination in September 1901 marked the end of much of Canton's political influence but did not dampen the city's affection for William and Ida McKinley.

William McKinley's rise paralleled Canton's rise as a major industrial city. Manufacturers of agricultural equipment, like Cornelius Aultman and Joshua Gibbs, saw the center of manufacture of farm equipment move to Chicago in the 1880s, but a number of other manufacturers brought wealth and jobs to the community. From 1888 when the Dueber-Hampden Watch Works was built until the 1930s, nationally and internationally known companies, like Canton Mine Door, Canton Manufacturing, Belden Brick, Canton Stamping and Enameling, Deibold Safe and Lock, and Hoover, built major factories. Timken Roller Bearing and Carnahan Steel earned Canton the designation of "the cradle of alloy steel." Wealthy businessmen built large homes and joined civic organizations. Eighteen banks opened between 1880 and 1920. According to a March 25, 1913, story in the *Canton Repository,* schoolchildren counted 1,043 products made in Canton. The city even had its own car manufacturing company. The Holmes was manufactured from 1919 to 1921.

Industry meant increased numbers of workers. Men came from all over the region to work in Canton factories. In 1910, "W.H.F." wrote from Canton to his friend "Ray" in Carlisle, Pennsylvania, that he "was working in a furniture factory making 25 cents an hour. Wages are much better out here than back there, but boarding is higher. Work is plenty now and anyone who wants to work can get it. There are over 200 shops and many sights to see here." More families meant an increased need for schools, churches, hospitals, and stores. The years between 1902 and 1922 saw the construction of 14 elementary schools, two high schools, two general hospitals, and a tuberculosis sanatorium. Indeed, the population of Stark County grew from 94,747 in 1900 to 177,218 in 1920. Correspondingly, Canton's population grew from 30,667 to 87,091 during the same period. By 1930, Canton had a population of 104,906.

Life in Canton, however, was not all work, study, and worship. The Grand Opera House and later movie theaters brought entertainment to the city. Local bands and singing societies provided musical entertainment. YMCA, high school, and company teams provided amateur sports opportunities. Of course, professional football originated in Canton during this time. Not all of Canton's citizens focused on sports and music. The city had 139 saloons in 1910. Indeed, Evangelist Billy Sunday found fertile ground for his 1912 crusade, claiming to convert 5,654 souls during his six-week stay.

Canton developed an extensive public park system, but the favorite recreation spot for most citizens was Meyers Lake. Meyers Lake provided amusement park rides, water sports, music and dancing, and a cool place to camp and picnic from the late 1890s until the 1970s.

I have had fun learning more about Canton, choosing postcards, and "eavesdropping" on the lives of the people who wrote them. I hope that you enjoy reading this book as much as I have enjoyed creating it. For the sake of consistency, all dates describing the postcards are postmark dates, not the dates they were originally printed.

—Gay Morgan Moore

One

William McKinley

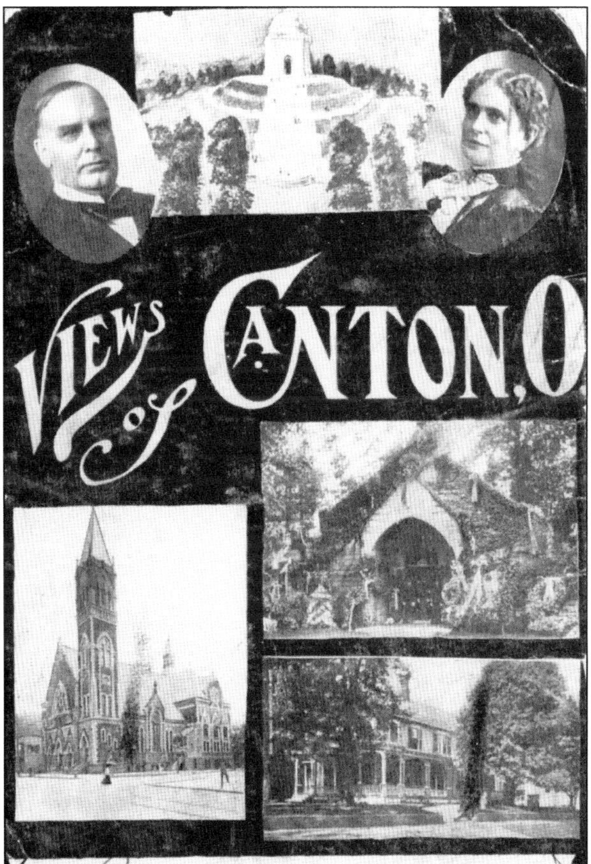

In 1906, Canton was preparing to dedicate the monument to Pres. William McKinley, who was assassinated in 1901. In addition to the president and the first lady, this card shows photographs of the Wertz vault where the president was originally interred, his home, the First Methodist Episcopal Church where he worshipped, and a drawing of the yet-to-be-completed monument.

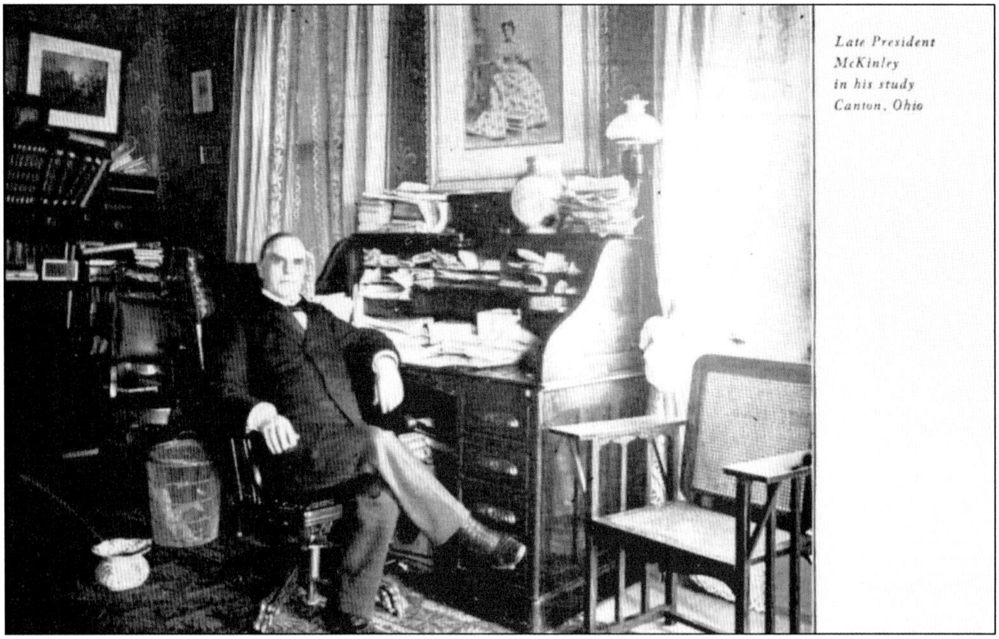

In 1867, following the Civil War during which he rose from private to brevet major, William McKinley arrived in Canton to practice law. By 1897, he had been county prosecutor, a U.S. congressman, governor of Ohio, and elected president of the United States. Along the way, he managed to marry the "belle of Canton," Ida Saxton. Ida's photograph is above his desk.

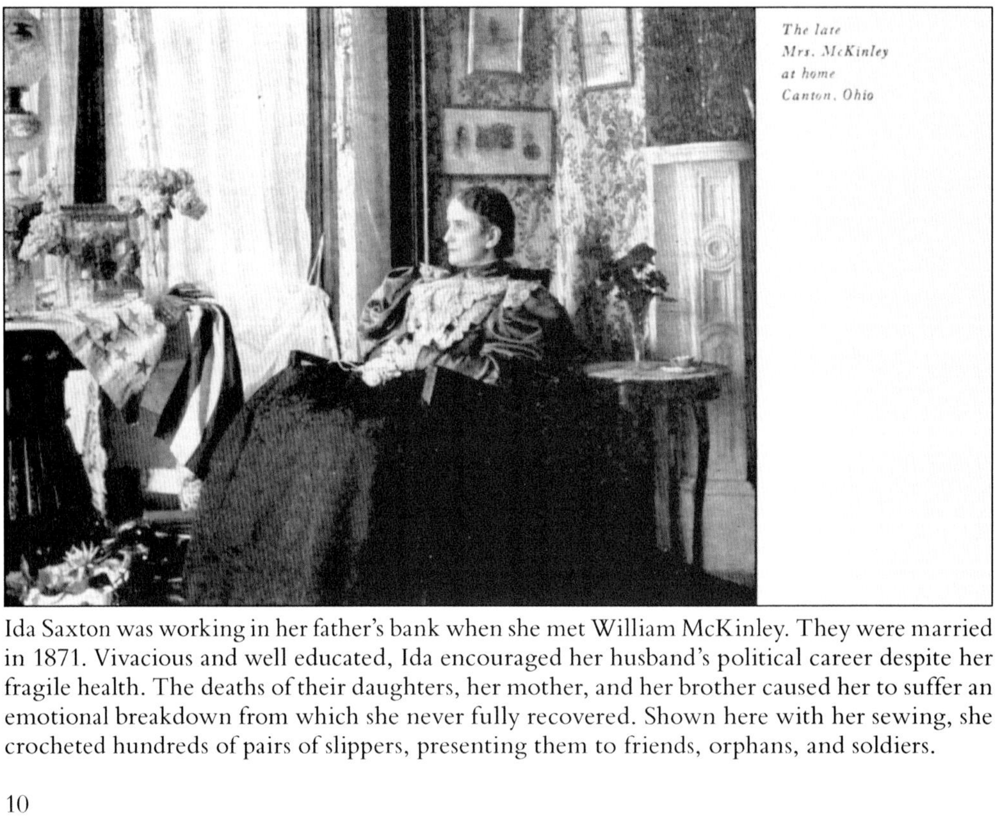

Ida Saxton was working in her father's bank when she met William McKinley. They were married in 1871. Vivacious and well educated, Ida encouraged her husband's political career despite her fragile health. The deaths of their daughters, her mother, and her brother caused her to suffer an emotional breakdown from which she never fully recovered. Shown here with her sewing, she crocheted hundreds of pairs of slippers, presenting them to friends, orphans, and soldiers.

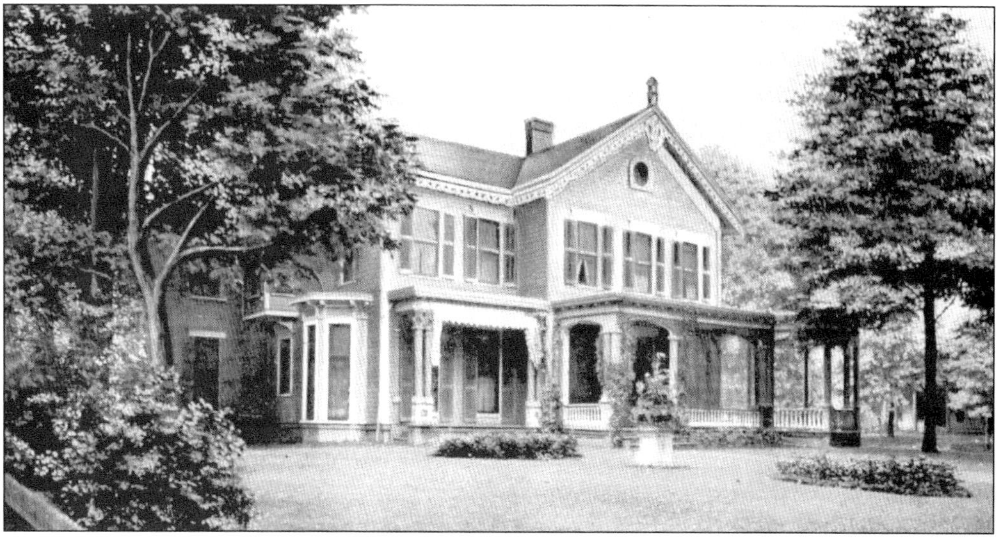

The McKinleys moved into this Victorian home on North Market Avenue shortly after their marriage. Following the deaths of their daughters, they moved to Ida's girlhood home, now the First Ladies Museum. They returned to this house shortly before his presidential campaign in 1896 and continued to return there throughout his presidency. The house was moved to Sixth Street in the 1920s and demolished in 1935 after it fell into disrepair.

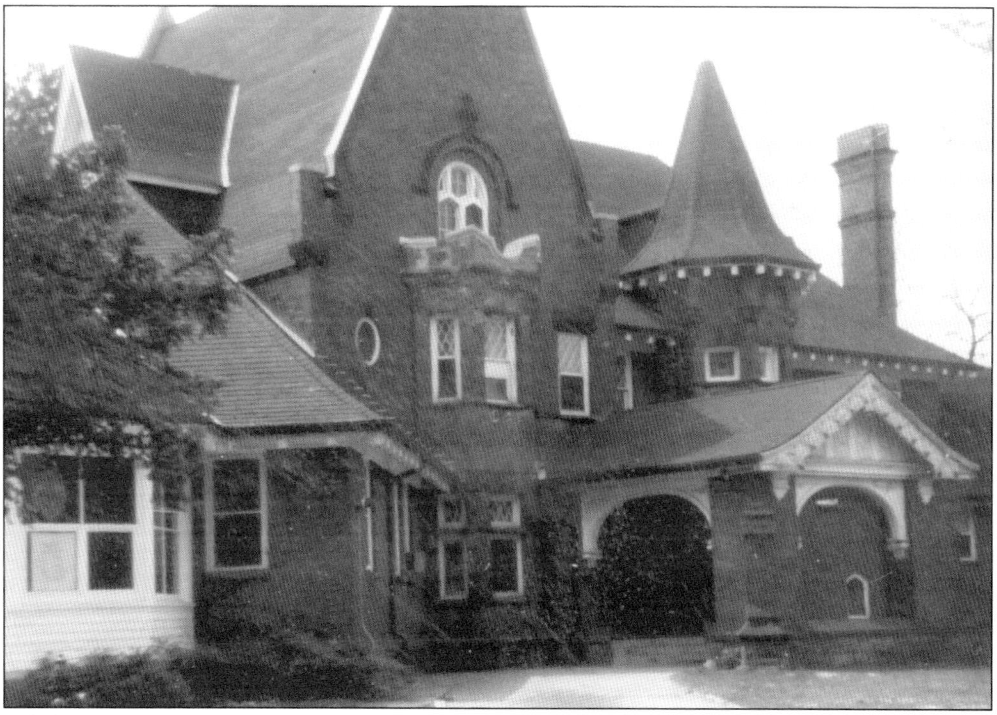

While McKinley was governor of Ohio, he signed legislation in 1897 creating the East Ohio Asylum for the Insane in Massillon. This home was the first building constructed on the site and was used for many years as the superintendent's residence. Called the McKinley Home, it may have also been used as McKinley's summer home after his election to the presidency. The home is still located on the grounds of the Massillon Psychiatric Center.

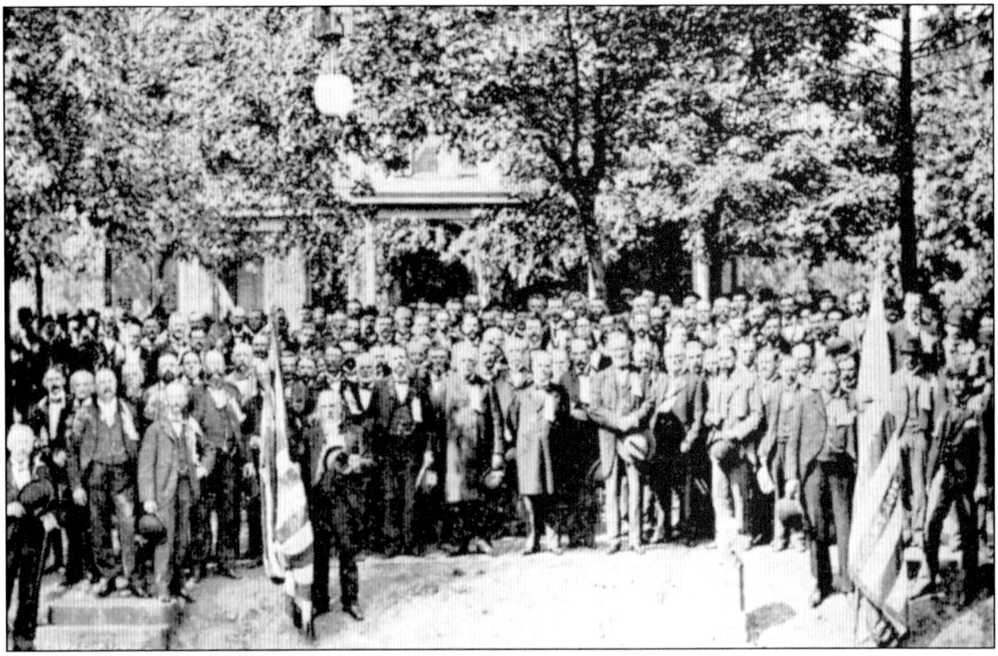

During McKinley's 1896 presidential "Front Porch Campaign," people, like the Vermonters, came from all over the country to hear him speak from the porch of his home. Mark Hanna, who orchestrated the campaign, arranged for special trains to arrive in Canton daily, except Sunday, from June until November. At the railroad station, visitors were met by a horse troop and the Grand Army Band and escorted to the McKinley residence.

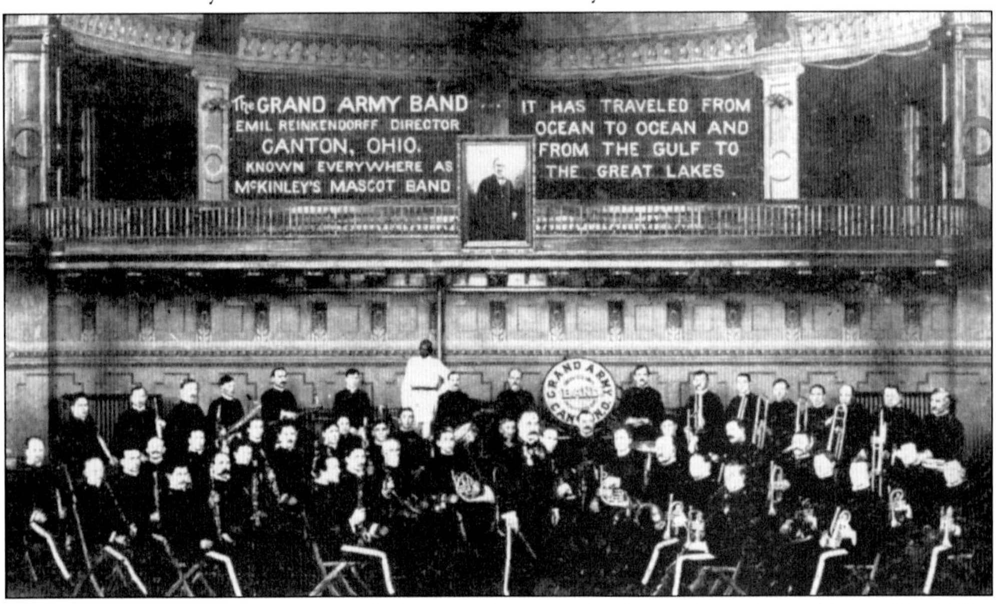

Known as McKinley's Mascot Band, the Grand Army Band was formed in 1866 by Civil War veterans. The band played in every McKinley political campaign, except the one he lost, traveling with him to the White House and "from ocean to ocean and from the Gulf to the Great Lakes." The Grand Army of the Republic (GAR) led McKinley's funeral cortege in 1901 and marched one last time for him at the dedication of the memorial in 1907. It was disbanded in 1927.

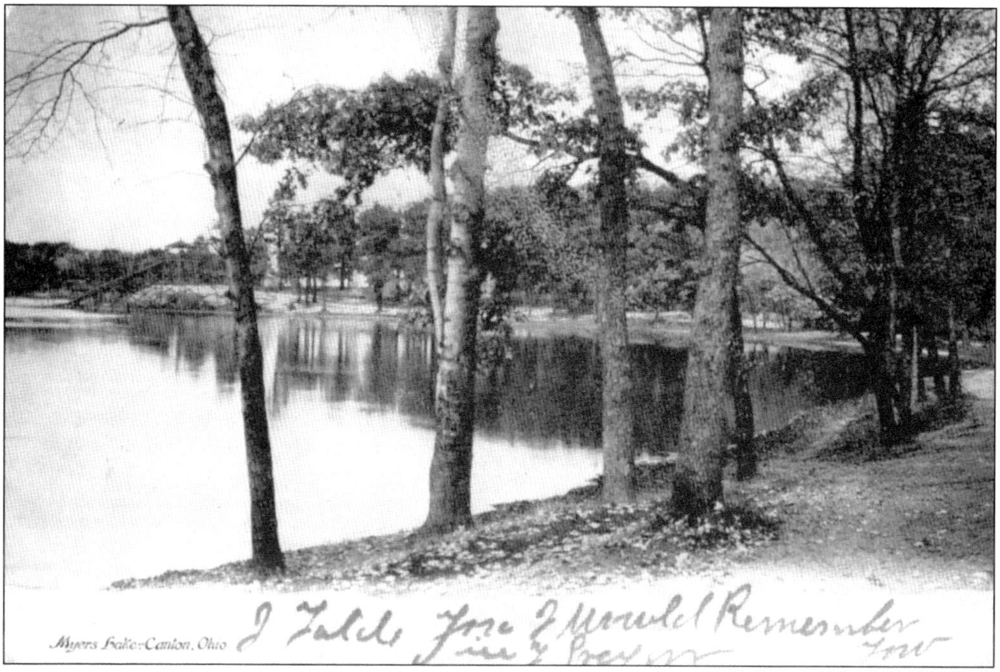

Ida and William McKinley liked to visit Meyers Lake when they were in Canton. In August 1901, they took a surrey ride through the park. Later a security guard reported seeing a man with two guns. When he told him that no firearms were allowed, the man said that he "did not pay attention to things like that." He ran away and police could not locate him. That man was Leon Czolgosz, who shot the president less than two weeks later.

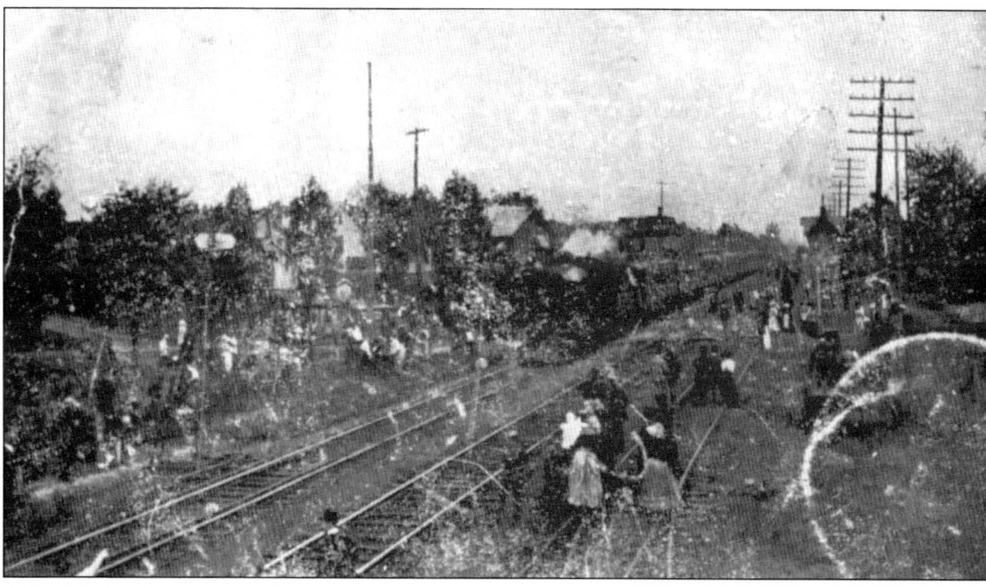

After his death on September 14, 1901, McKinley's body was returned to Canton via train. The Associated Press reported, "The entire population of the little city and thousands from all over Ohio, the full strength of the National Guard . . . 5,000 men in all, the governor, lieutenant governor, and a justice of the supreme court . . . were at the station to receive the remains." This picture was taken as the train crossed East Fourth Street.

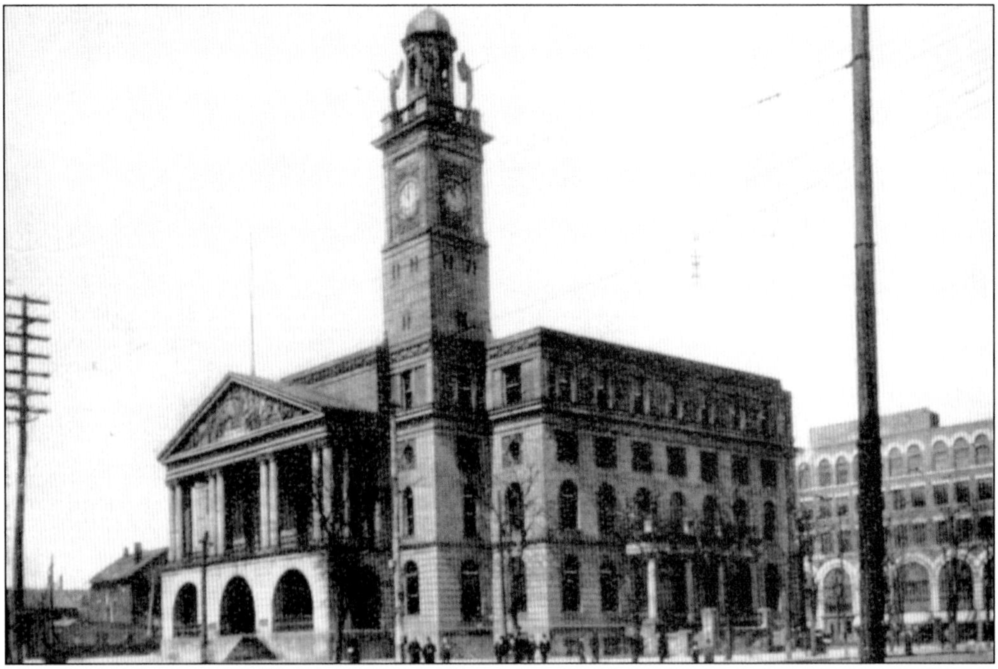

William McKinley lay in state in the Stark County Court House on the evening of September 18 and into the morning of September 19, 1901. Thousands passed by offering their respects. Hundreds were still in line as the doors were shut and the body was moved to the First Methodist Episcopal Church for the funeral. An Associated Press reporter remarked on the darkened and discolored features of the president, who had died of gangrene following a gunshot wound.

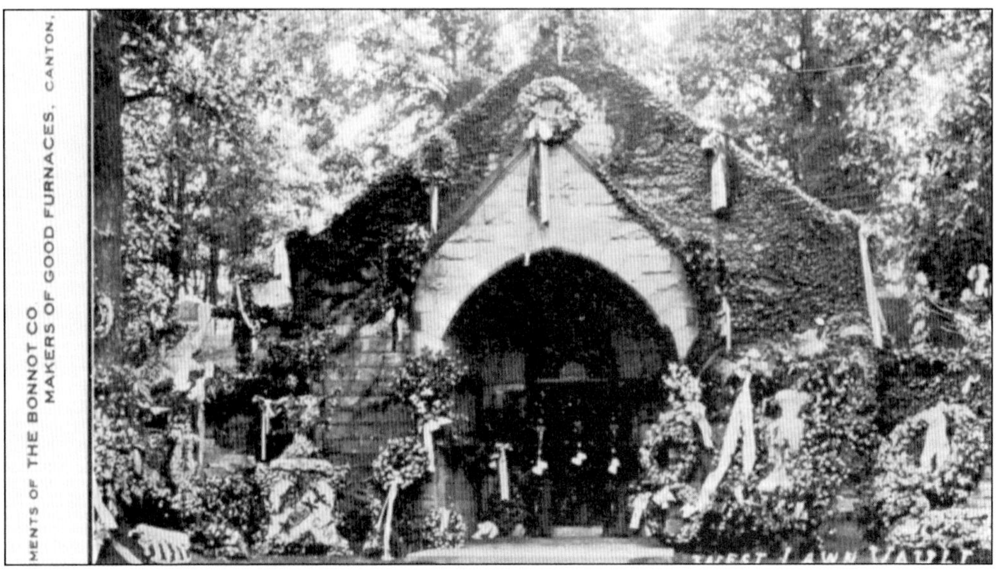

Following the funeral, during which Pres. Theodore Roosevelt gave the eulogy, McKinley was interred in the Wertz vault in West Lawn Cemetery. An account of the day stated that the vault was nearly obstructed by the many floral tributes. Ida McKinley, who had been at her husband's side when he died and had accompanied his body back to Canton, did not attend the funeral, as was the custom of the day.

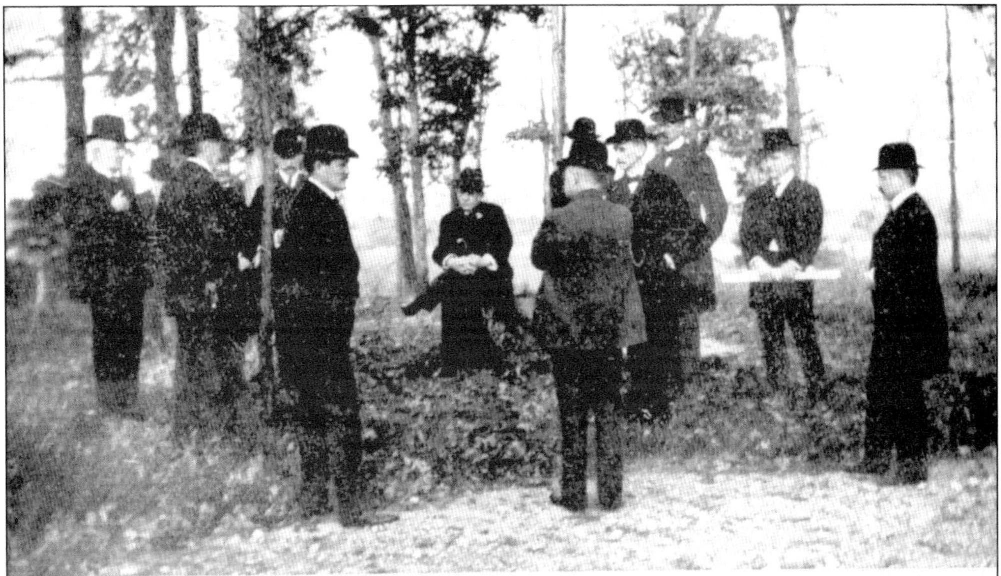

McKINLEY NATIONAL MEMORIAL TRUSTEES, SELECTING SITE FOR MONUMENT. No. 21

From Left to Right—Cornelius N. Bliss, Wm. A. Lynch, Henry C. Payne, Alexander H. Revell, Myron T. Herrick, Marcus A. Hanna, Wm. McConway, John G. Milburn, Wm. R. Day, Charles W. Fairbanks, Fred. S. Hartzell, George B. Cortelyou.

Friends and cabinet members met on the day of McKinley's funeral to decide on the site for his memorial. Pictured from left to right, they included interior secretary Cornelius Bliss, postmaster general William Lynch, Chicago businessman Henry Payne, Alexander Revell, Ohio politician Myron Herrick, Sen. Mark Hanna, William McConway, Sen. Charles Fairbanks, Secretary of State William Day, Frederic Hartzel, and McKinley's secretary George Cortelyou.

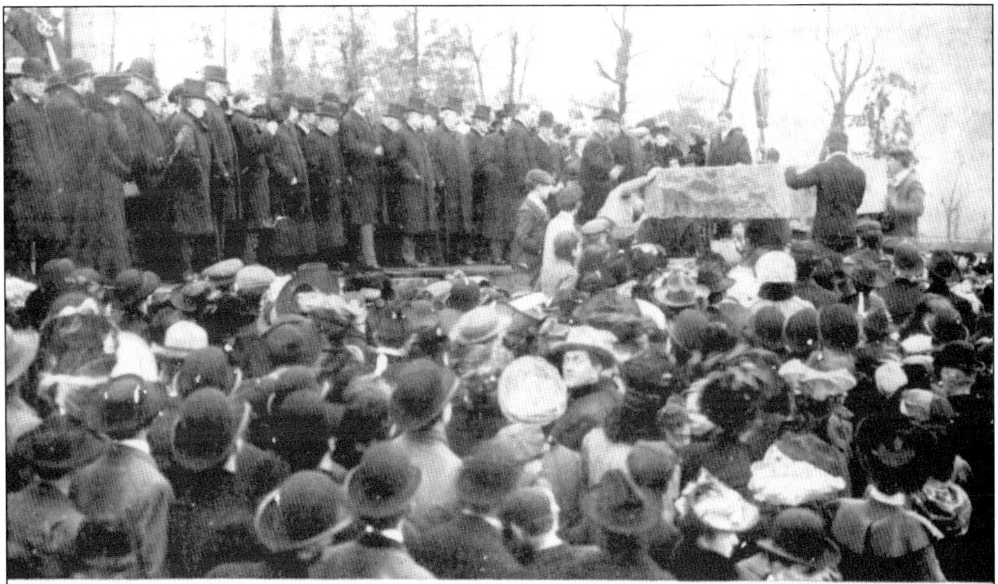

Corner-stone Laying Ceremonies, McKinley Monument, Canton, Ohio, November 16, 1905 No. 14

On November 16, 1905, the five-ton cornerstone of the McKinley Monument was laid. Ida McKinley attended the ceremony and watched as some of the president's personal belongings were placed in the stone.

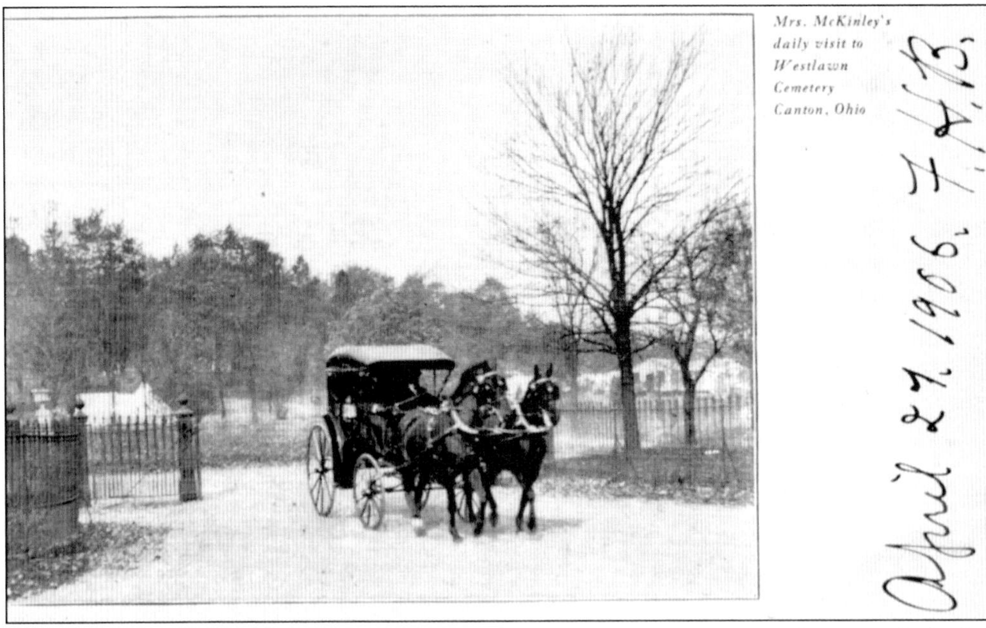

Ida McKinley visited the cemetery daily until her death on May 26, 1907, four months before the dedication of the memorial to her late husband. She was also interred in the Wertz vault until after the monument was completed.

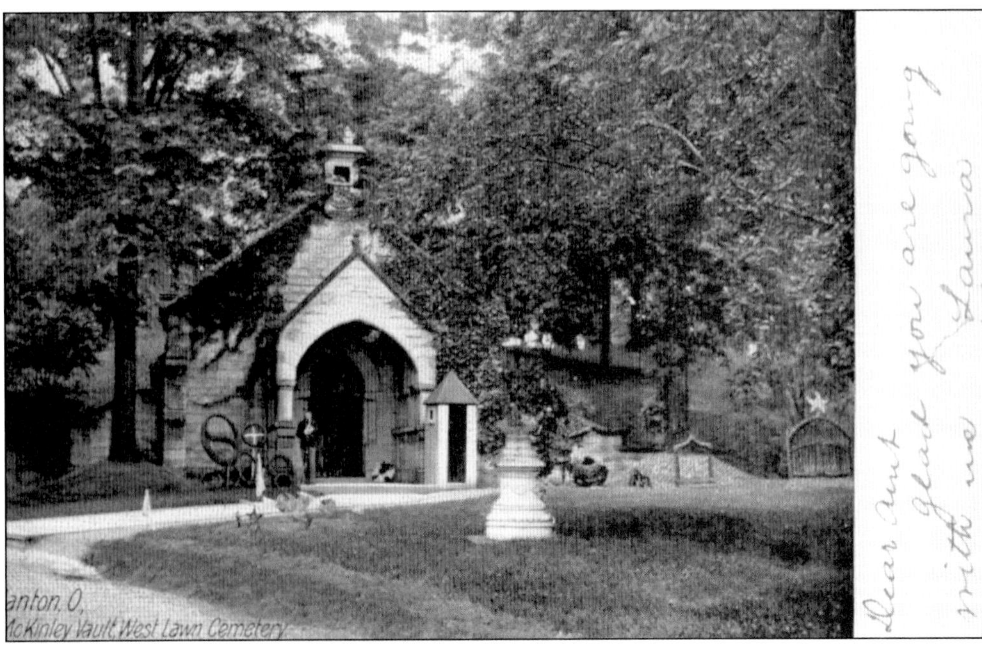

The Wertz vault near the Fourth Street entrance to the West Lawn Cemetery was the temporary resting place of Pres. William McKinley and later his wife, Ida, prior to the completion of the monument. "It was guarded day and night by soldiers detailed by the Government for the purpose."

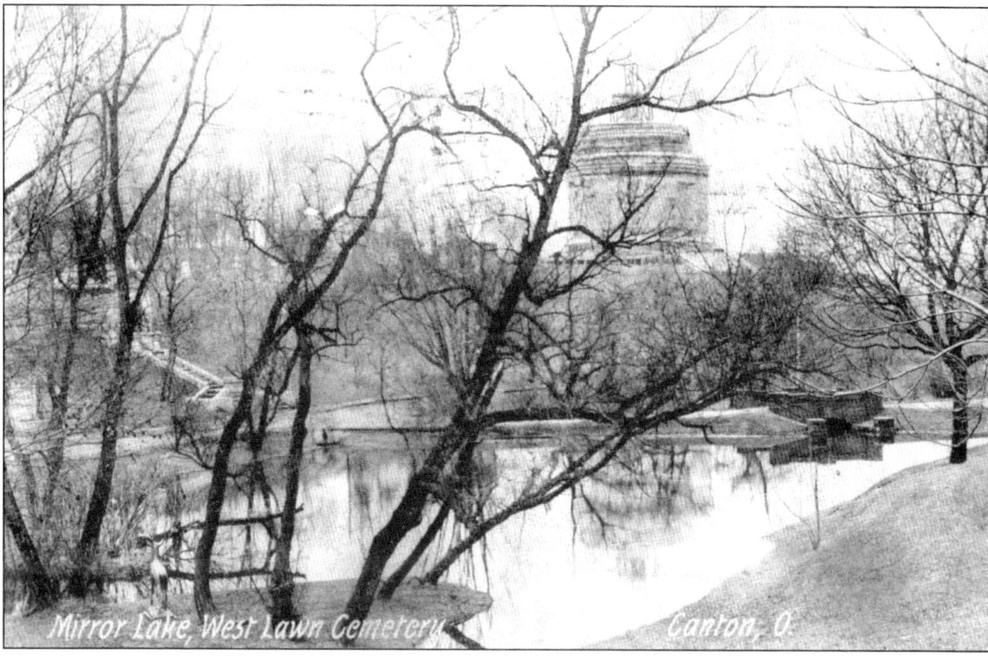

This view from the West Lawn Cemetery shows the McKinley Monument under construction. From 1905 until its completion in 1907, craftsmen, some volunteers, came from many areas of the country to help build the memorial. Materials from nine different states arrived in Canton by rail and were brought to the site by horse-drawn wagons. Later craftsmen have marveled at the skill and workmanship that went into the monument's construction.

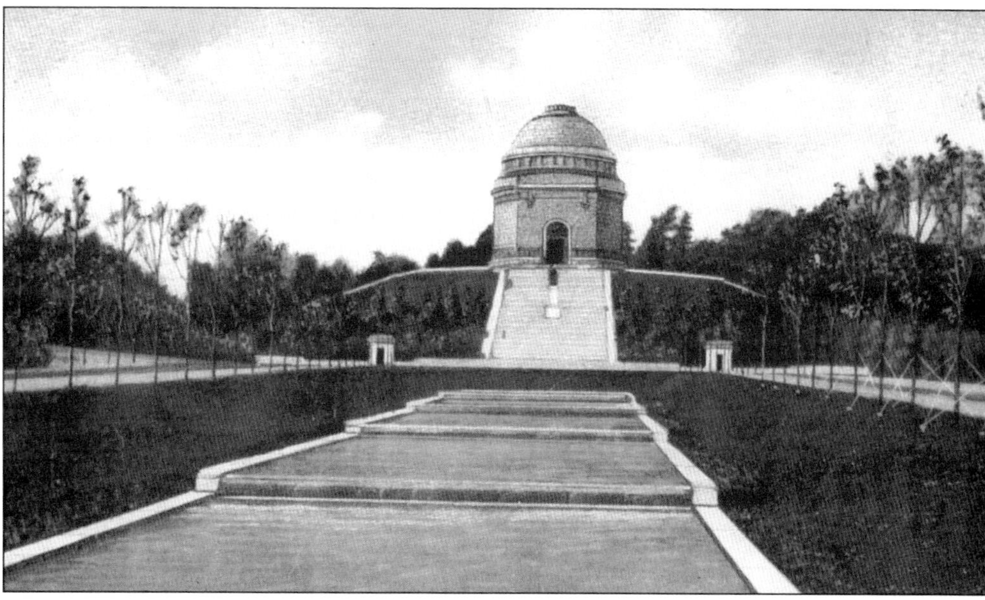

In a way, William McKinley chose the site for his memorial. He had often visited the site and thought it would be a fitting place for a military memorial. Designed by Harold Van Magonigle of New York City, the monument cost $586,848.92. The majority of the funds came from small donations, including those from schoolchildren. Small banks were issued across the country by the McKinley National Memorial Association to collect donations.

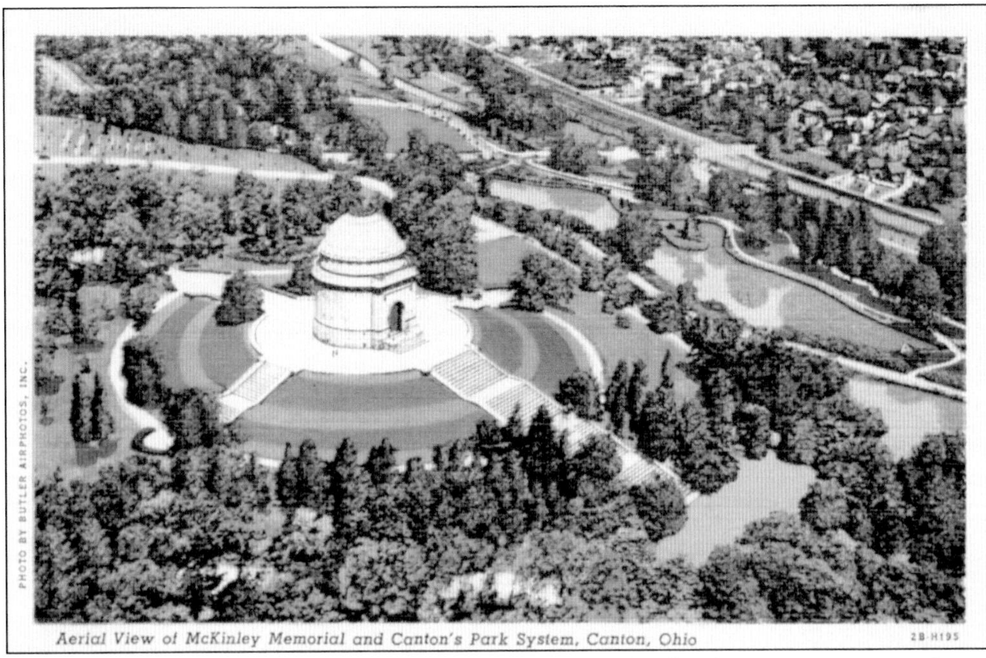

Constructed of Massachusetts pink granite and locally made bricks, the monument sits at the top of a 108-step stairway. The entire site is incorporated into a cross-hilted sword, symbolizing the martyred president. The main approach to the memorial is the blade of the sword, the plaza is the guard, and the tomb is the hilt. The side and rear approaches form the arms of the sword.

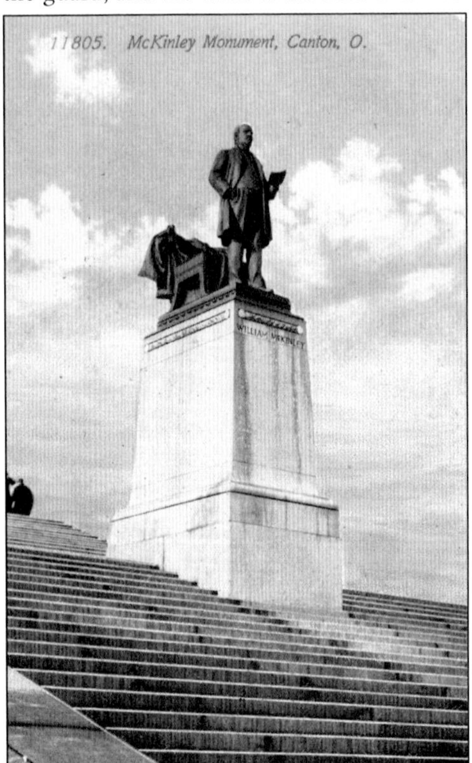

The nine-and-a-half-foot statue midway up the monument steps sits on a 13-foot pedestal. Cast in bronze by Charles Henry Neihaus, it depicts William McKinley, wearing his characteristic frock coat and vest, delivering his last speech in Buffalo, New York, on September 6, 1901. The statue was unveiled by Helen McKinley, the president's sister, during the dedication of the monument.

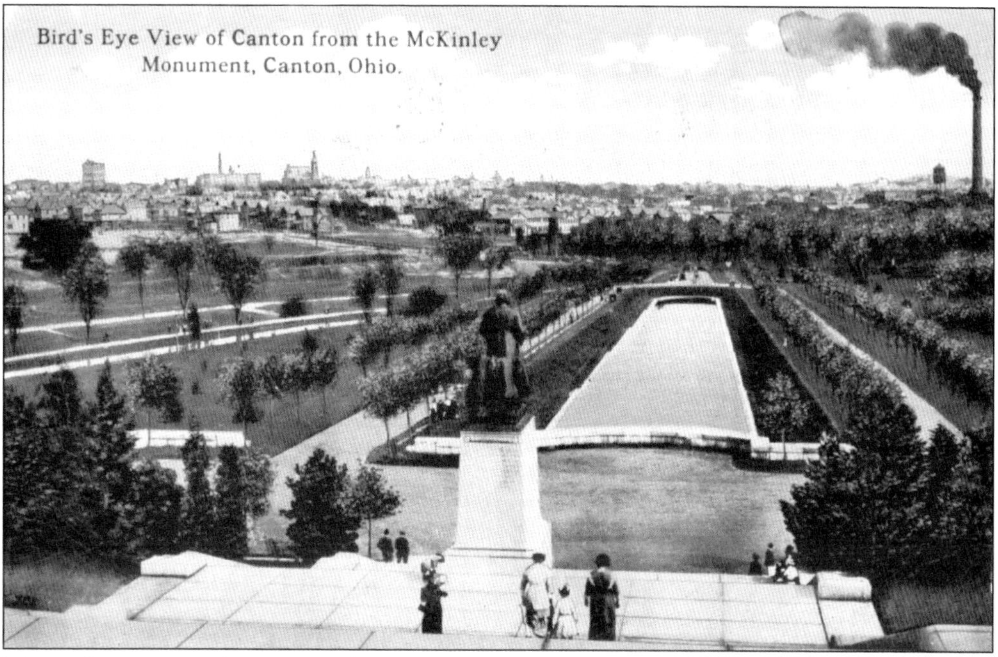

"C.E.L." wrote to Edna Yossie of Willink, New York, in August 1911 describing the memorial as a "fine monument" from which "you can see a long distance." The reflective long water concrete lagoon measured 575 feet. It was filled in 1951 due to erosion problems.

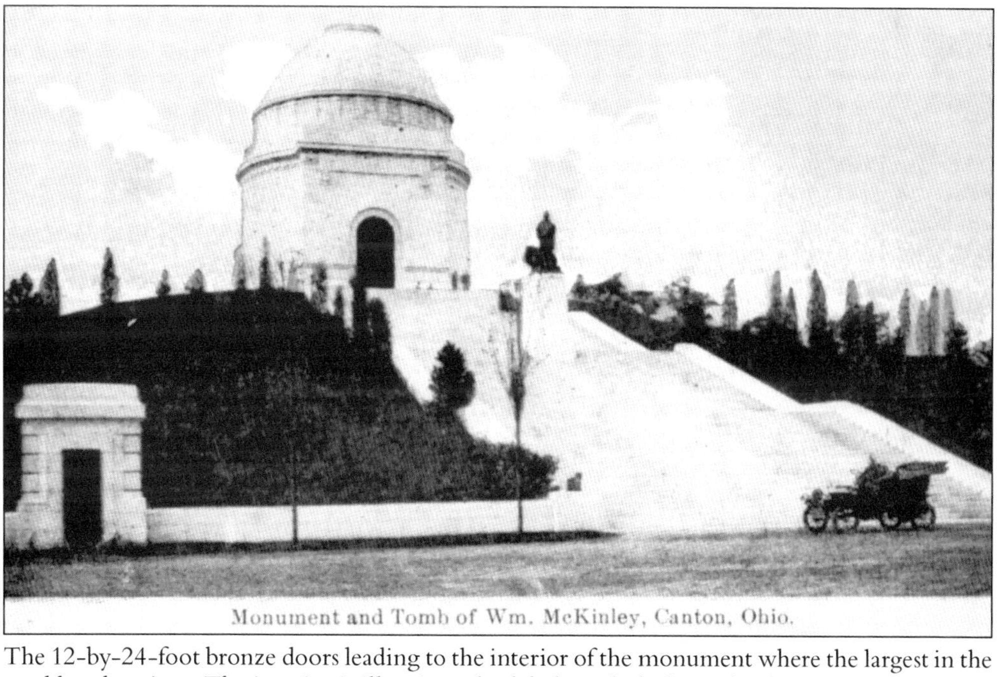

The 12-by-24-foot bronze doors leading to the interior of the monument where the largest in the world at that time. The interior is illuminated solely by a skylight in the dome. The inscription at the base of the dome is a quotation from McKinley's last speech: "Let us ever remember that our interest is in concord not conflict and that our real eminence rests in the victories of peace not war."

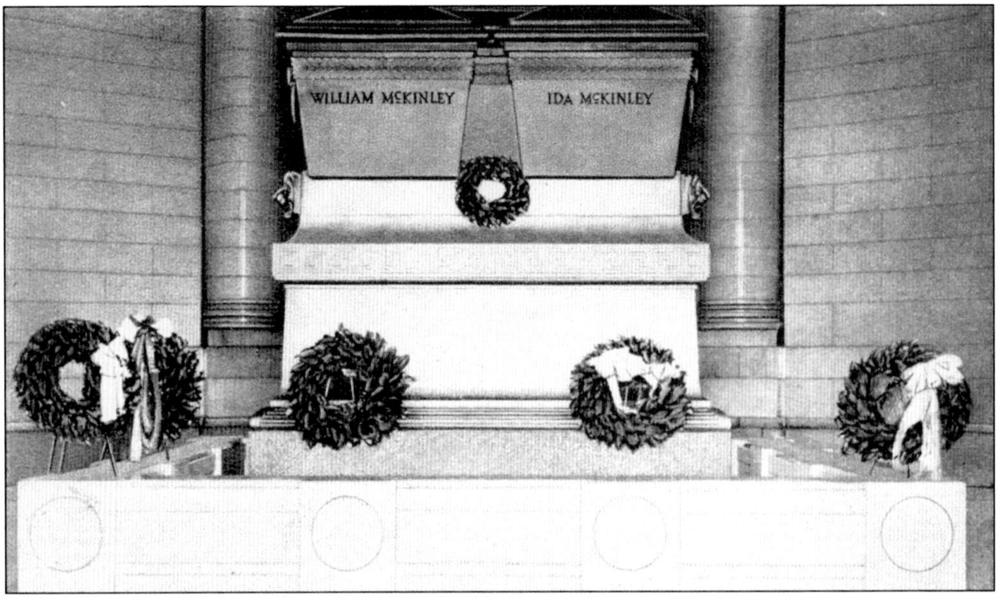

The 50-ton double sarcophagi were carved from Vermont green granite, while the black granite base and floor tiles were from Wisconsin. The bodies of Pres. William and Ida McKinley were not moved from the Wertz vault to the monument until October 10, 1907. At the same time, the bodies of their daughters, Katherine and Ida, were moved from West Lawn Cemetery to niches in the north wall of the monument.

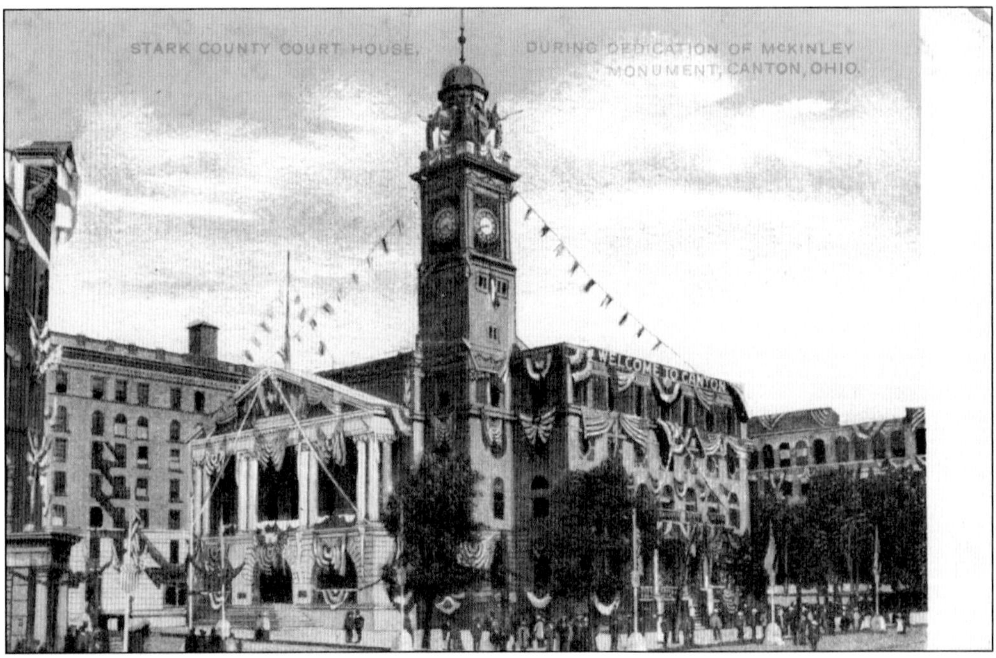

The Stark County Court House was the focal point for much of the celebration surrounding the dedication of the McKinley memorial on September 30, 1907. Pres. Theodore Roosevelt headed the official party. It is estimated that 50,000 people travelled to Canton to attend the dedication. "Nina" wrote to Mary Spencer of Shreve, Ohio, on September 29 that they were having a "fine time . . . a large crowd today and thousands more tomorrow."

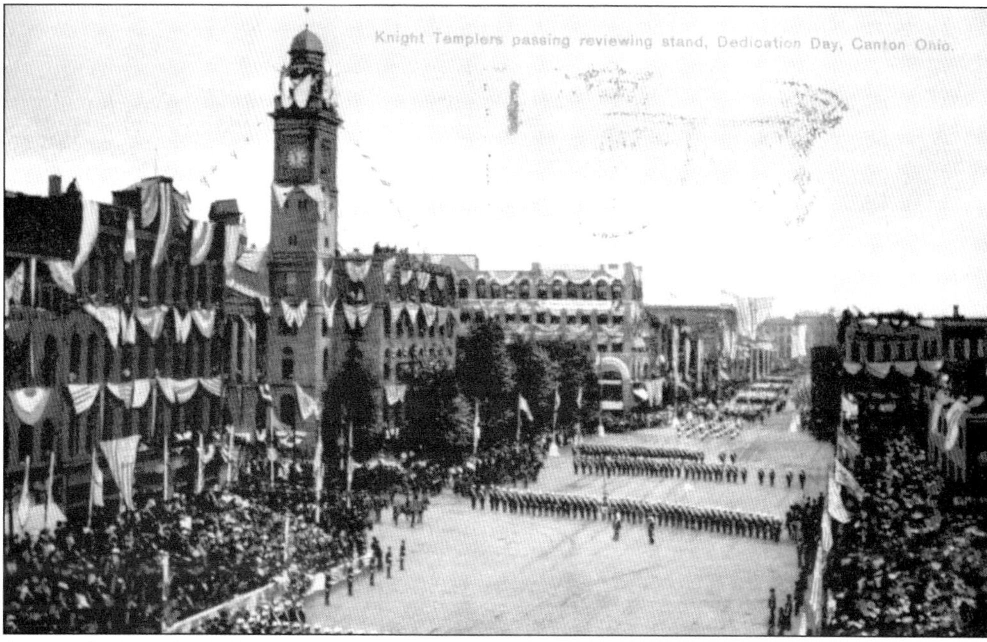

"L.R.S." described the monument dedication parade to Mrs. William Browne of Derby, Connecticut. "The parade was two hours long and composed of 7 to 8,000 people. It was a wonderful sight to see all these people walking as though it was the greatest thing on earth."

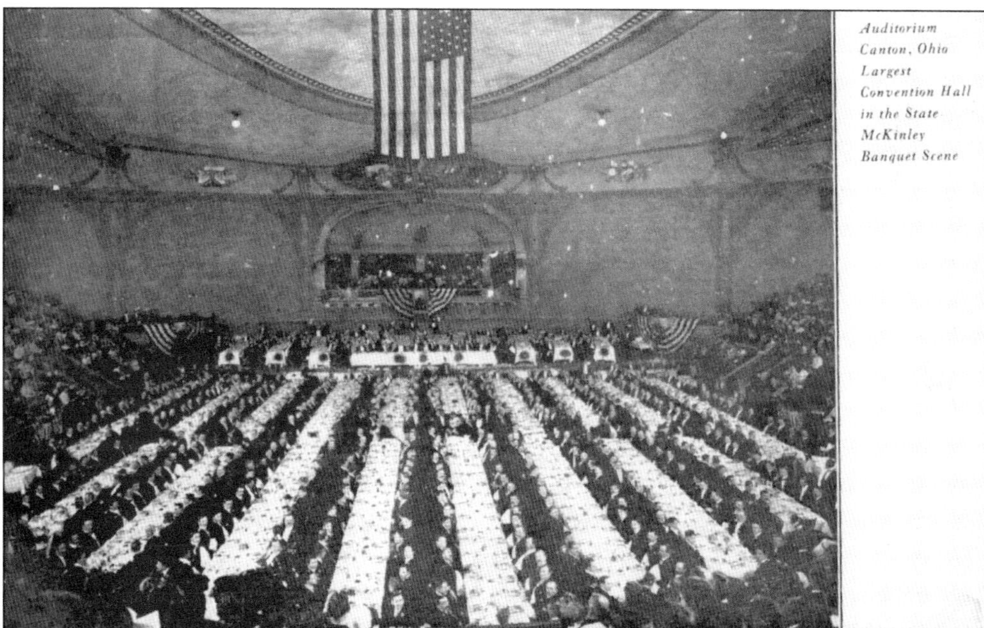

Following the parade, Pres. Theodore Roosevelt and other dignitaries attended a luncheon at the Canton Auditorium. This pre-1907 photograph of the auditorium is probably not the actual dedication day luncheon, but instead shows an earlier State McKinley Day Banquet. The governor made William McKinley's birthday a state holiday on January 29, 1902.

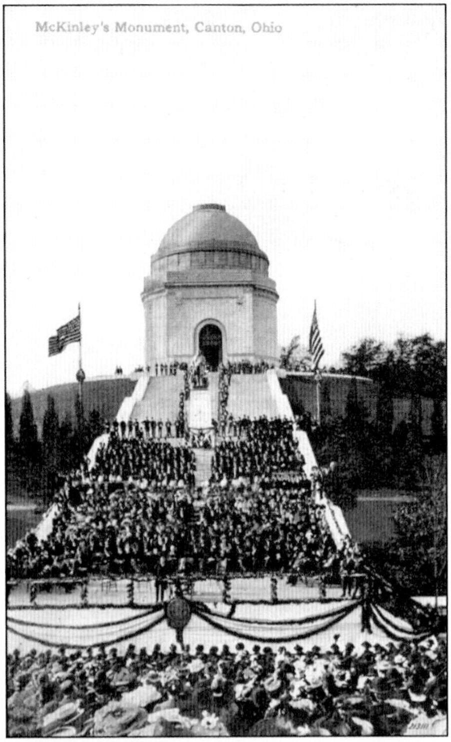

William Day, president of the McKinley National Memorial Association, opened the dedication ceremony. The Grand Army Band and the 150-voice Canton Singers' Club led the crowd in the "Star Spangled Banner." James Whitcomb Riley read an original poem, Helen McKinley unveiled the statue, and Pres. Theodore Roosevelt was the featured orator. The program concluded with the band and the chorus leading the crowd in singing "America."

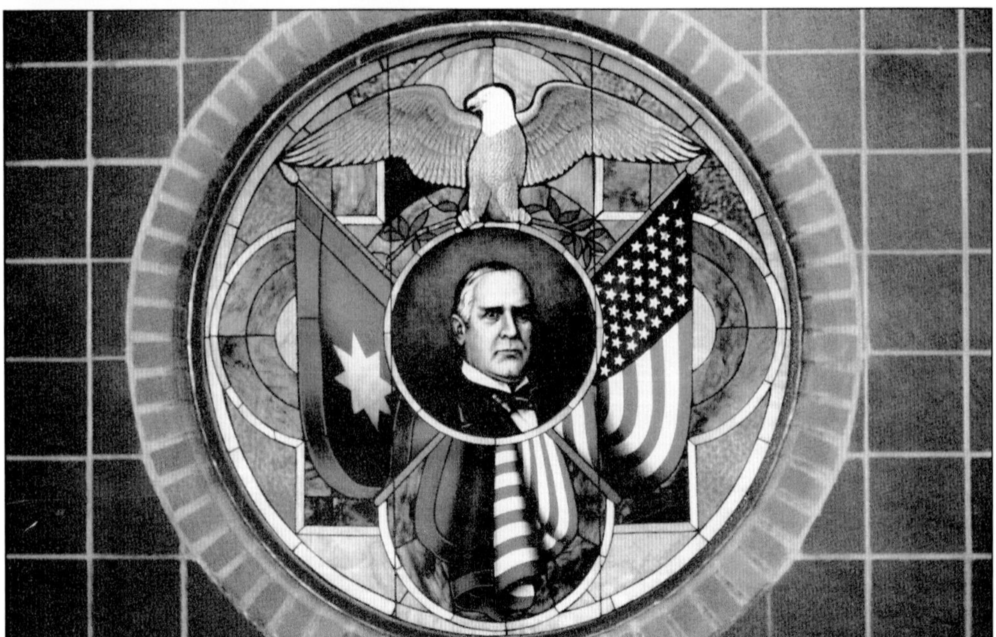

Given by a member of the McKinley family to the Salvation Army, the McKinley Window was placed in the chapel. When the Walnut Street building was demolished, the window was sent to the Salvation Army Archives in New York City. When a new Salvation Army headquarters was built on Market Avenue, the organization requested its return. The window is now in the diagonal wall facing Ida McKinley's childhood home.

Two

Street Scenes

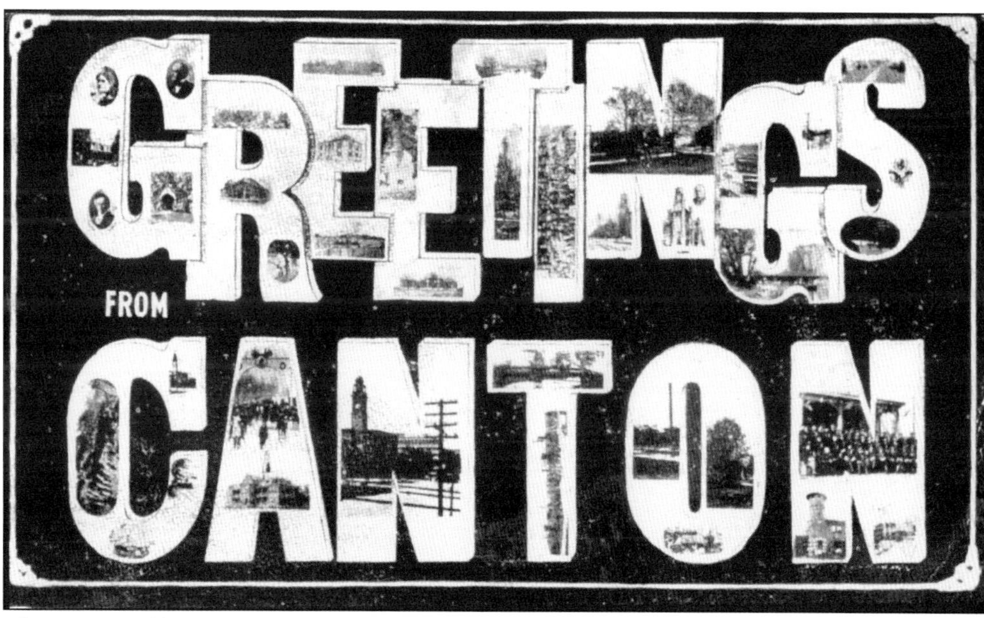

This 1907 card has images associated with McKinley, including one of the arches erected during his "Front Porch" presidential campaign, his home, the Wertz vault, the monument, and pictures of the president, his wife, and his mother. It also has pictures of the auditorium, public library, courthouse, Aultman Hospital, Cherry Street School, Central High School, First Methodist Episcopal Church, and First Lutheran Church.

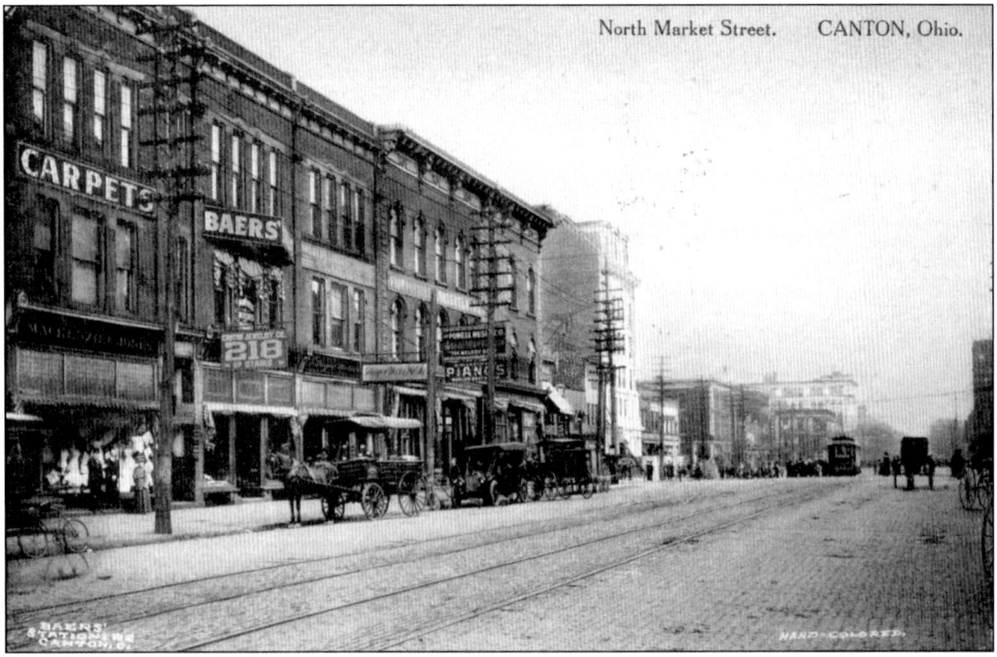

This 1911 view of North Market Street shows a streetcar and an early automobile, as well as several horse-drawn carts and carriages. From 1884 until 1889, horse-drawn streetcars ran up and down Canton's major streets. At the end of each line, the driver would have to unhitch the horses and bring them to the other side of the car and hitch them up for the return trip.

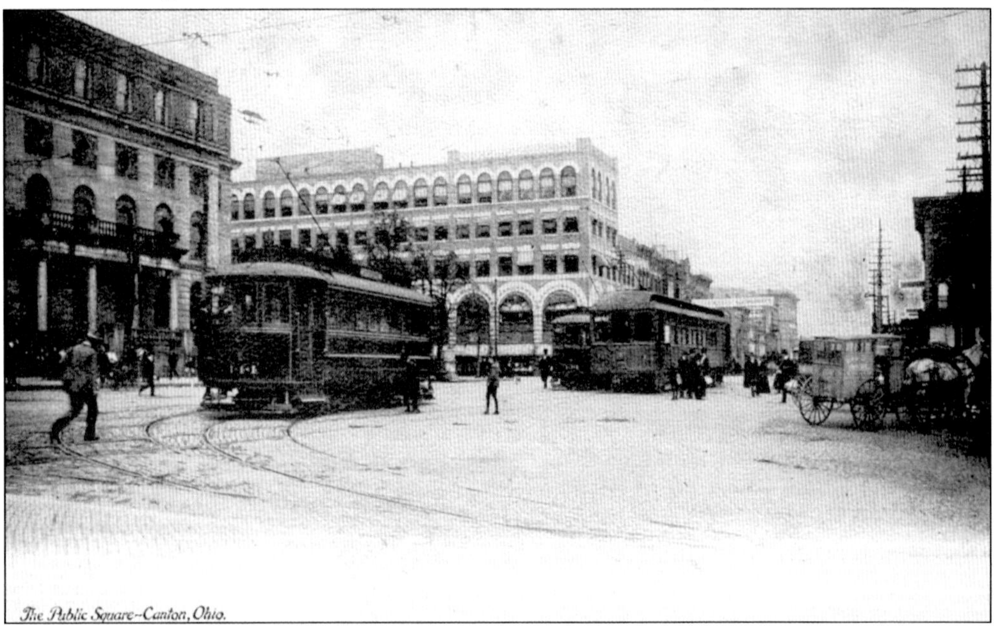

Electric streetcars arrived in Canton in 1889. The grinding wheels and clanging bells could be heard for blocks. As shown in this 1907 image, the tracks were located in the middle of the street, forcing the riders to watch for oncoming carriages and cars as they jumped on and off. Reportedly, not even these dangers prevented even the most prominent citizens from trying to get on and off without paying the fare.

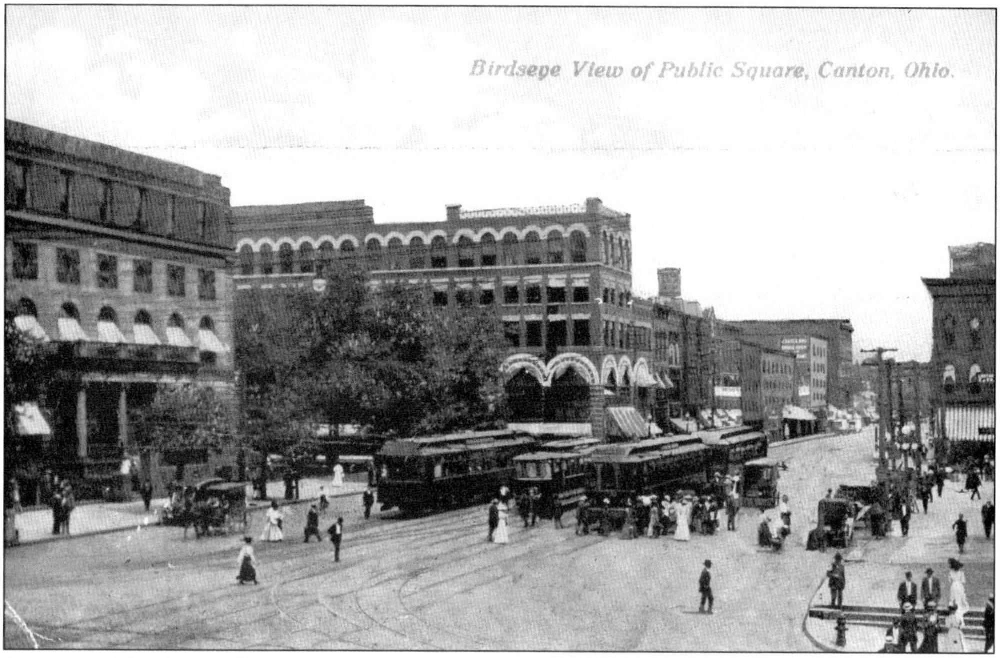

Streetcars, like the smaller one in the center, moved along Canton's major streets. The interurbans, like the two larger cars, went further into the suburbs, to Meyers Lake, and Massillon. Later they provided service to Alliance, New Philadelphia, Akron, and Cleveland. The height of the streetcar era was in the early 1920s. As cars and buses became more prevalent, the streetcars had fewer riders. Streetcar service ended in 1931.

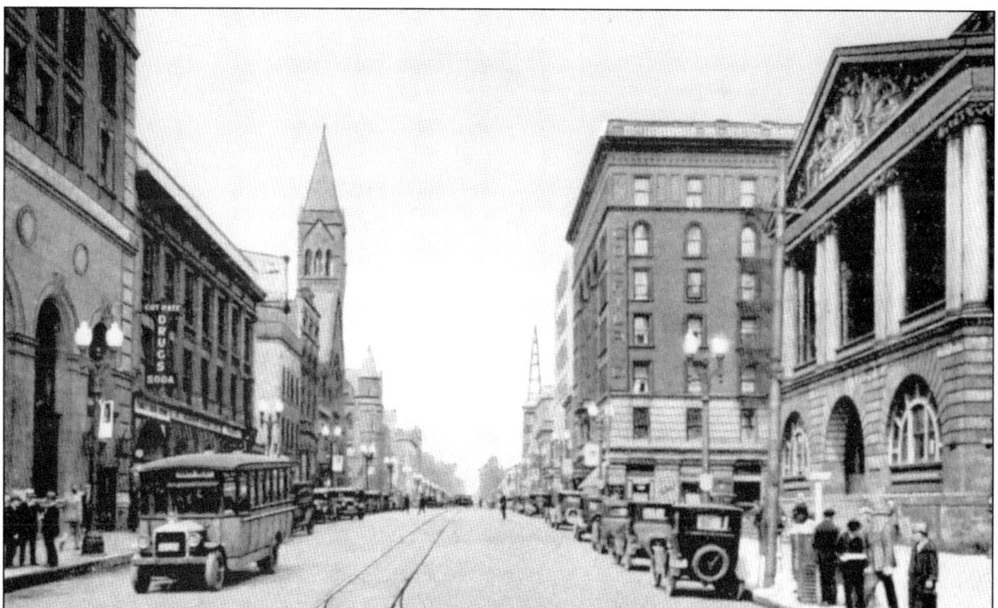

This view of West Tuscarawas Street from the square shows a jitney, one of Canton's first buses. The first jitney was the *Hoodlebug*, owned by A. H. "Tony" Wilson. Built on a one-cylinder Cadillac chassis, the jitney held 12 passengers who paid 10¢ to ride from the square up Market Street to what is now the Canton Civic Center.

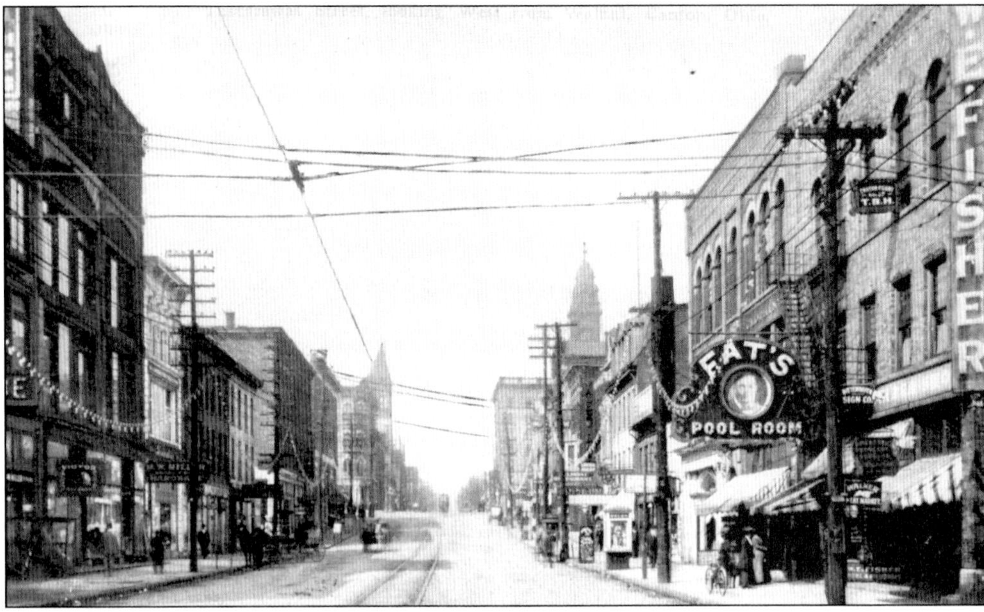

Located on West Tuscarawas Street, Fat's Pool Room was one of 139 saloons doing business in Canton in 1910. However, New Berlin (North Canton) was "dry." "B.B." wrote to his friend Harry Awyer of Paris, Ohio, in 1911 that although he had never seen "such a dry town in all my life. . . . It wasn't very dry and quiet last night here at the house when I came home from Canton."

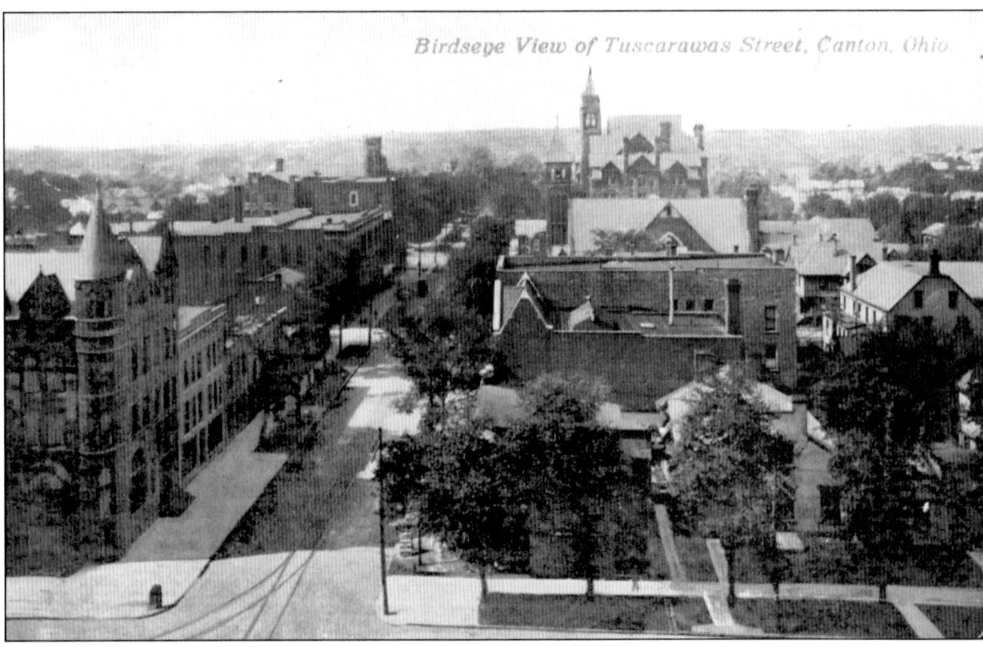

The Central Savings Bank was on the corner of West Tuscarawas Street and Cleveland Avenue before Stern and Mann Company built its department store on the opposite corner in 1926. Also visible is the square steeple of the Christ United Presbyterian Church on the south side of the street and the steeple of the Trinity Lutheran Church and bell tower of Central High School on the north side.

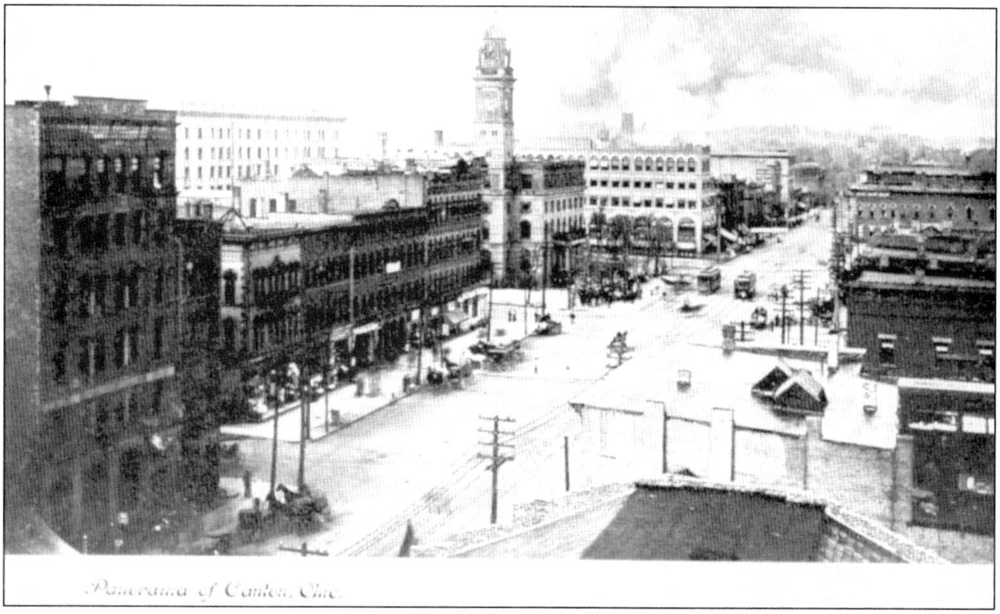

Visible in the left foreground, the City National Bank was one of the 18 banks organized in Canton between 1880 and 1920. Constructed in 1895, it was the tallest building in Canton. It is one of the few buildings from that era still standing today. It features different style windows on each floor, brass doors, marble interior floors and panels, and a marble staircase from the first to the top floor.

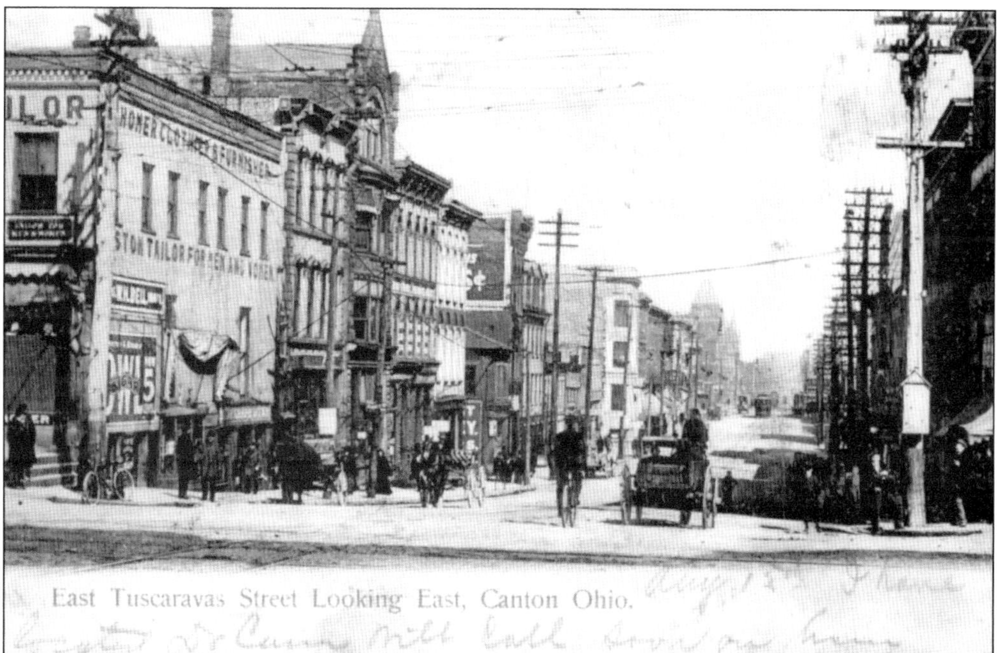

Looking east from Market Avenue, East Tuscarawas Street in this pre-1906 view is a hub of activity. Note the bicycles and streetcar in the distance as well as the horse-drawn vehicles. The street had electrical service, as evidenced by the many electrical poles. The spire of the First Lutheran Church is visible at the far end of the street.

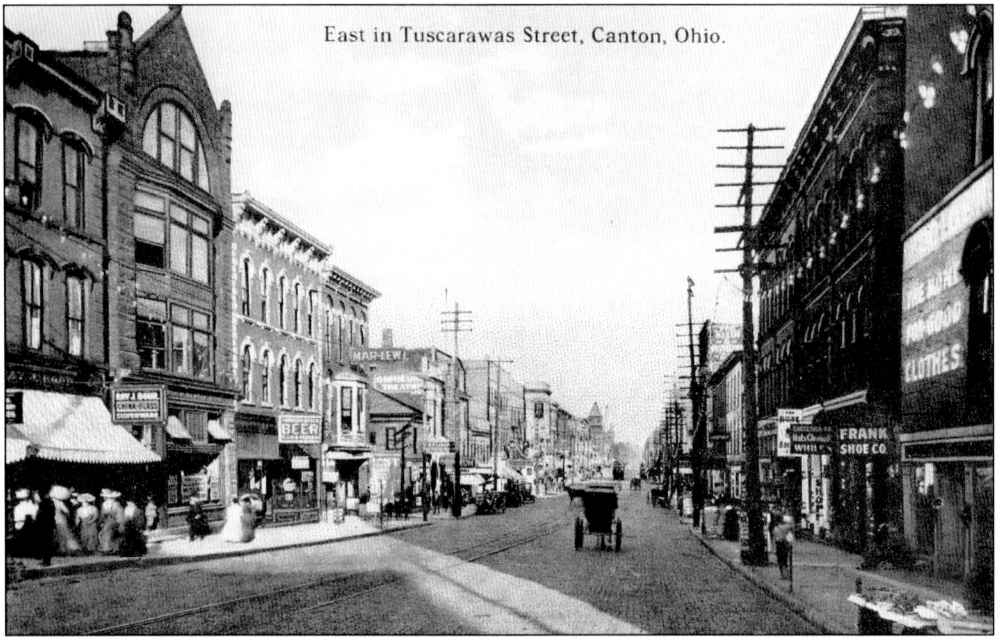

Frank Case built the Dime Savings Bank in the heart of the many businesses located on East Tuscarawas Street in 1905. The bank, designed by Guy Tilden with a rounded facade, is visible in the middle of the north side of the street. When the bank was organized in 1895, one could open an account for 10¢ and would receive interest on $1 left in the account for 30 days or more.

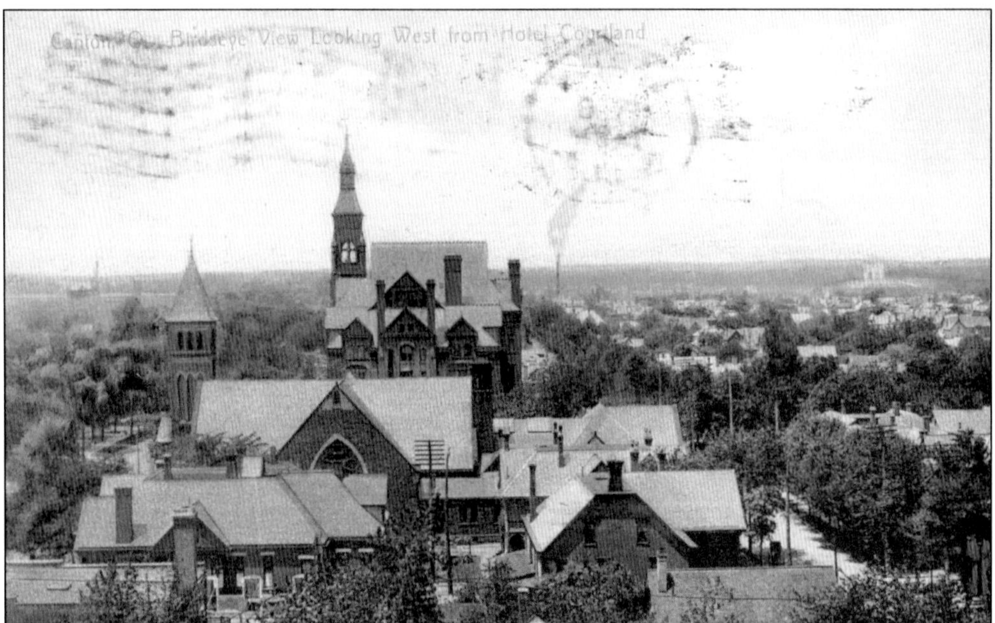

Looking west from the Courtland Hotel in 1909, one could see the Central High School bell tower and the spire of the Trinity Lutheran Church, as well as the McKinley Monument, the Dueber-Hamden Watch Factory on the far left, and tree-lined residential areas.

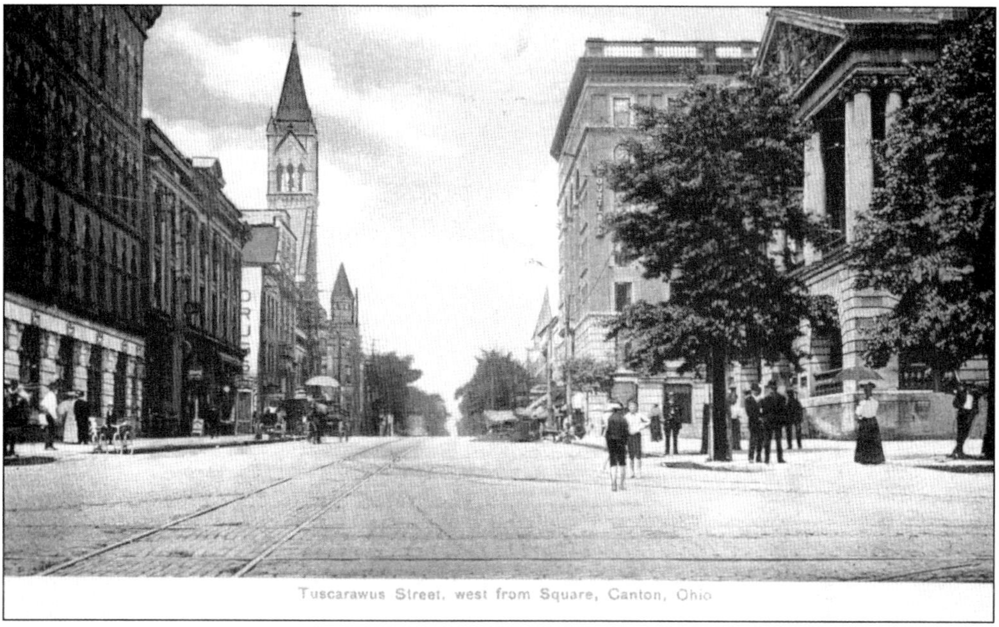

Standing on the south side of the courthouse in 1907, one could see the Courtland Hotel, A. E. Stocker Cigar Store, News Exchange, Bowman Brothers Drugs, and the Canton State Bank. On the opposite side of the street were the First National Bank, Schafer Building, Savings and Loan Company, First Methodist Episcopal Church, and Central Savings Bank.

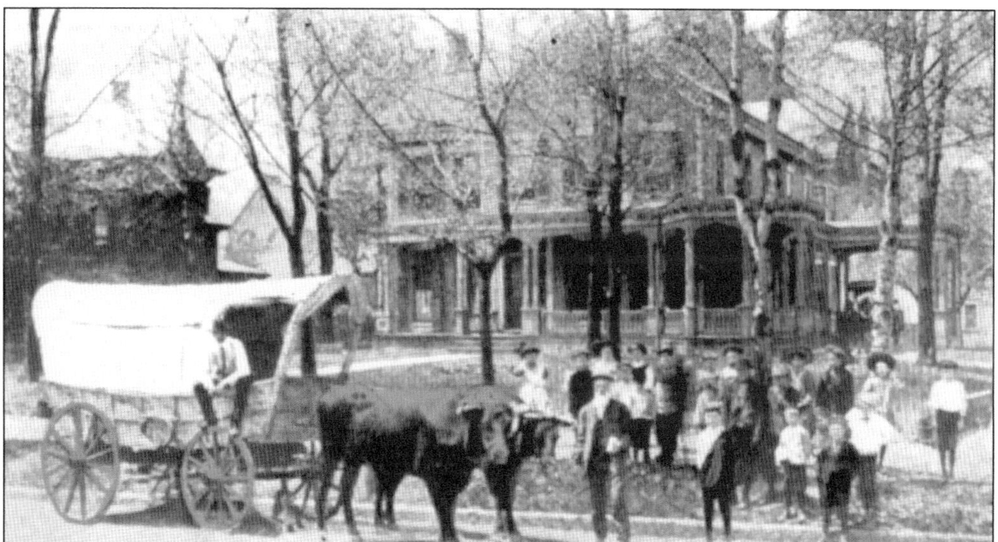

Ezra Meeker, shown here in front of the McKinley home in his Conestoga wagon, traveled the Oregon Trail from Indiana to Puget Sound in 1852. In 1906, he decided to raise funds to commemorate the trail by traveling eastward and charging admission to view his wagon. He arrived in Washington, D.C., in November 1907. He made additional trips by wagon, car, rail, and eventually at age 94 in an airplane.

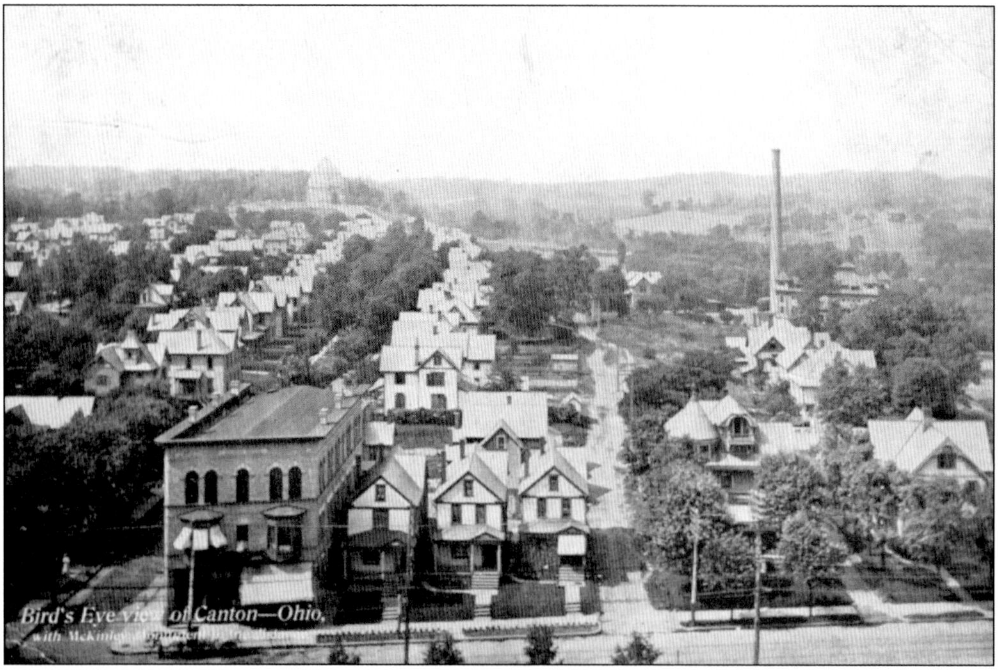

This card shows the northwestern residential area of Canton around 1910. The McKinley Monument is in the background. Notice that the city did not extend past Monument Park.

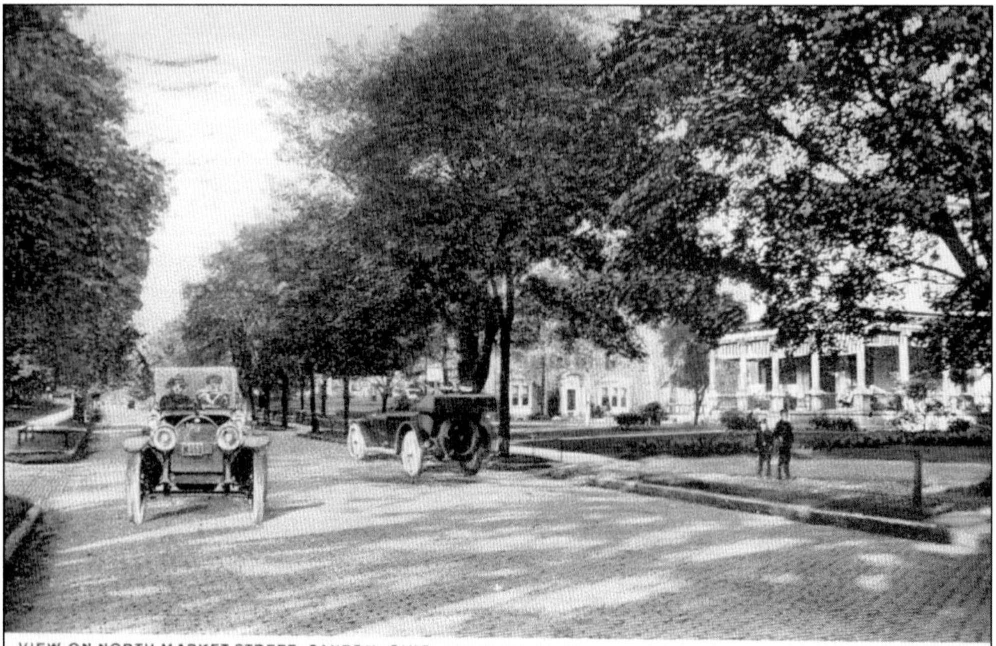

North Market Avenue was Canton's most fashionable address in the early 20th century. Many of the city's wealthy businessmen had impressive homes along this street, including the Renkert, Belden, Case, Aultman, and Harter families.

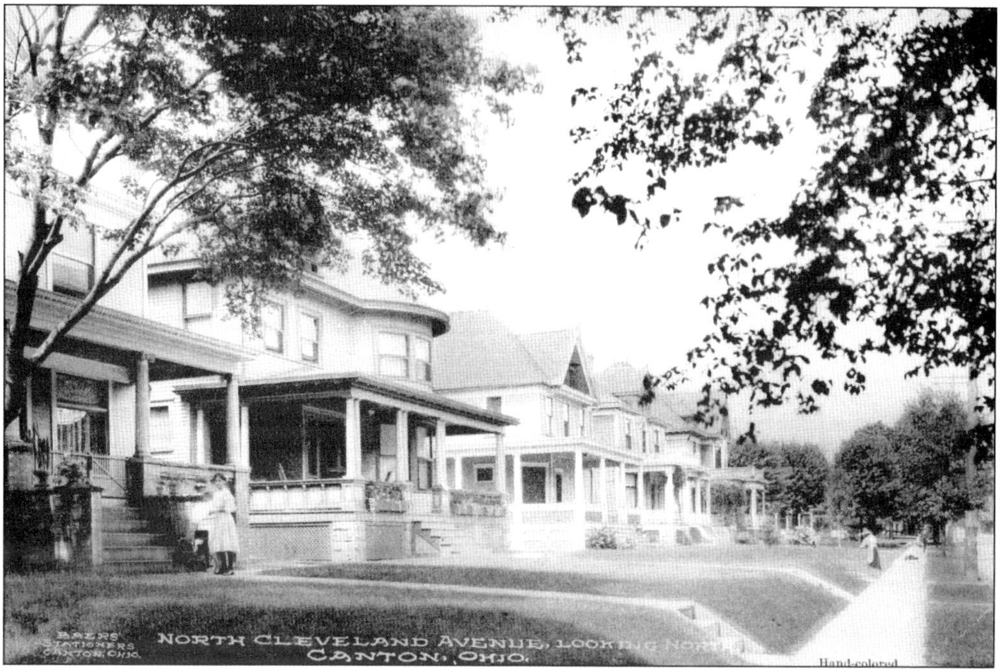

While not as grand as those on North Market Avenue, North Cleveland Avenue had many lovely homes, as shown in this 1910-era card.

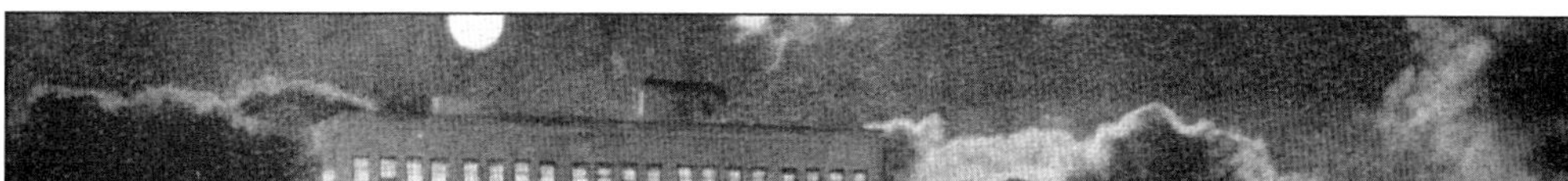

The offices of the *Canton Daily News* were located on the east side of the square. The paper was founded in 1833 by John Bernard as the *Stark County Democrat*. In 1926, the editor, Donald Mellett, was murdered following a series of articles on official corruption in Canton. The paper was purchased in 1930 by the *Canton Repository*, whose staff moved into the facility owned by the *Canton Daily News* on South Market Avenue.

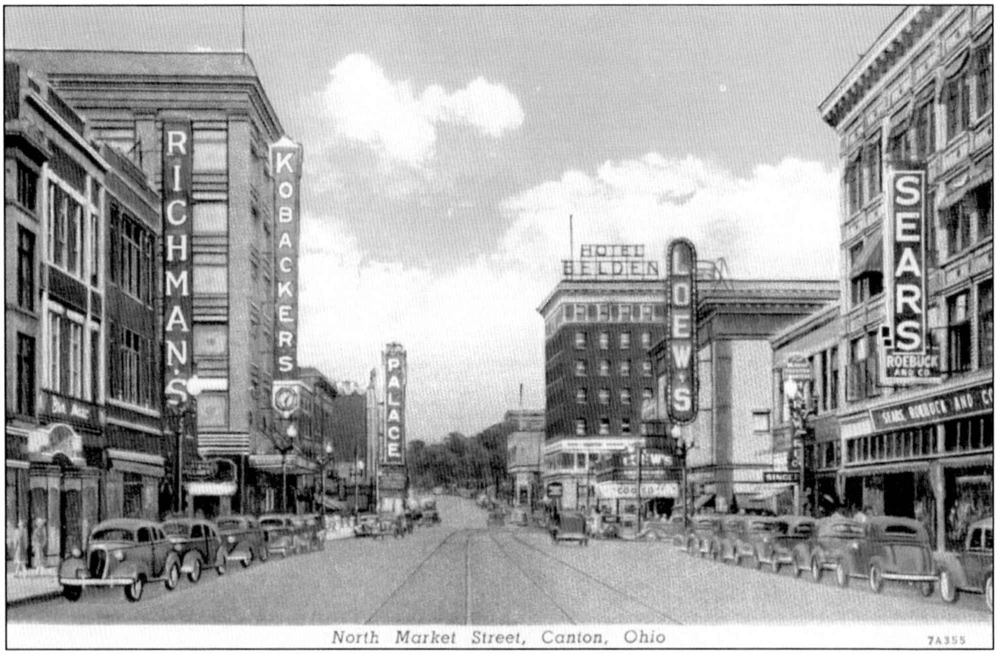

As this 1930s view of North Market Avenue shows, downtown was the hub for shopping and entertainment. The C. N. Vicary Building (right foreground) housed Vicary's Clothing and the Canton Actual Business College on the upper floors. Sears and Roebuck occupied a portion of the building from the 1930s until the 1950s. Across the street the 1920s Richman Brother's Building housed their clothing store. The adjacent Bon Marche clothing store opened in 1927.

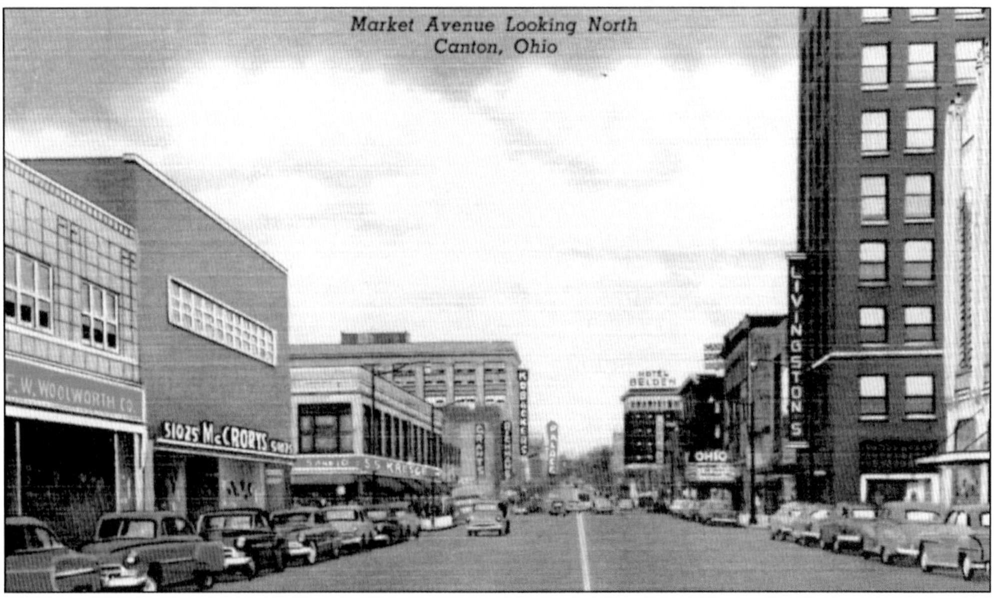

Midway down the right side of Market Avenue was the Ohio Theater. Built in 1913 by lumber dealer Phil Bernower and his partner Valentine Ney, it was originally called the Alhambra. The first theater in Canton constructed specifically as a motion picture house, it was one of several theaters built in that period. The Niarchos Restaurant located next door was known for its fountain drinks and ice-cream sundaes.

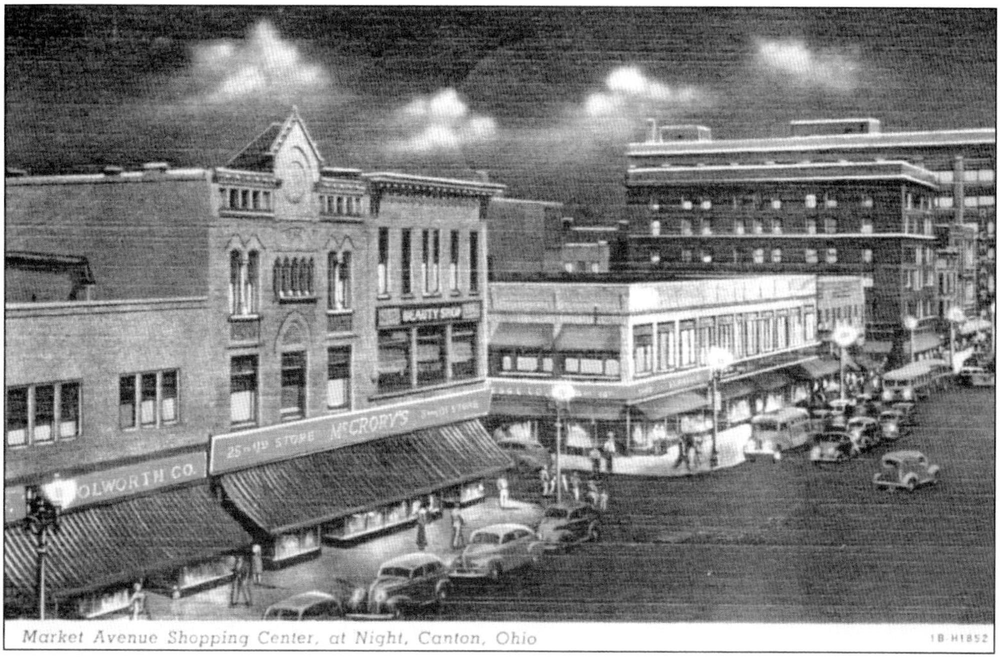

Prior to 1930 when the paper merged with the *Canton Daily News*, the McCory Building was the home of the *Canton Repository*. The oldest Ohio newspaper retaining its original name, it was founded in 1815 by John Saxton. The *Canton Repository* remained under Saxton ownership for 70 years. John Saxton was an abolitionist and staunch Republican. He lived to see his granddaughter Ida married to another Republican, William McKinley.

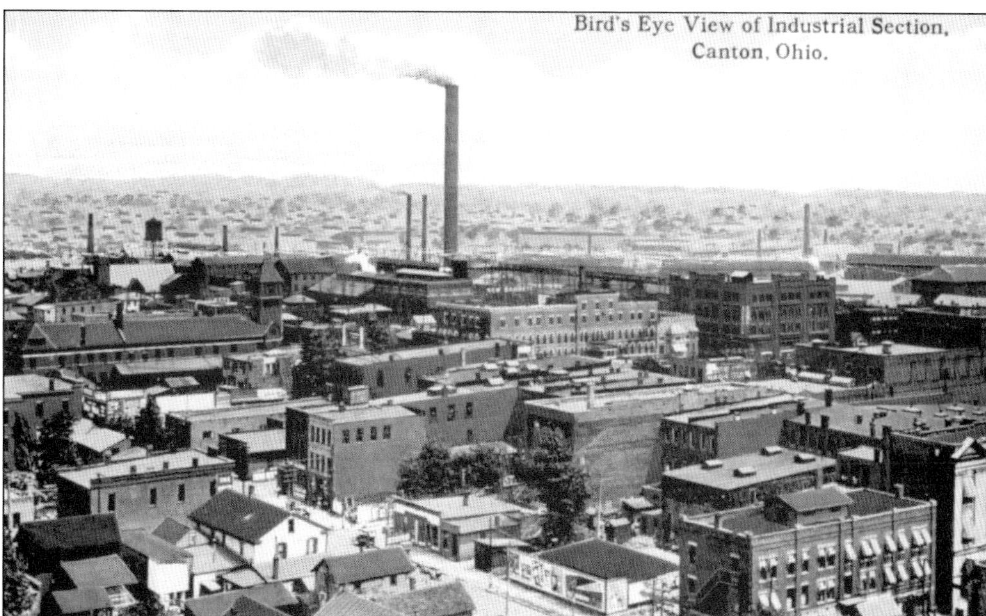

Notice that the city did not extend far past this early industrial area. The Barnett Hotel on Cherry Street is visible below the large smokestack.

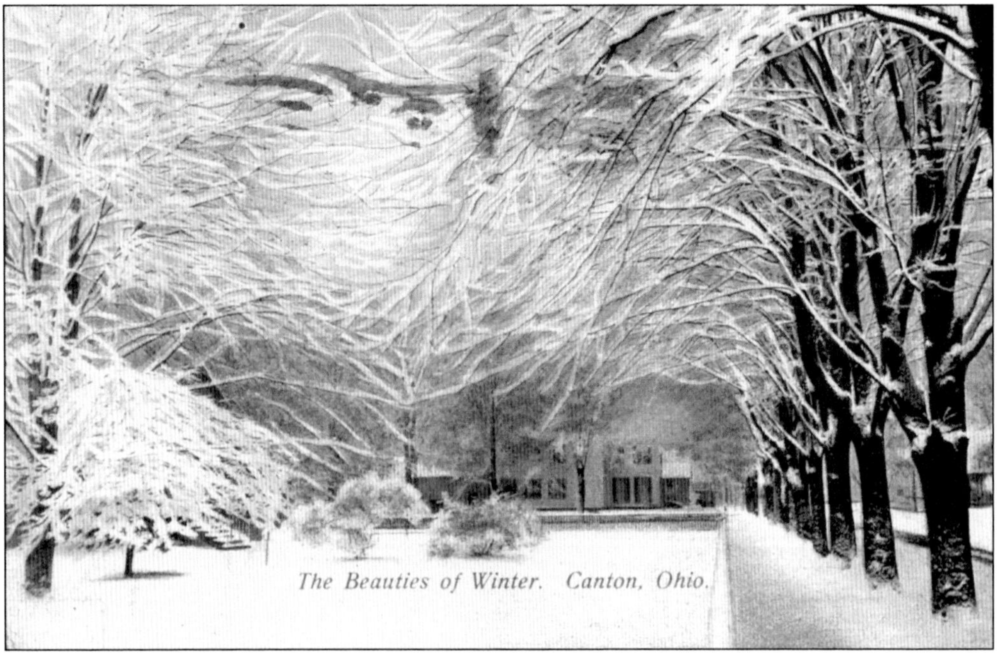

In February 1910, "Edna" wrote to Sallie Grove in Hamilton Square, New Jersey, that Canton was experiencing a snowstorm and it was "awful cold." On April 19, 1901, Canton experienced a 15½-inch snowfall, virtually paralyzing the city. Streetcar and train services were halted, stranding many passengers. Telegraph and telephone lines were downed by strong winds and heavy snow.

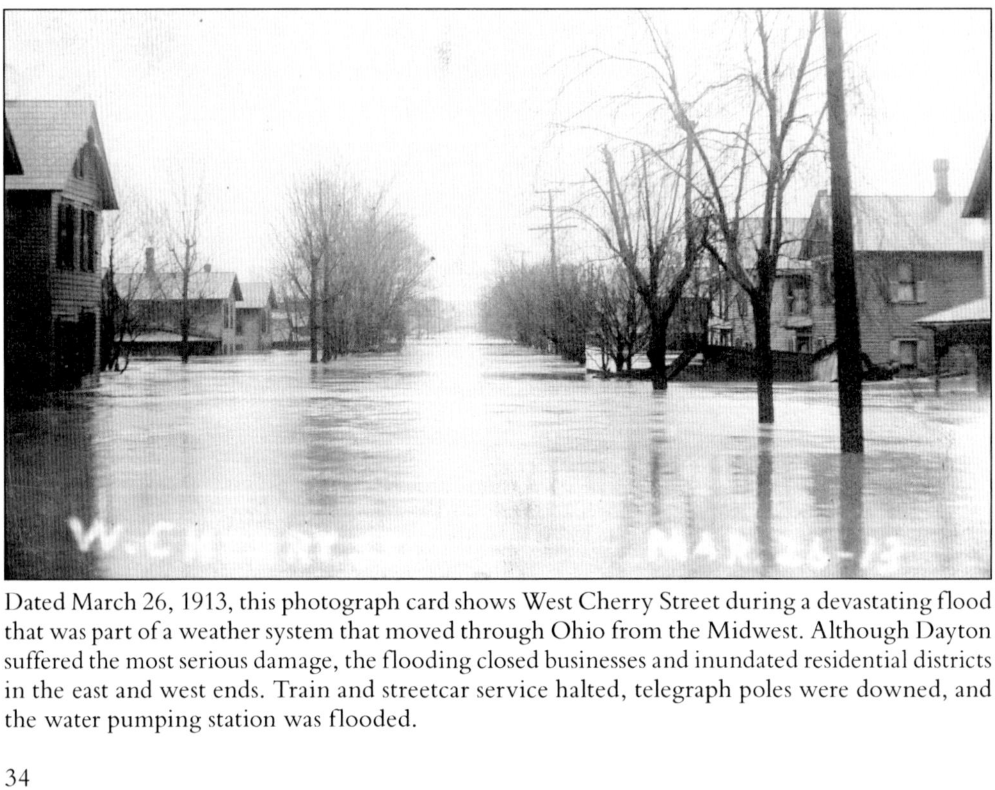

Dated March 26, 1913, this photograph card shows West Cherry Street during a devastating flood that was part of a weather system that moved through Ohio from the Midwest. Although Dayton suffered the most serious damage, the flooding closed businesses and inundated residential districts in the east and west ends. Train and streetcar service halted, telegraph poles were downed, and the water pumping station was flooded.

Three

GOVERNMENT AND CIVIC FACILITIES

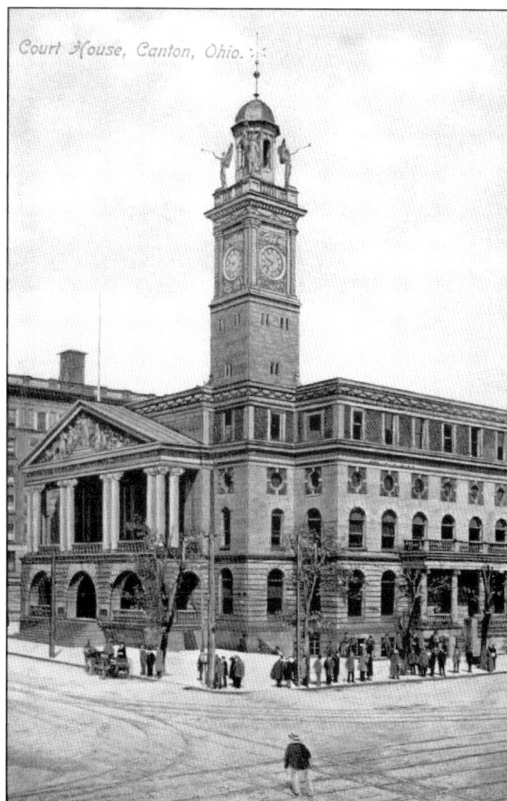

Built in 1895 over the shell of the second courthouse, the Stark County Court House is an excellent example of classical American public building design. The building, with its four gilded trumpeters of justice atop the clock tower, marks the center of town. Many residents recall when Santa's igloo was set up on the square each Christmas. There the old gentleman heard many Christmas wishes.

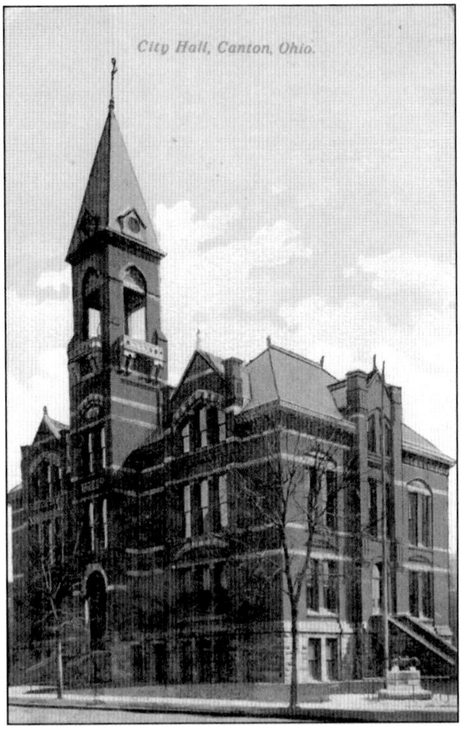

Located on the Cleveland Avenue site of the current city hall, this city hall was built in 1884 at the same time as the adjacent central firehouse and city market. Typical of High Victorian–style architecture, the building featured several different varieties of stone and brick. The central tower housed the city bell, which was used as a fire signal. The jail holding both men and women was located in the basement.

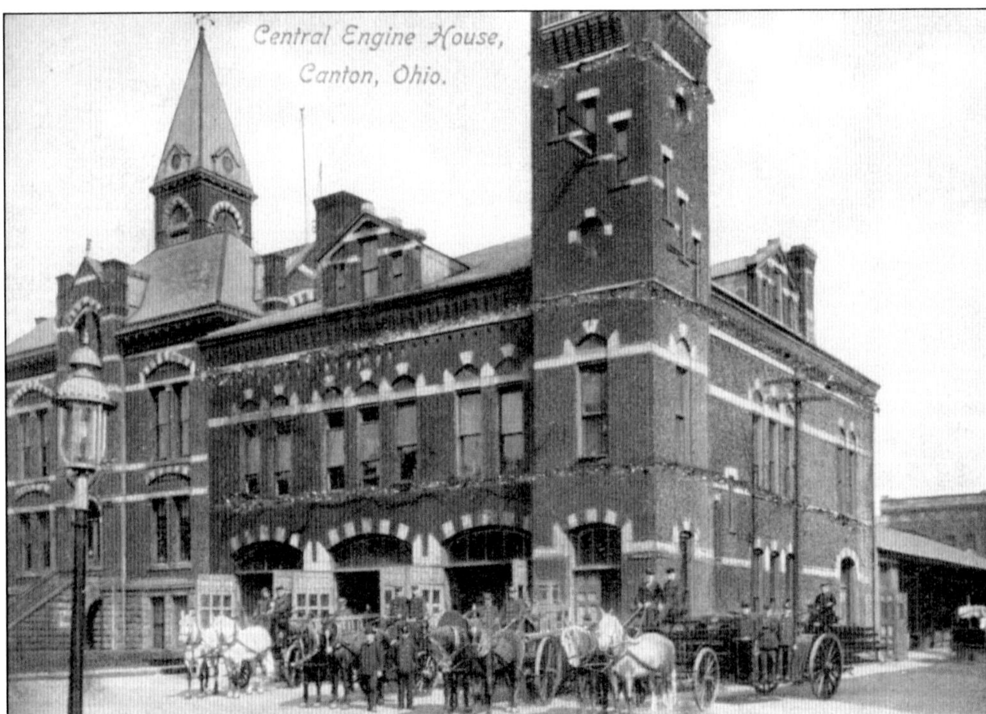

Built on a Cleveland Avenue site next to Canton City Hall, the Canton Central Fire House featured a loud bell in the tower that alerted the horses. The alarm tripped the stall gates, and the horses trotted out to stand in front of their designated apparatus.

Constructed in 1894, utilizing the varied brick and stone materials that gave High Victorian–style public buildings their characteristic appearance, the Canton Post Office was located on Cleveland Avenue on the site of the current Frank T. Bow Federal Building. At the time of construction, Canton had 21 postal carriers, 15 postal clerks, and a special delivery messenger.

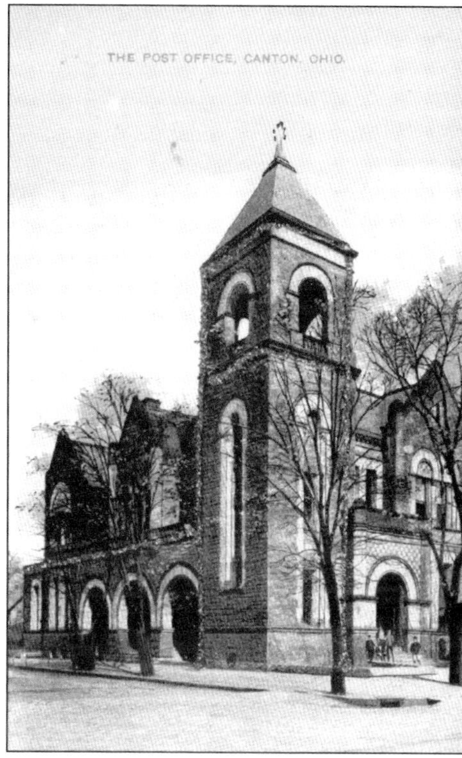

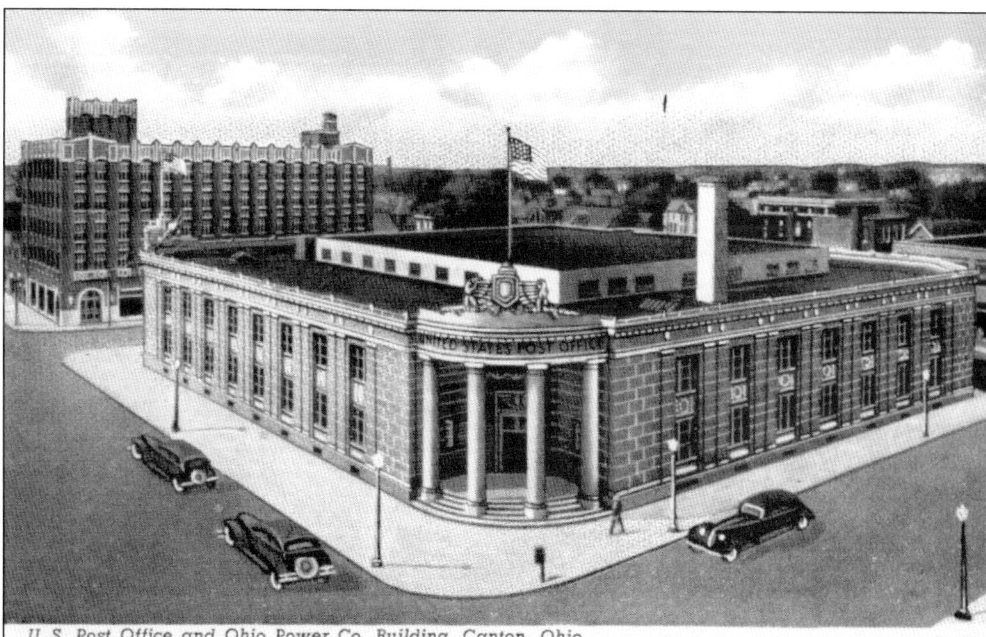

By the late 1920s, the 1894 Canton Post Office was no longer adequate. However, the stock market crash and the start of the Great Depression delayed construction until 1932. Designed by Canton architect Charles Firestone, the building lobby features murals by Glenn Shaw depicting the steel industry. The building was named for longtime congressman Frank T. Bow.

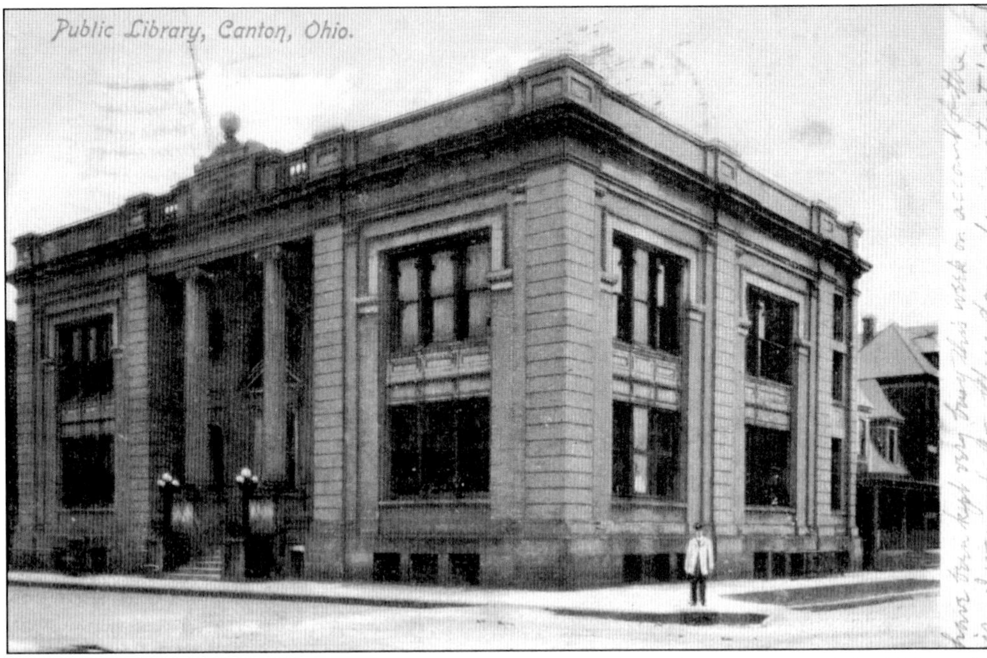

Designed by Canton architect Guy Tilden, the Canton Public Library was built in 1903 as the result of a $60,000 gift from Andrew Carnegie. The motto "Open To All" is in the multilighted window over the entry door. Located on Third Street, the building was used as a library until 1980. It currently houses the Timken Foundation.

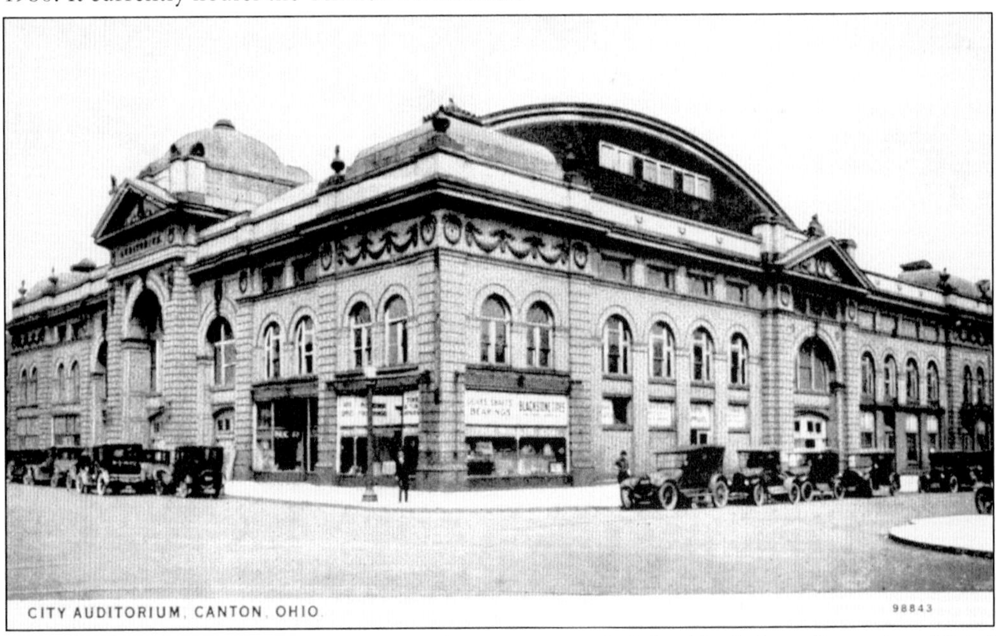

Dedicated in 1903, the Canton City Auditorium occupied the block from Second to Third Streets on Cleveland Avenue. Built at a cost of $180,000, it was the scene of many cultural and civic events, including performances by Enrico Caruso and Jasha Heifetz. Seven-day bicycle races and revival services led by Aimee McPherson were among other events held there. It was closed in 1938 and was demolished in 1956.

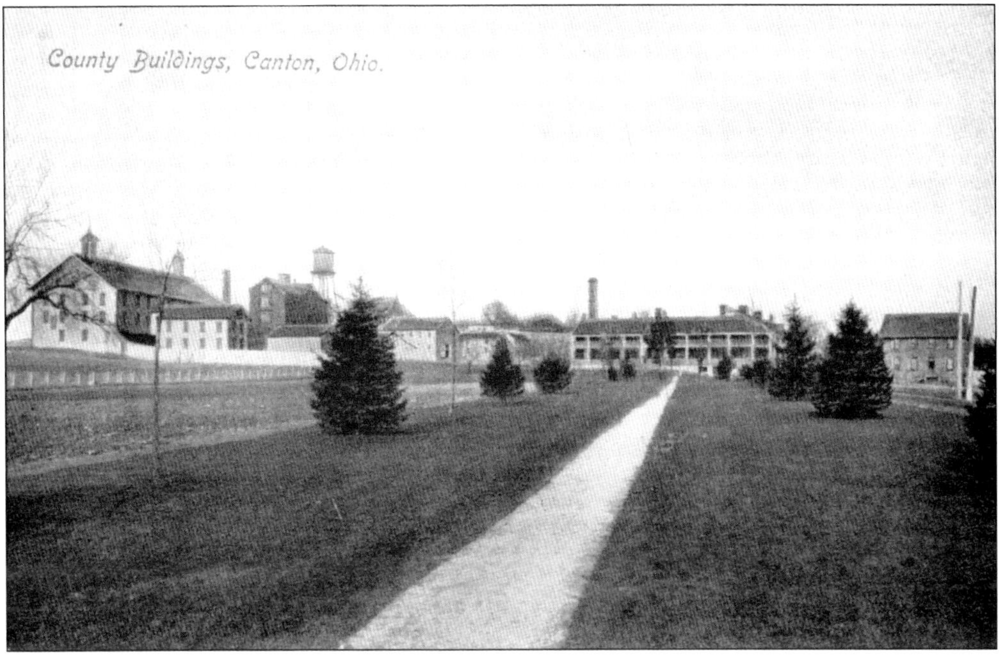

This card is an early view of the Stark County Home. The land for the county home was purchased in 1833. At its peak the property was bounded by Cleveland Avenue, Thirtieth Street, Market Avenue, and Twenty-fifth Street. Over the years, it was used as a home for orphans, the mentally ill, the poor, stranded immigrant workers, the disabled, and the elderly. The home was primarily a farm worked by the residents.

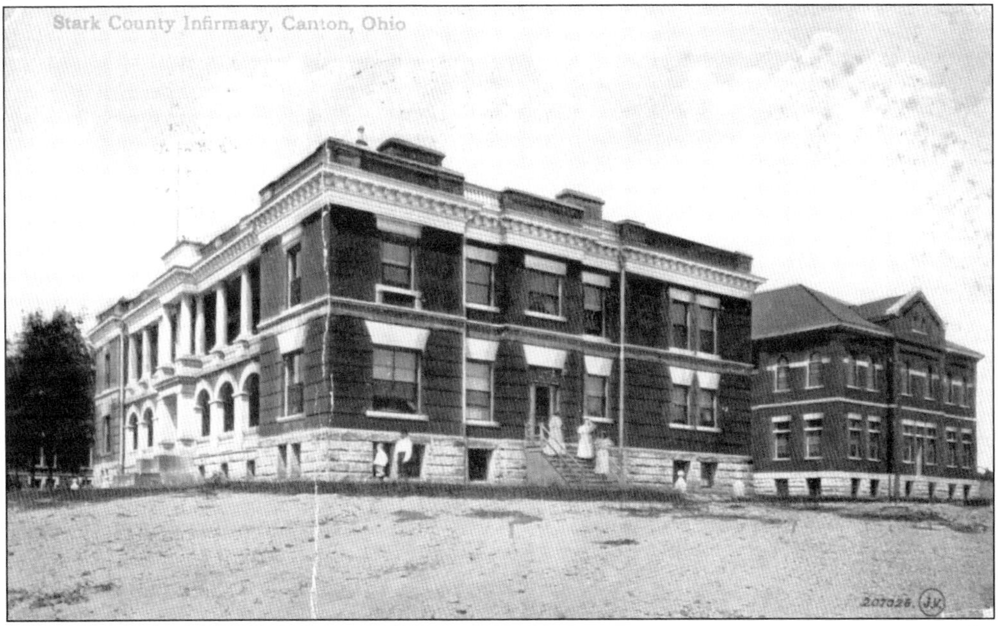

In 1860, the Stark County Home was renamed the Stark County Infirmary. In the 1870s, the facility was greatly improved and several new buildings were added closer to Cleveland Avenue, including this one pictured in 1921. Much of the property is now occupied by Malone College, the First Christian Church, and the Canton Christian Home.

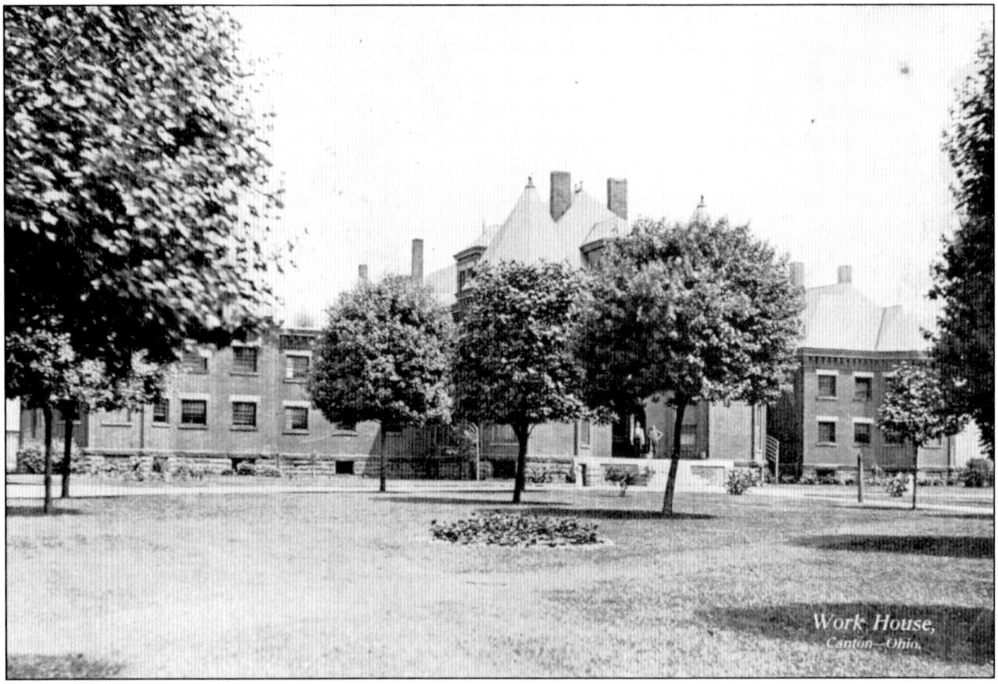

This 1907 card shows the Stark County Work House. Built in 1890, during the height of Canton's industrial and civic growth, the Stark County Water and Animal Control Departments now occupy the Mahoning Road site.

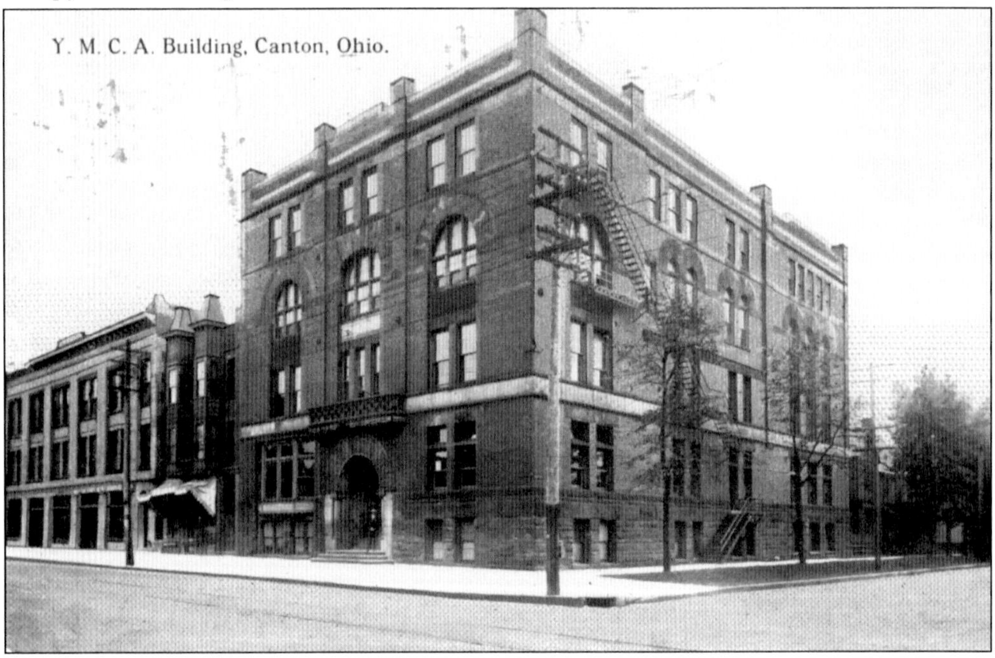

Constructed in 1886 on the Second Street site of the current Central YMCA, the "Y" offered youth and adult organized sports. Basketball teams were formed just a few months after the game's invention. Volleyball and handball were popular, and in 1899, the first indoor pool in the county opened there. The organization also offered evening vocational and business classes.

When the new YMCA opened in 1915, it was the second-tallest building in Canton. In addition to organized physical activities and swimming, the "Y" offered Bible studies, Sunday school, vocational training, community education, and a music lecture series, as well as English and "Americanization" classes to new immigrants. It was also a residence for young workingmen.

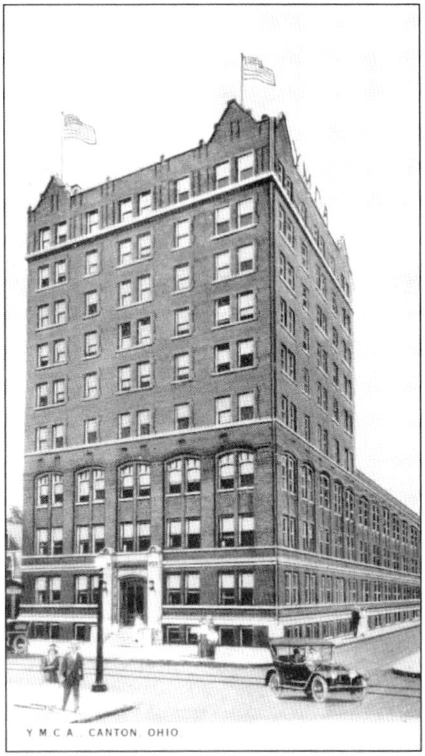

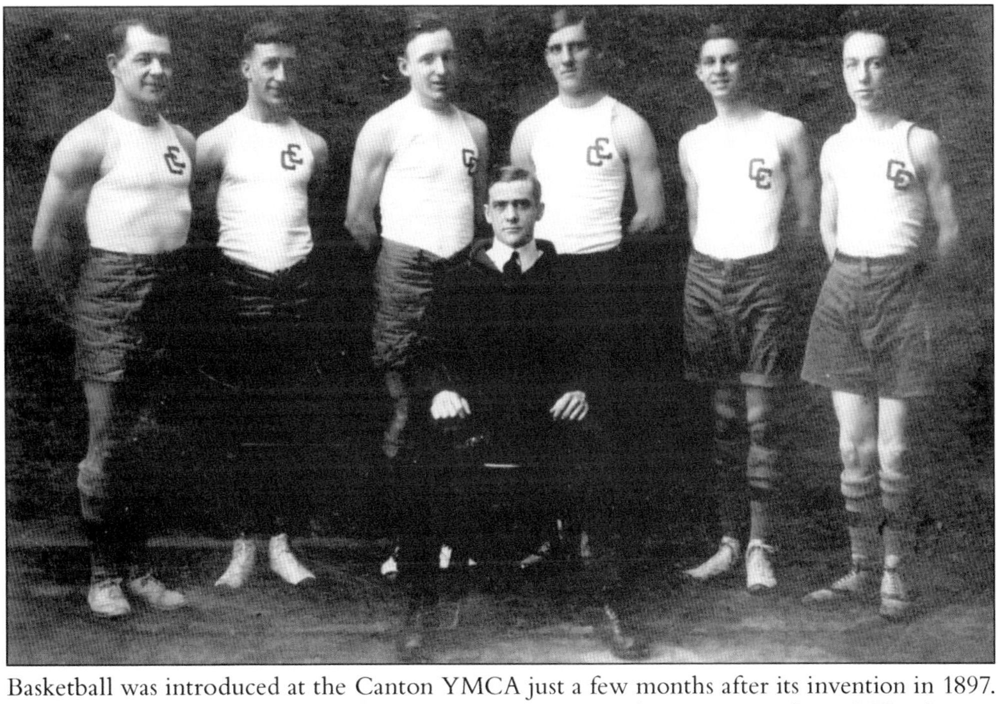

Basketball was introduced at the Canton YMCA just a few months after its invention in 1897. The sport was immediately popular, and many young men's teams were formed like the one pictured here in 1914. Boys' teams were formed soon after, somewhat of a rarity for that time. By 1900, girls were also included.

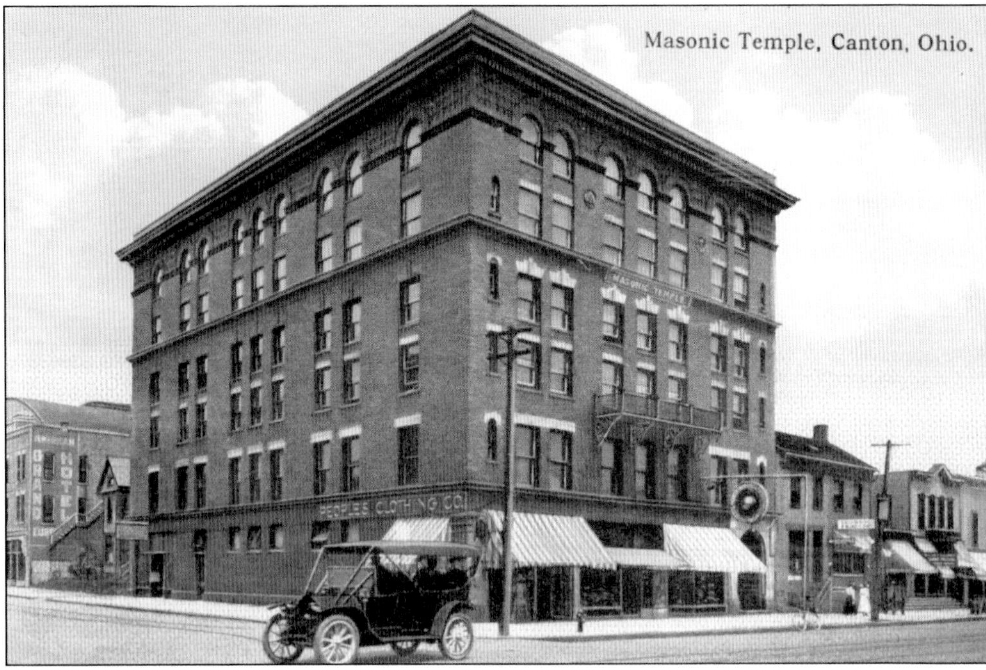

This 1915 card shows the Masonic temple and People's Clothing Company on North Market Avenue. Owned by M. F. Taylor and sons, the store was described in a 1907 city publication as having "elegant show windows and excellent light . . . with an almost endless variety of goods." Taylor was described as one of Canton's "most prominent merchants and financiers. He is highly esteemed in social circles and secretary of the Masonic Association."

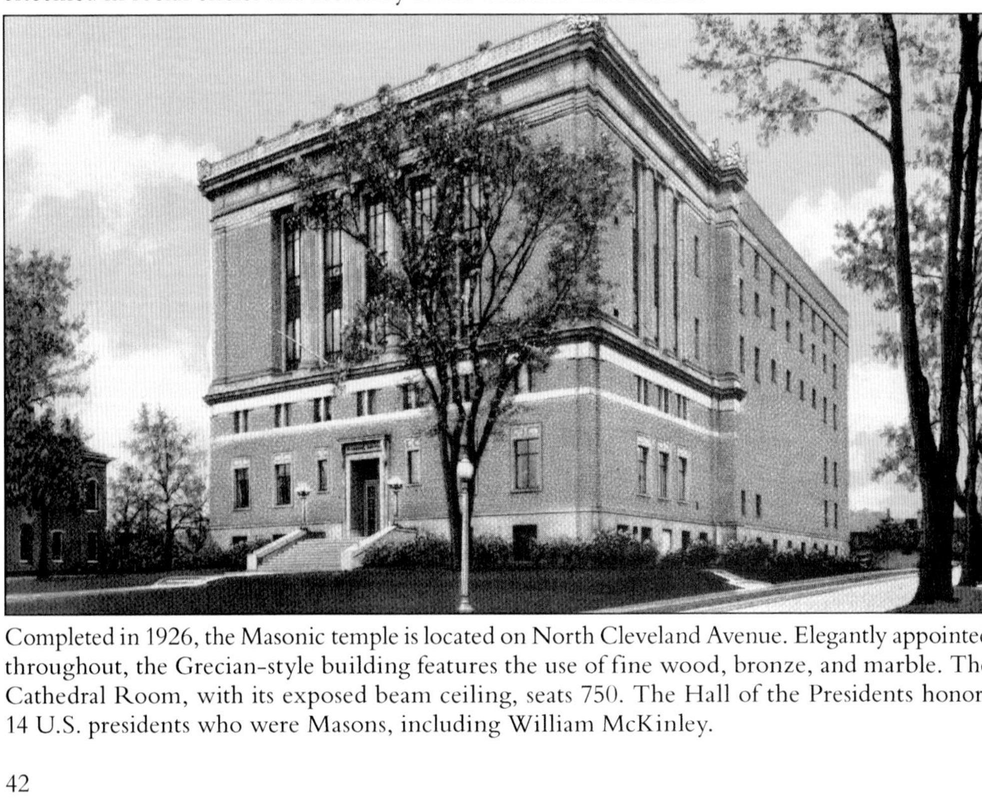

Completed in 1926, the Masonic temple is located on North Cleveland Avenue. Elegantly appointed throughout, the Grecian-style building features the use of fine wood, bronze, and marble. The Cathedral Room, with its exposed beam ceiling, seats 750. The Hall of the Presidents honors 14 U.S. presidents who were Masons, including William McKinley.

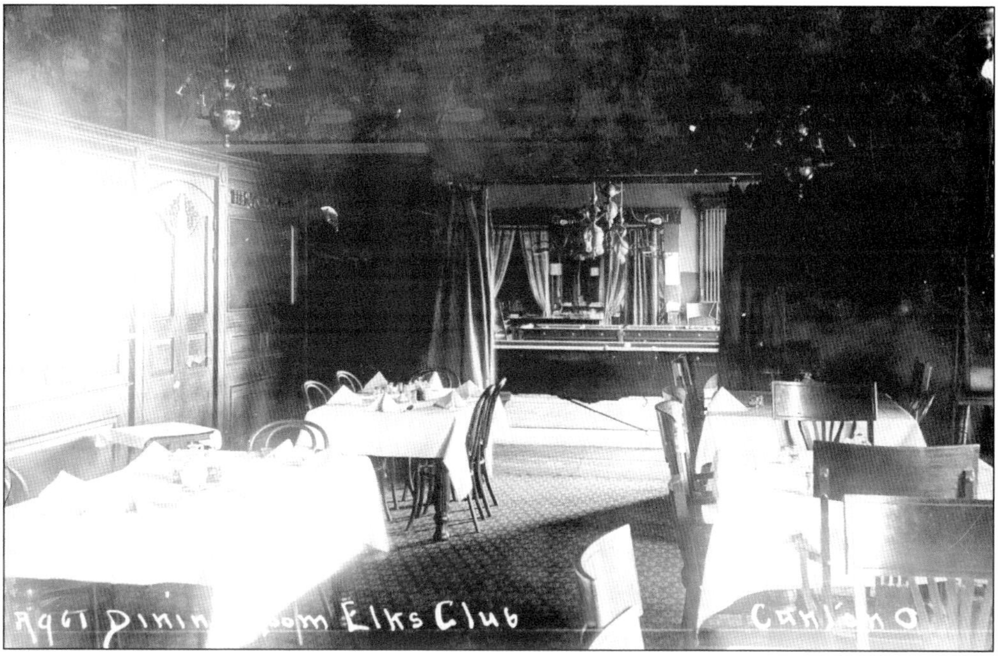

The Canton Lodge of the Benevolent and Protective Order of Elks was organized in 1887. The organization attracted business and professional men, as well as office workers and managers. The organization was known for its charitable work with veterans, support of the Salvation Army, and its clinic for those with cerebral palsy. The chapter was also well known for its excellent dining room.

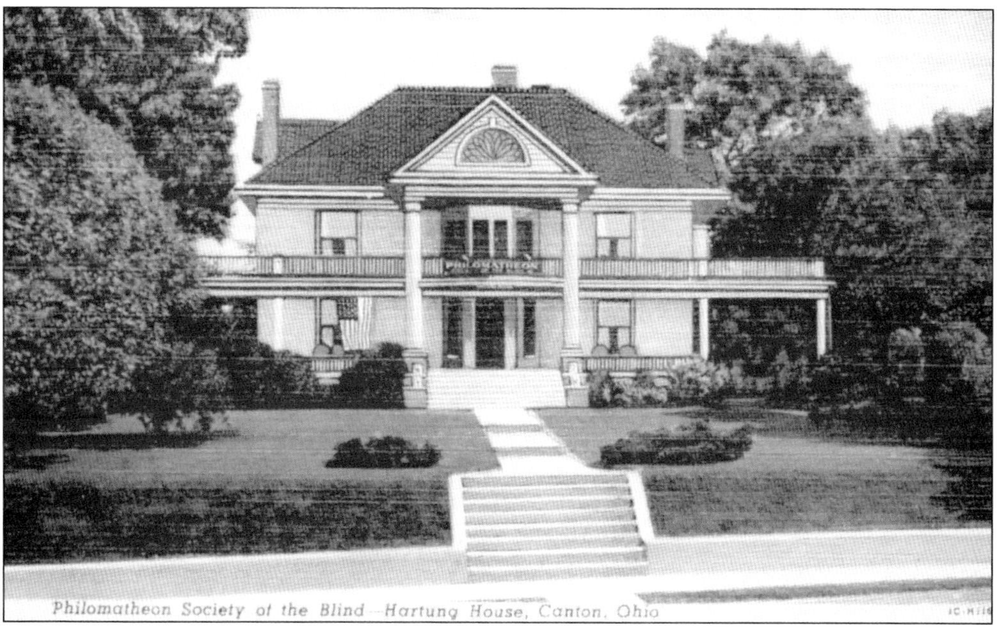

Built in 1909 for businessman Lewis Hartung, this home was one of the mansions that used to line West Tuscarawas Street. The house became the Philomatheon Home in 1951. It "was owned and operated by the blind for the blind." In April 2001, the 270-ton, 4,200-square-foot house was moved to Wertz Avenue. It is now the home of the Canton Preservation Society.

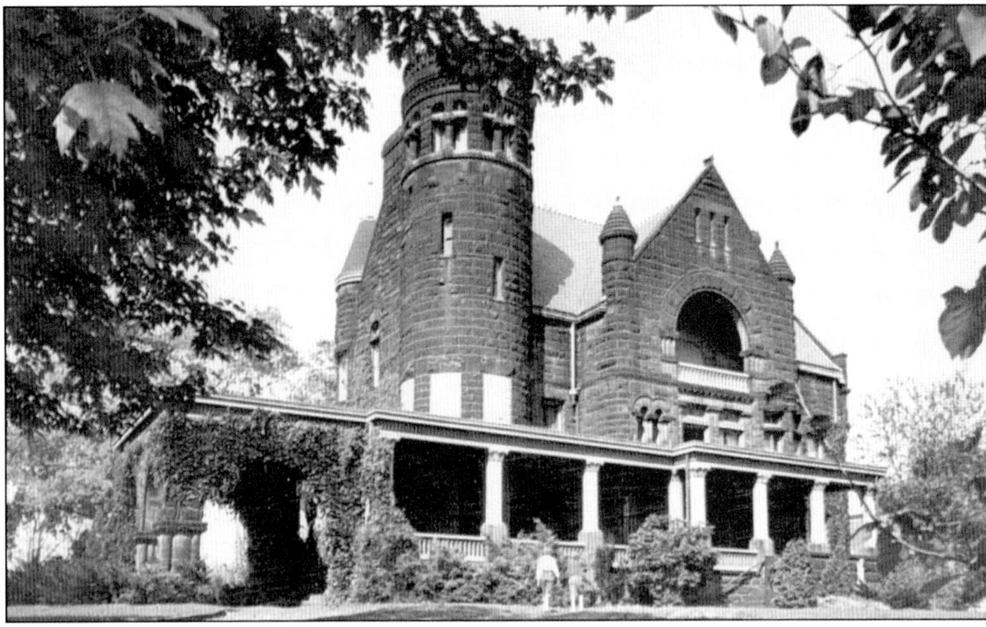

Frank Case, owner of the Harvard Dental Company, hired Guy Tilden to design his Richardson Romanesque mansion on North Market Avenue. Built between 1898 and 1902, the home featured gas and electric lights, water and natural gas heat, and an elevator. A subsequent owner, F. W. Pryor, donated the home to the Canton Art Institute in 1940. It served the institute until 1970 and was demolished in 1990.

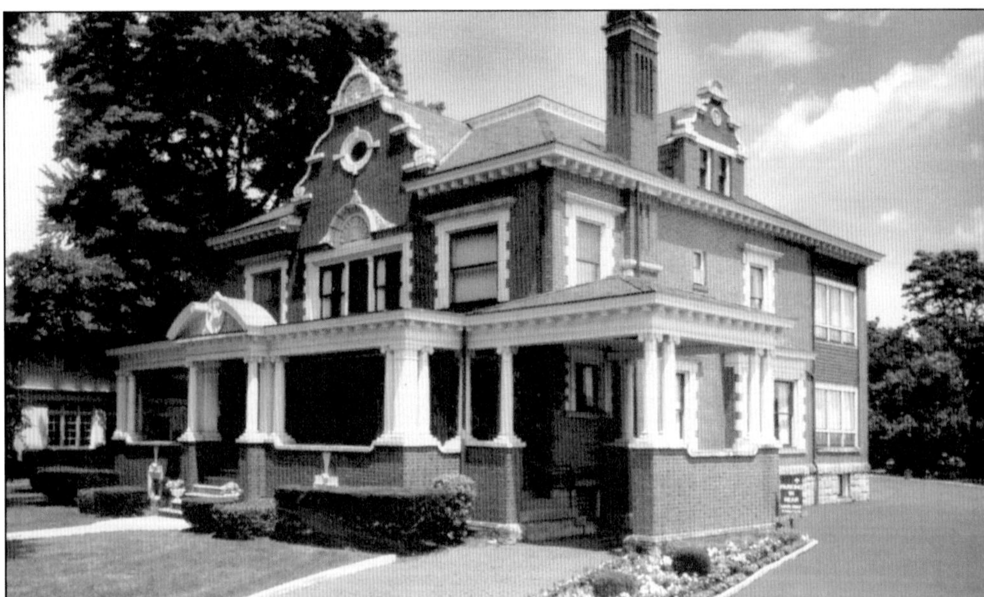

Built on North Market Avenue by Harry Renkert in 1908, the exterior of the home and driveway are constructed entirely of brick and tile from his Metropolitan Paving Brick Company. Renkert wished to demonstrate the value and durability of his products for uses other than paving. The exterior of the home is unchanged since its construction and has housed the Greater Canton Amateur Sports Hall of Fame since 1979.

Four

Business and Industry

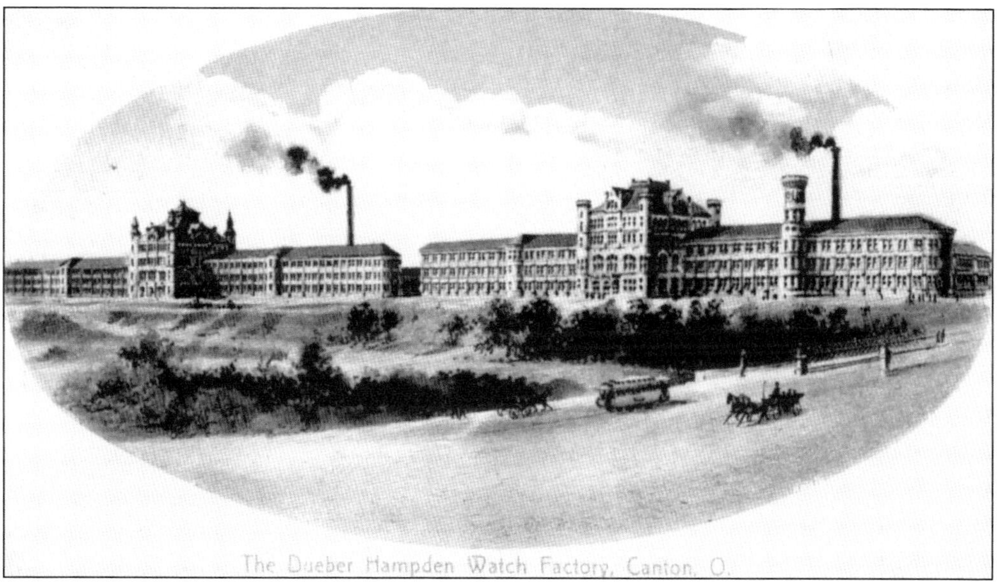

In 1886, John Dueber announced that the first city to raise $100,000 would be the location of his new Dueber-Hampden Watch Factory. A number of Canton businessmen, including opera house owner Louis Schaefer and the Meyers family who donated the land, were instrumental in bringing the company to Canton. Completed in 1888, the company eventually employed 3,000 workers, effectively doubling Canton's population.

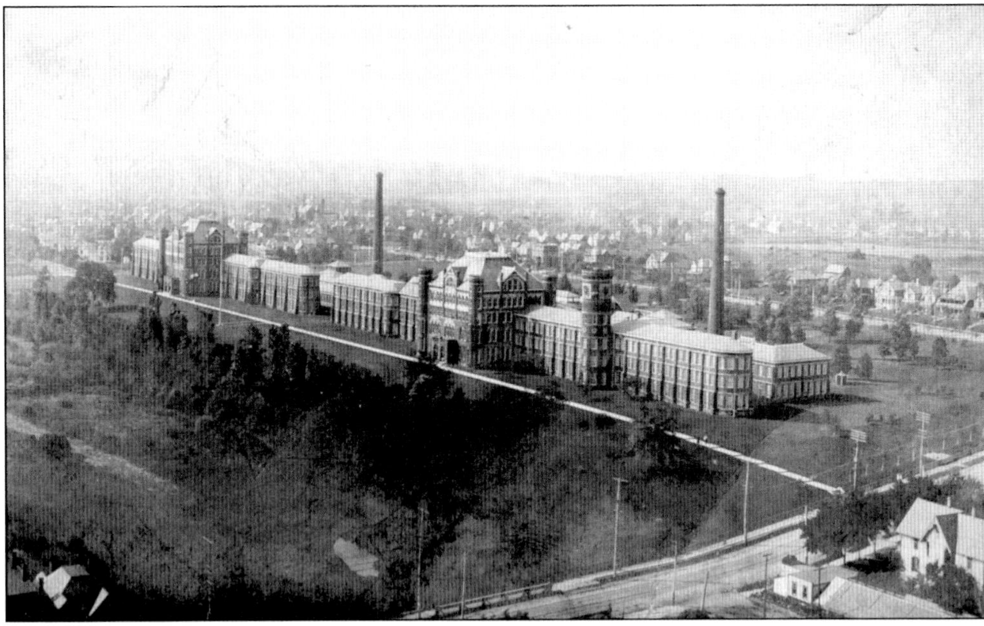

This pre-1907 photograph shows the Dueber-Hampden factory bordered by West Tuscarawas Street and the current site of Interstate 77. The factory occupied two 1,100-foot-long buildings. Known for elaborately engraved watches, Dueber had the floor and workers' clothing cleaned daily for gold shavings for resmelting. In 1930, the watch works, including all the machinery and equipment, was sold to the Soviet Union.

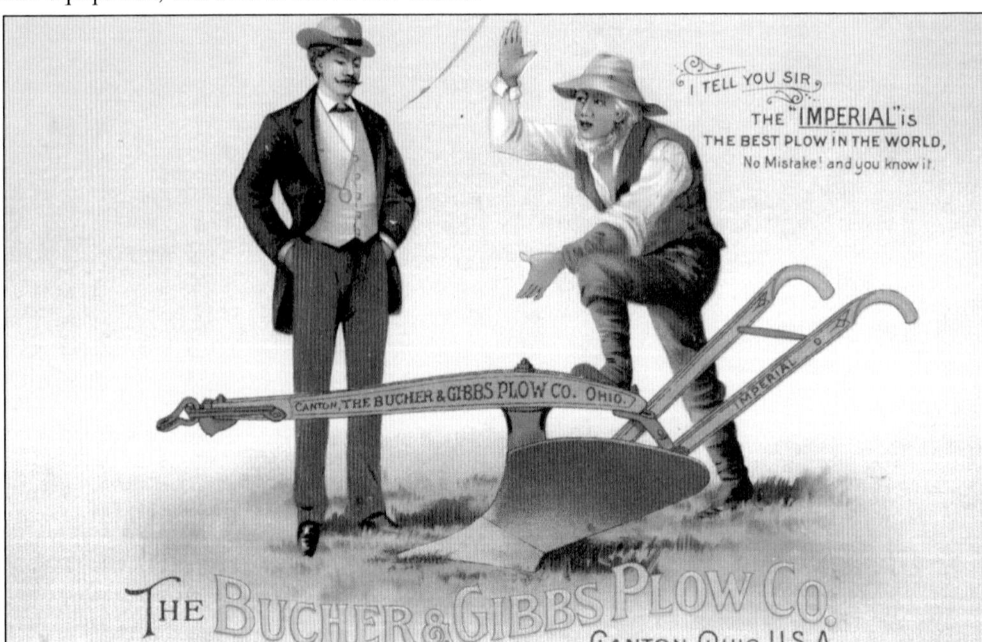

Stark and the surrounding counties are known for their rich soil. Indeed, early Canton was built to support agriculture. Joshua Gibbs, a barrel maker and blacksmith, came to Canton in 1824. In 1836, he invented the Imperial Plow. His business grew rapidly, and although he held patents on other farm equipment, the plow was the mainstay of his company.

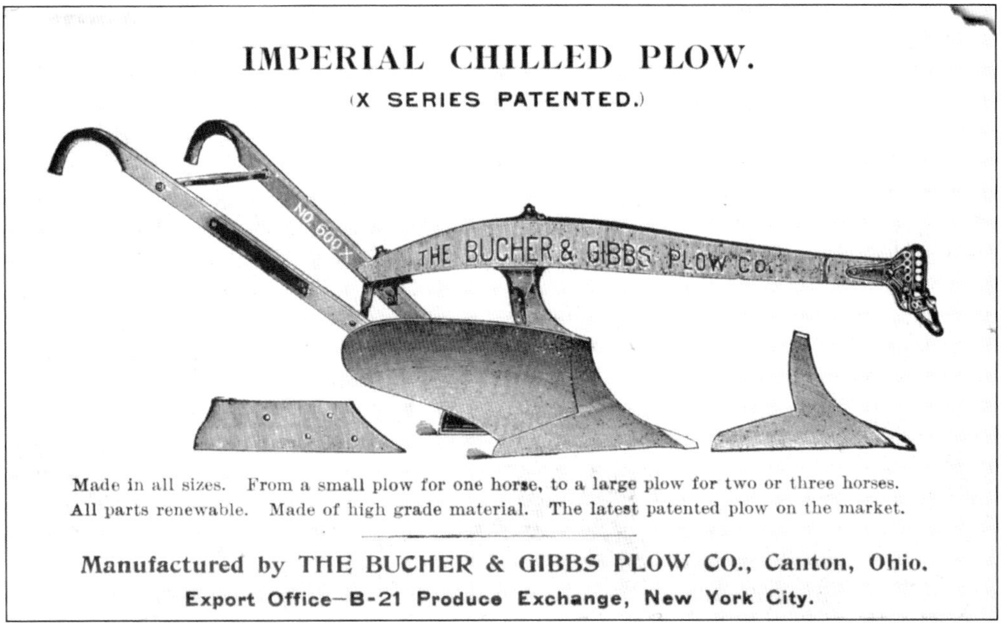

In 1870, Joshua Gibbs's son, Lewis, formed a partnership with John Bucher, founding the Bucher and Gibbs Plow Company. They shipped their products to both domestic and foreign markets. Another Canton manufacturing pioneer, Cornelius Aultman also made his fortune manufacturing farm equipment. In 1860, C. Aultman and Company was the world's largest manufacturer of reapers and mowers.

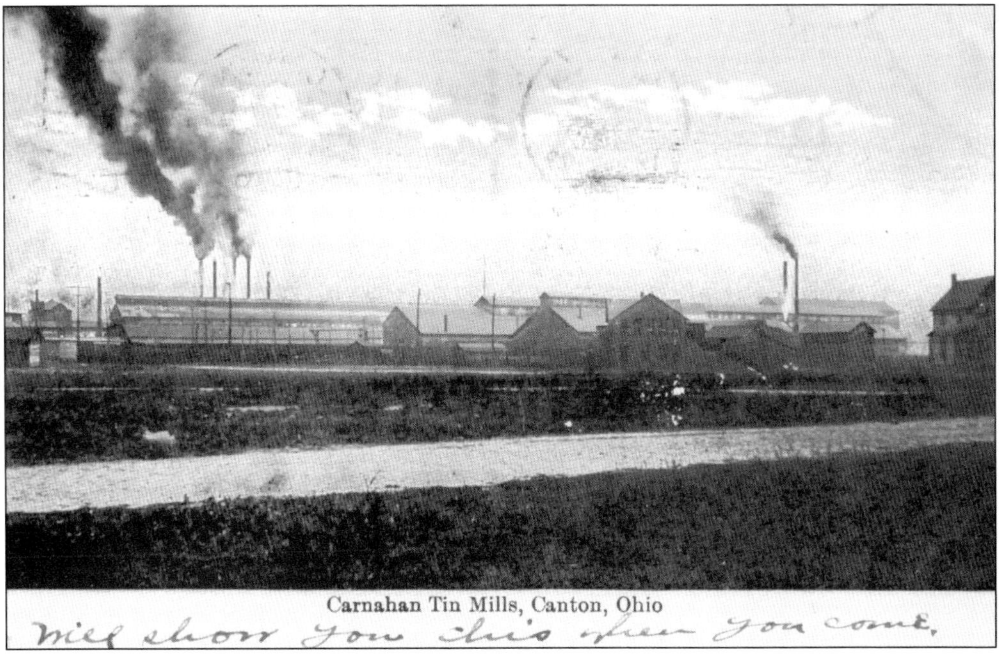

John E. Carnahan came to Canton in 1897. Given six acres by Daniel Hoover on Fifteenth and Henry Avenue, by 1903 he established the Carnahan Tin Plate Mill, Carnahan Stamping and Enameling, and United Steel Company. The mill and United Steel became the Republic Steel Corporation. Carnahan also helped found Hercules Motor Corporation.

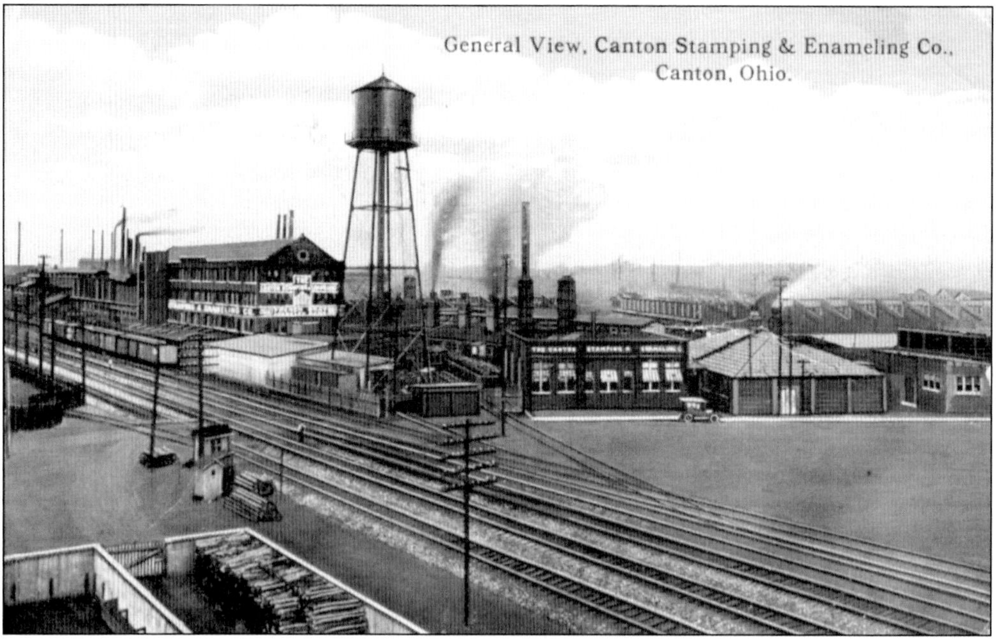

Canton Stamping and Enameling was founded in 1907. Originally Carnahan Stamping and Enameling, the company manufactured enameled tin called graniteware. By the 1920s, Canton was the largest producer of enameled ware in the United States, with several Canton companies accounting for 20 percent of the total production.

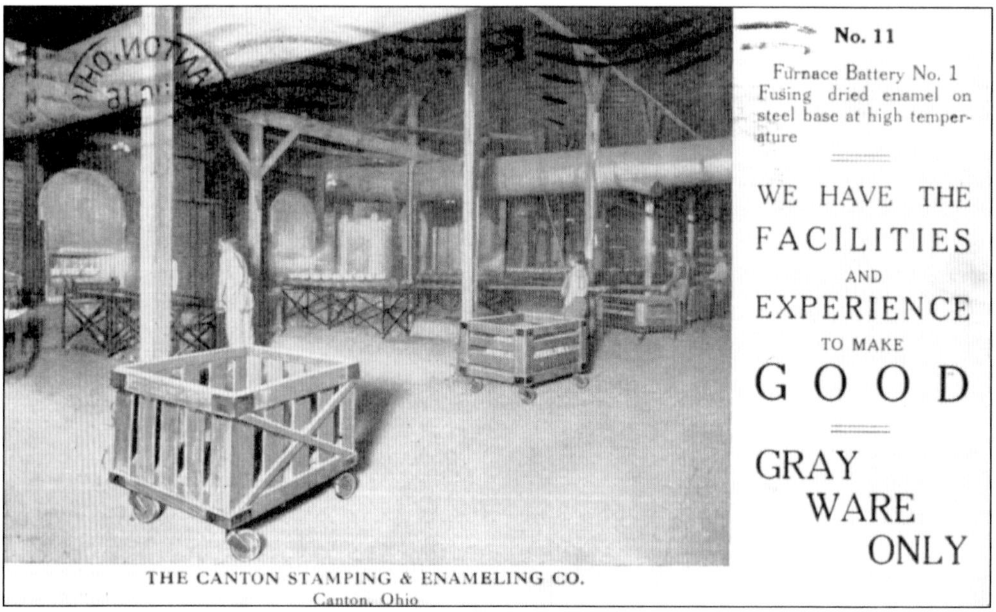

In the 1930s, Canton Stamping and Enameling was the world's largest producer of gray enameled ware, manufacturing over 100,000 pieces per day. The company made several hundred items, the most popular of which were dishpans, cooking pans, mixing bowls, teakettles, coffeepots and percolators, washbasins, and commodes.

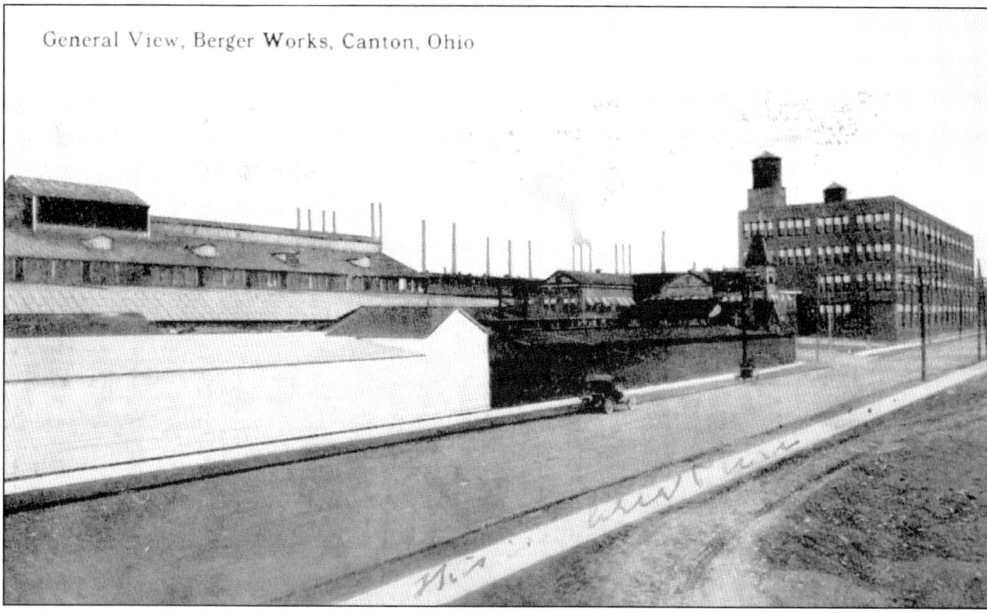

John and Wilson Berger, Edward Langenbach, and Herman Klorer formed the Berger Manufacturing Company in 1886. By 1893, the company employed 125 people and was Canton's largest tin fabricating firm with sales offices across the United States. By 1901, the company was making 61 different products and had capital of over $5 million. The firm continues to operate as Republic Storage Systems from its 1900 Belden Avenue site.

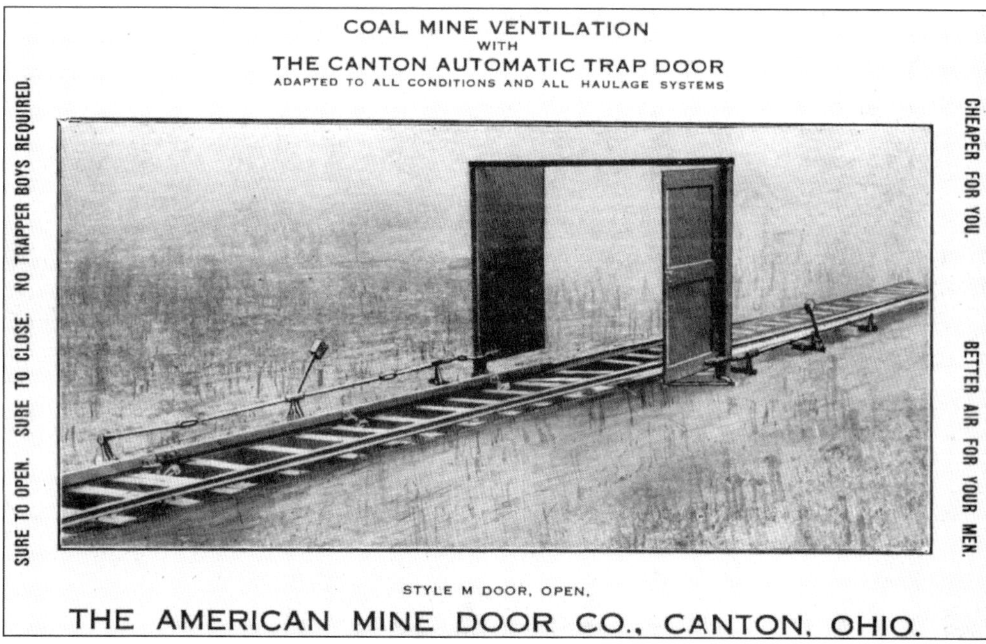

Newton Bowman incorporated the American Mine Door Company in 1905, manufacturing automatic mine doors that replaced makeshift doors used in coal mines. Eventually the company's products, known for their safety, economy, and elimination of child labor, were used by 80 of the largest coal operators in the world. By his death in 1934, Bowman held 125 patents, almost all of which dealt with mining applications.

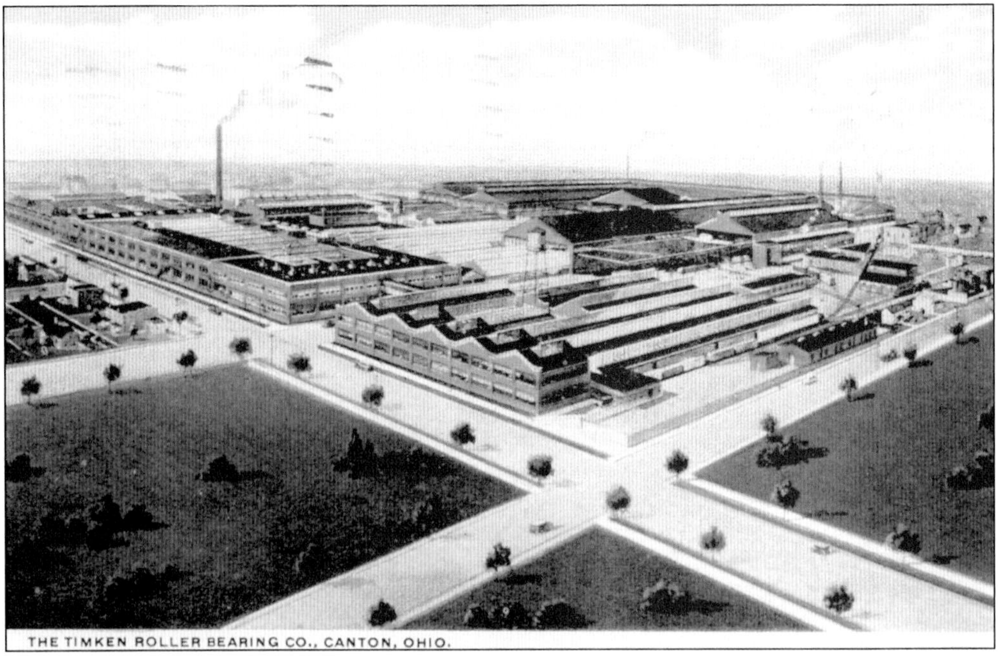

In 1901, Henry Timken and his sons, Henry H. and William, moved their successful roller bearing manufacturing firm from St. Louis to Canton. Their first plant, located on Dueber Avenue, employed approximately 40 people making bearings and axels for carriages, wagons, and the emerging automobile industry. By 1901, the Timken Roller Bearing Company employed 1,200 workers. This early-1920s picture shows the company after it began making steel.

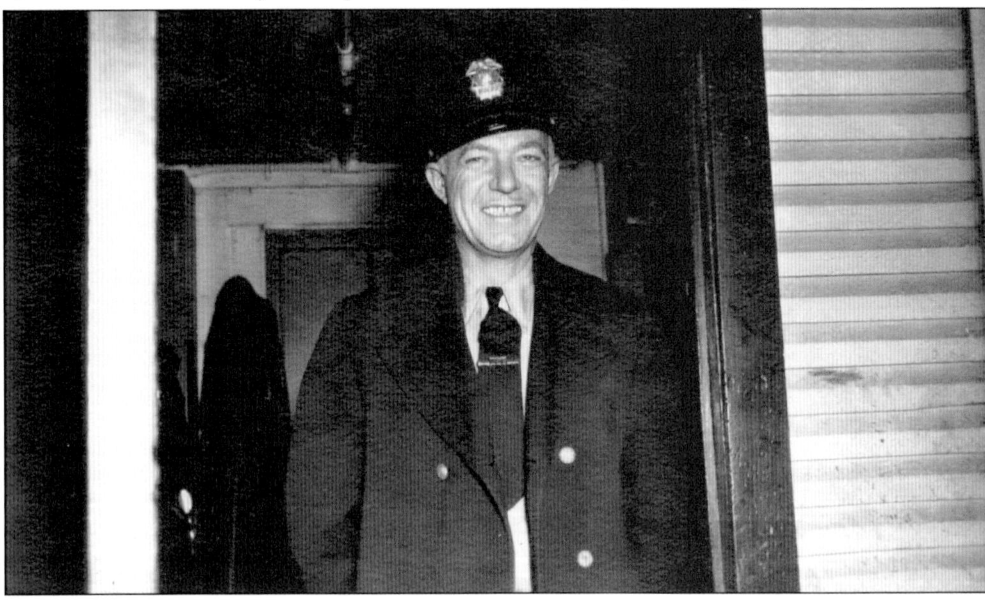

The reverse of the next three cards showing three unidentified Timken employees state, "Working For Victory at Timken." According to Kimberly Kenney in *Canton: A Journey Through Time*, during World War II, Timken employed 18,000 people, up from 8,000 before the war. Working 48 hours a week, Timken workers produced submarine deck guns, railroad cars, and aircraft propeller blades.

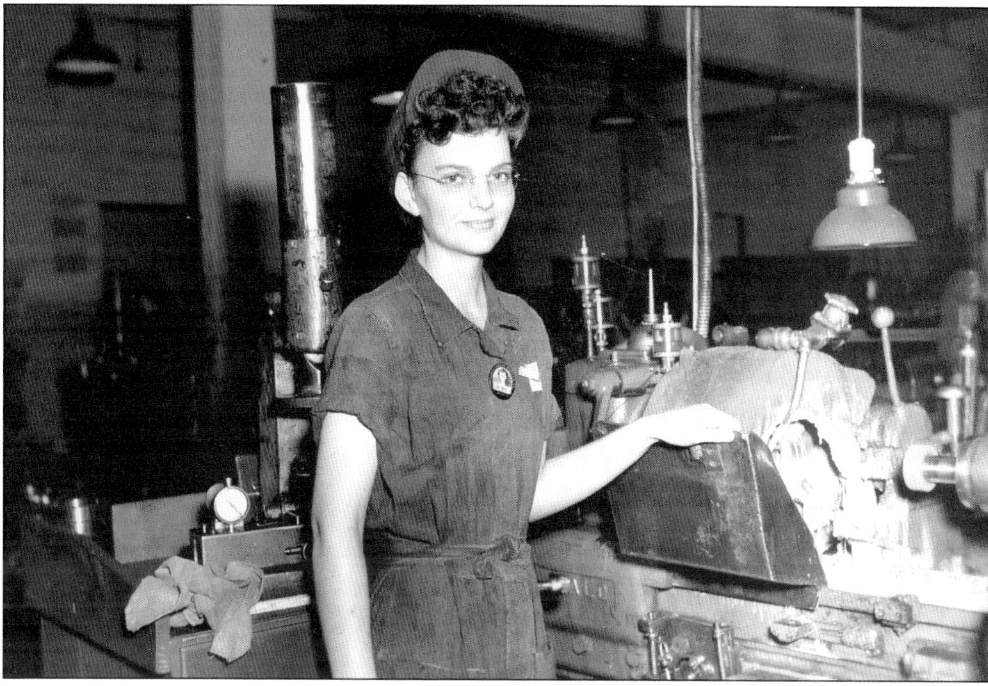

As men were called into military service, women entered the manufacturing workforce. At the height of wartime production, Canton's major manufacturers employed 15,082 women. Half of the Timken engineering staff was female by the end of the war. Timken Vocational High School students made ball bearings in a glass-enclosed facility across from the school. Eighteen blind persons were also employed in Timken offices.

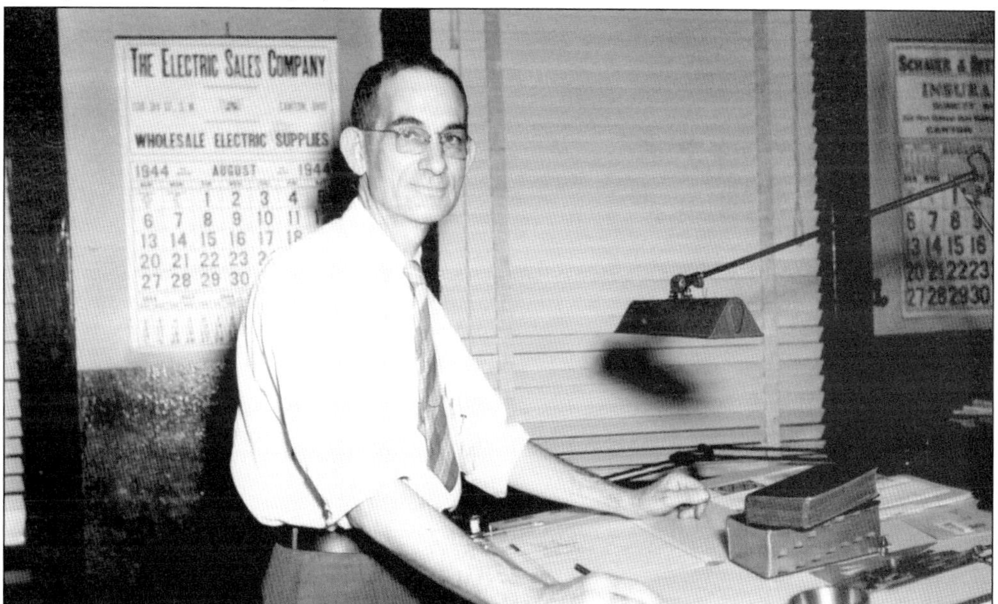

Timken bearings and steel tubing could be found in nearly every piece of military hardware. The company's wartime production included an innovative seamless tubing gun barrel that could fire 7,000 rounds without showing any signs of wear.

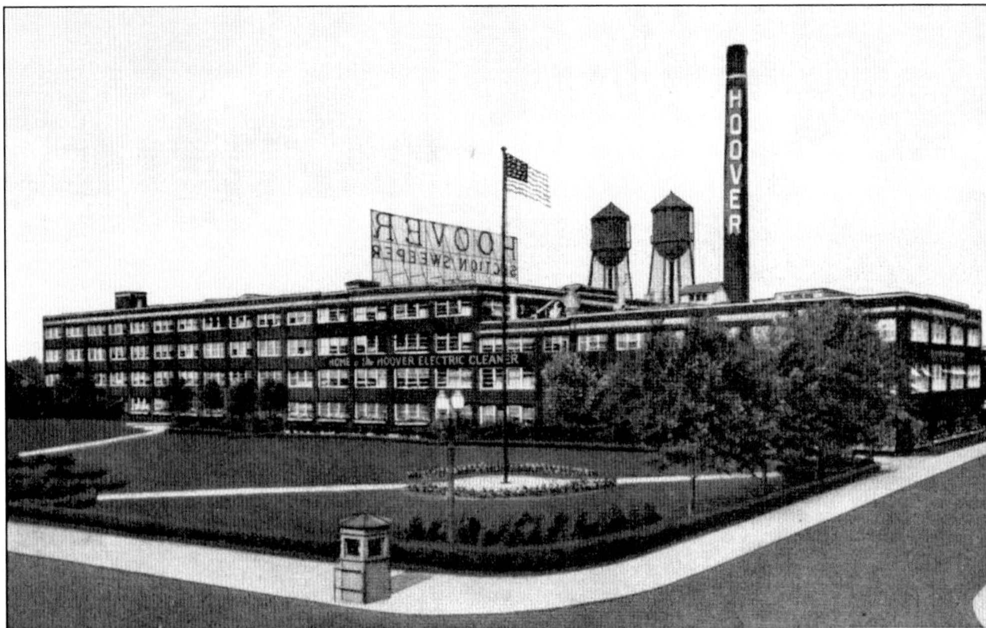

Home of the Hoover Electric Sweeper, North Canton, Ohio

In 1908, William Hoover, who had begun his career in the leather business, bought his wife's first cousin's patent for the upright vacuum cleaner. As president of the Electric Suction Sweeper Company in New Berlin (North Canton), he made many improvements to the design. By 1922, the company was renamed the Hoover Company and occupied this building on the North Canton square.

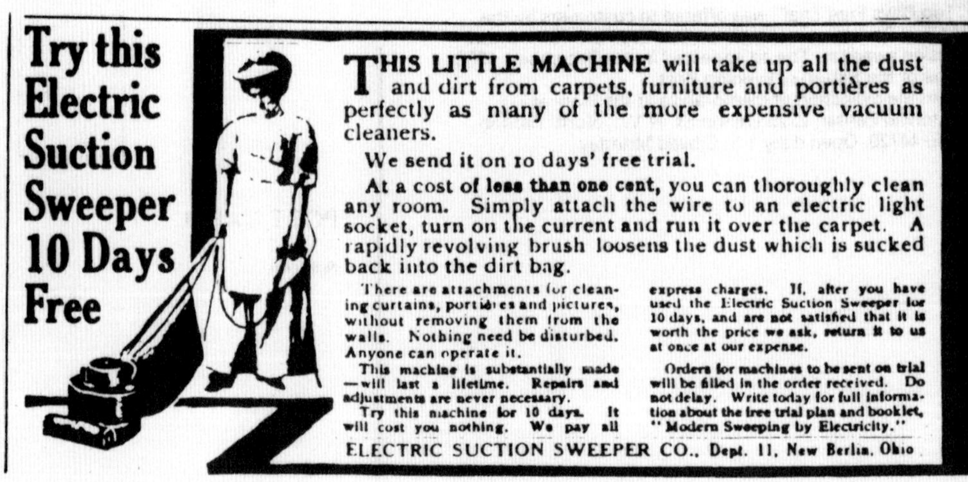

THE FIRST HOOVER COMPANY SUCTION SWEEPER AD

Product innovations and creative marketing eventually made Hoover Company the largest vacuum cleaner manufacturing company in the world. In 1911, the company opened a factory in Canada and another in England in 1919, where the cleaner quickly dominated the market. Many people in England still refer to vacuuming as "Hoovering."

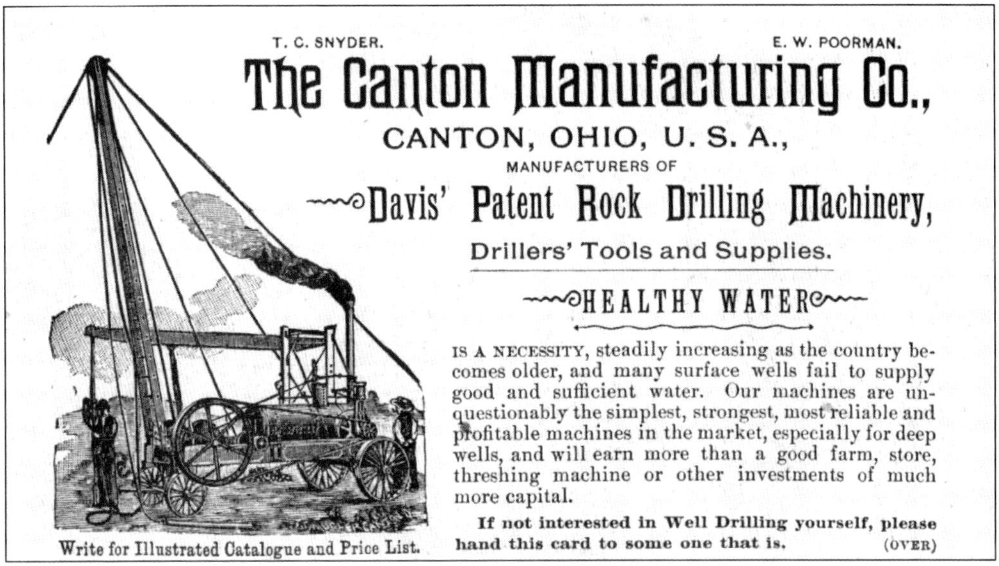

The Canton Manufacturing Company was one of the industries in Canton making heavy equipment for manufacturing and residential use. By World War I, Canton factories were making over 1,000 products.

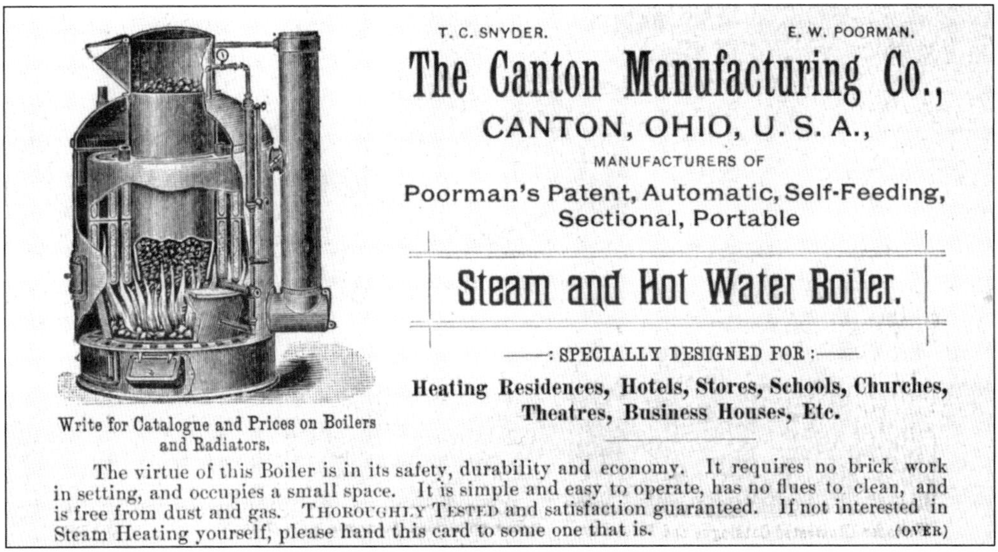

This advertising card for the Canton Manufacturing Company encourages enterprising businessmen to go into the water drilling business with their Davis Patent Rock Drilling Machinery. This machine "will earn more than a good farm, store, threshing machine or other investments of much more capital."

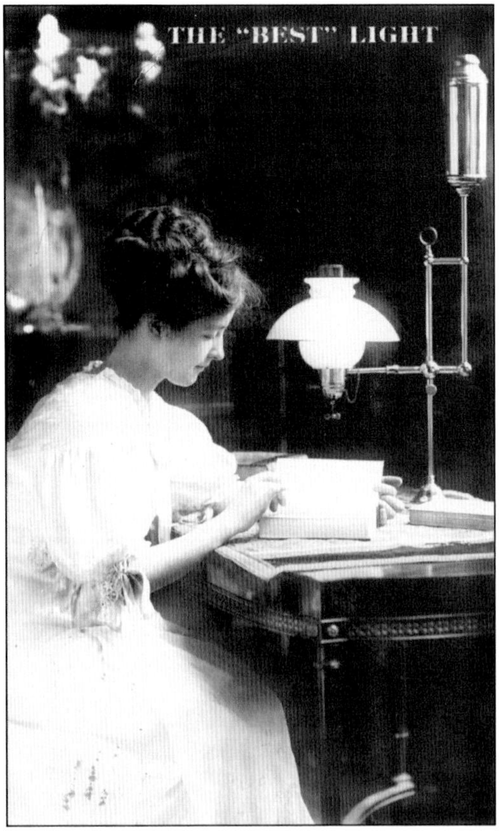

In 1911, the Best Light Company sent out this advertising card to the Baustians of Sunnyside Farm in Minden, Iowa. Founded in 1870 by Martin L. Best, the company made gasoline lamps for indoor and outdoor use. Employing over 100 workers in 1907, its products were sold in foreign and domestic outlets. The advertisement on the back claims that "the light is superior to electronic light."

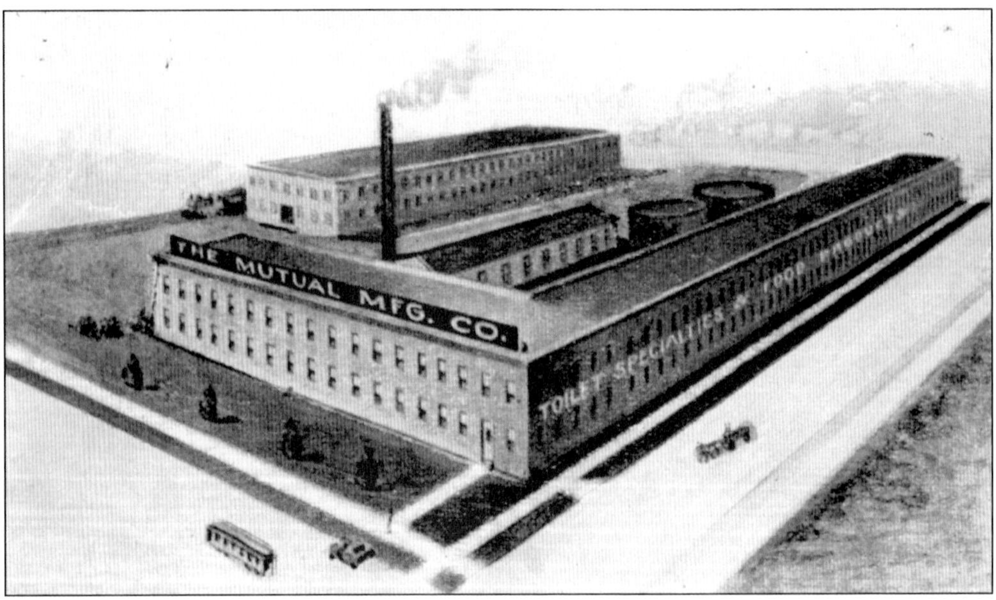

Although the date on the card is not legible, the Mutual Manufacturing Company sent it informing Elizabeth Dell in Greenville that the Mutual Wagon and salesman J. W. Davis would visit next week. The company sold remedies for "every emergency, guarding your health in your home," as well as "toilet specialties and food products."

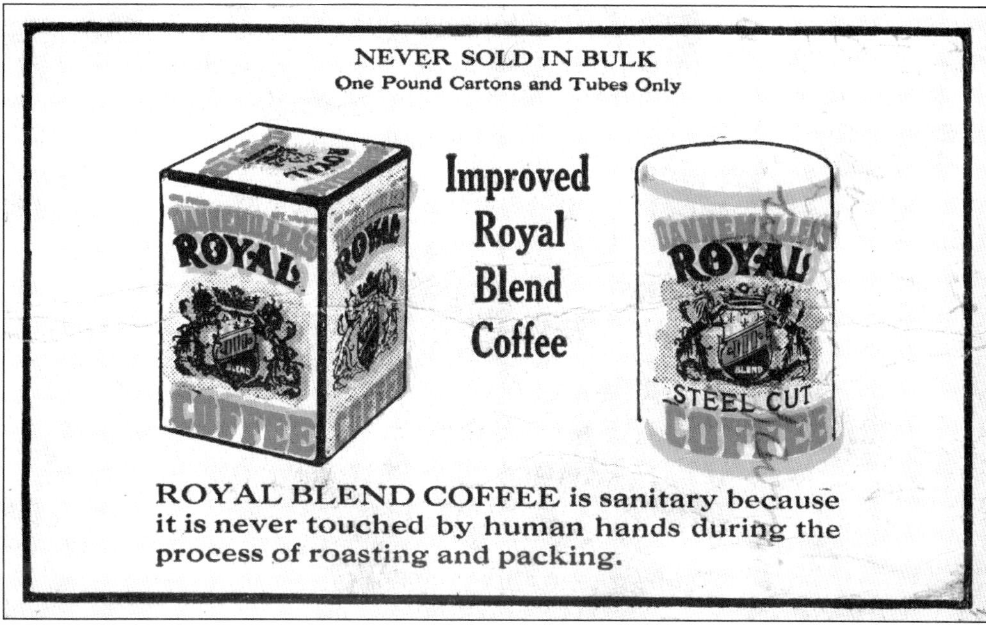

William Dannemiller entered the grocery business in 1869. Located on the corner of Cherry and Second Streets, railroad sidings on Second Street allowed products to move efficiently to and from the warehouse. As advertised by this 1922 calendar card, Dannemiller Royal Blend Coffee was roasted and packaged on-site. It was a popular brand in much of the Midwest and one of Dannemiller's important house brands.

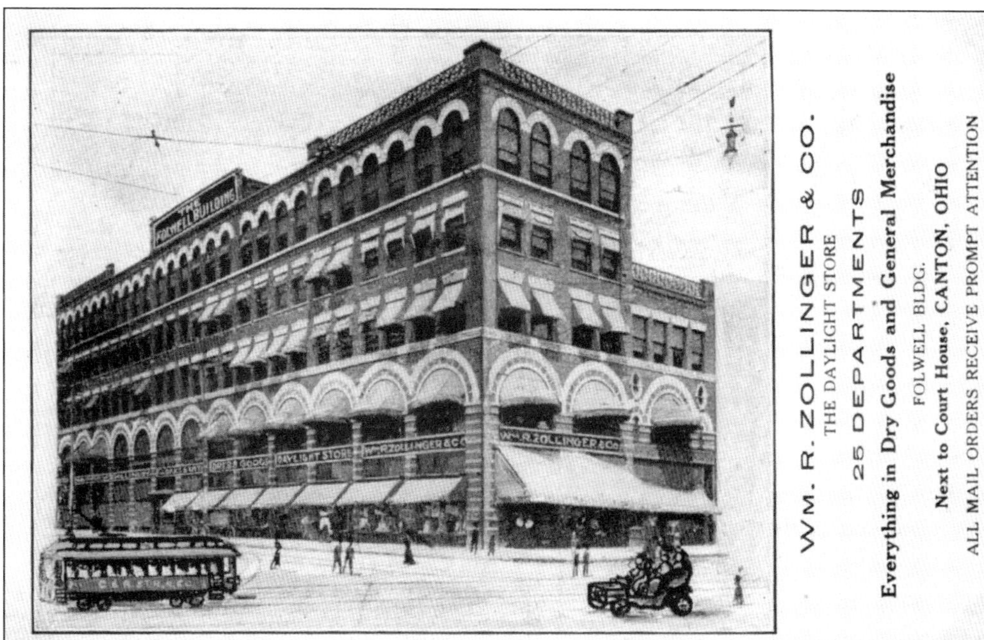

Located in the Folwell Building on North Market Avenue across from the courthouse, William R. Zollinger Company had many large windows and advertised as the Day Light Store. Zollinger's had "Everything in Dry Goods and General Merchandise" in "25 Departments." It also had a mail-order business.

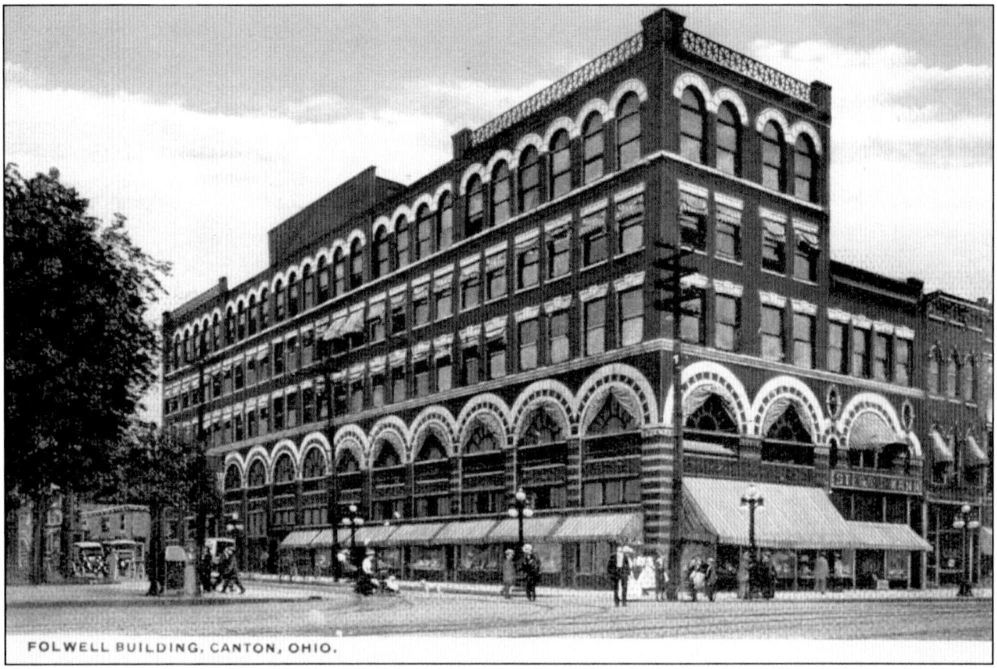

Brothers W. H. and N. T. Folwell partnered with William Zollinger and built the Folwell Building in 1900. With its distinctive arched windows and location north of the courthouse, the building figures prominently in many postcards of Canton's public square. J.C. Penny's occupied the building from 1934 until the early 1960s.

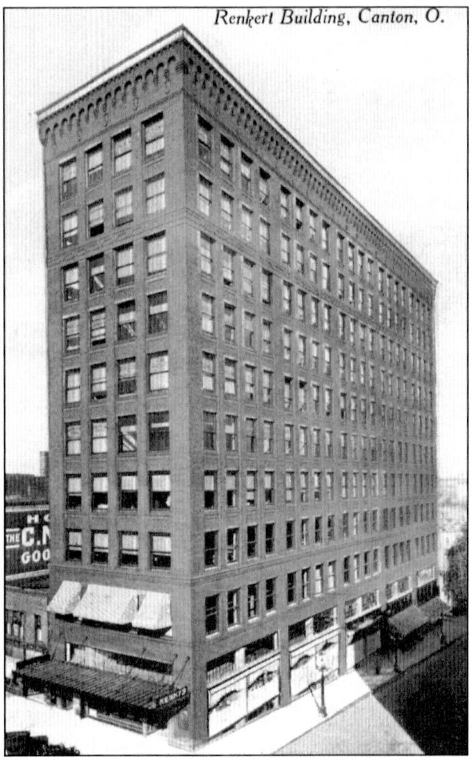

The 11-story Renkert Building on North Market Avenue was Canton's first skyscraper. Built by Harry Renkert in 1912, it is constructed entirely of paving bricks and tile from Renkert's Metropolitan Paving Brick Company. Headquartered in this building, by 1917 the company was the largest paving brick company in the world. Kenny's Department Store, known for elaborate Christmas display windows, occupied the lower four floors for many years.

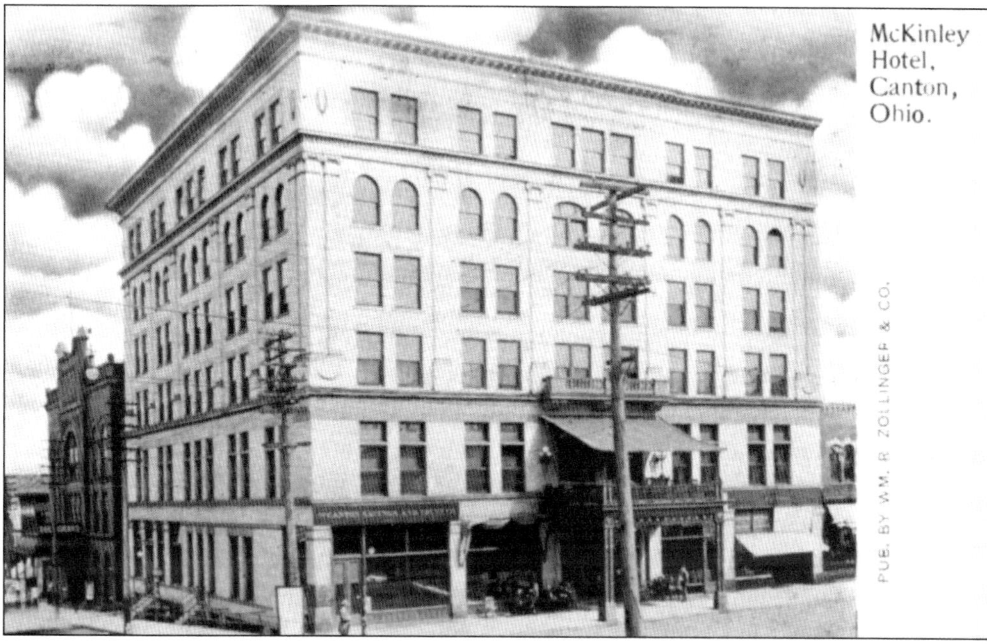

The Grand Opera House was located on Third Street next to the McKinley Hotel. Built in 1890 by Louis Schaefer, the Grand had a seating capacity of 1,300, the latest in electric lighting, steam heat, and luxurious appointments. The theater hosted many nationally known entertainers. *Ben Hur* was staged complete with horses, and Maude Adams played Peter Pan. The Ziegfeld Follies and John Phillips Souza also played the Grand.

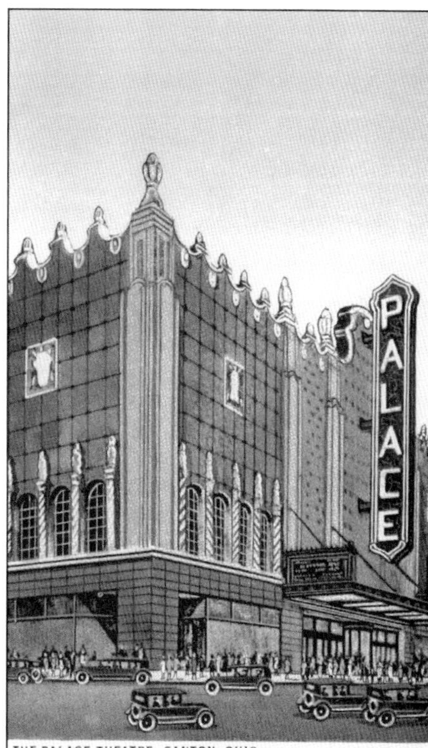

Opened in 1926, the Palace Theater is an example of Chicago architect John Eberson's "Atmospheric" theaters. The 1,800-seat interior resembles a Mediterranean garden. The ceiling decoration features light gradation from darkness to dawn in a star-filled sky. Built by Harry Ink, who made his fortune from the sore throat remedy Tonseline, the company's trademark giraffe is discretely incorporated into the design of one of the interior panels.

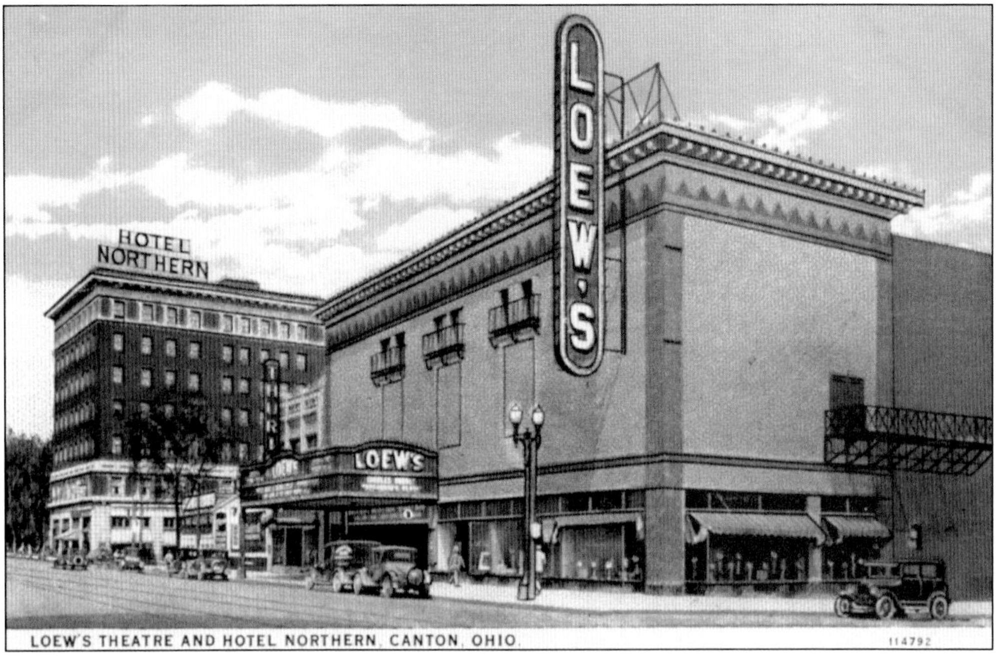

Built in 1925 on North Market Avenue, the 2,200-seat Loew's Theater was one of the grand movie houses built in many cities with the advent of talking pictures. In the 1920s, for 50¢ one could go to the Palace or Loew's and see a feature film, several vaudeville acts, a newsreel, a comedy short, previews of coming attractions, and hear an organ concert.

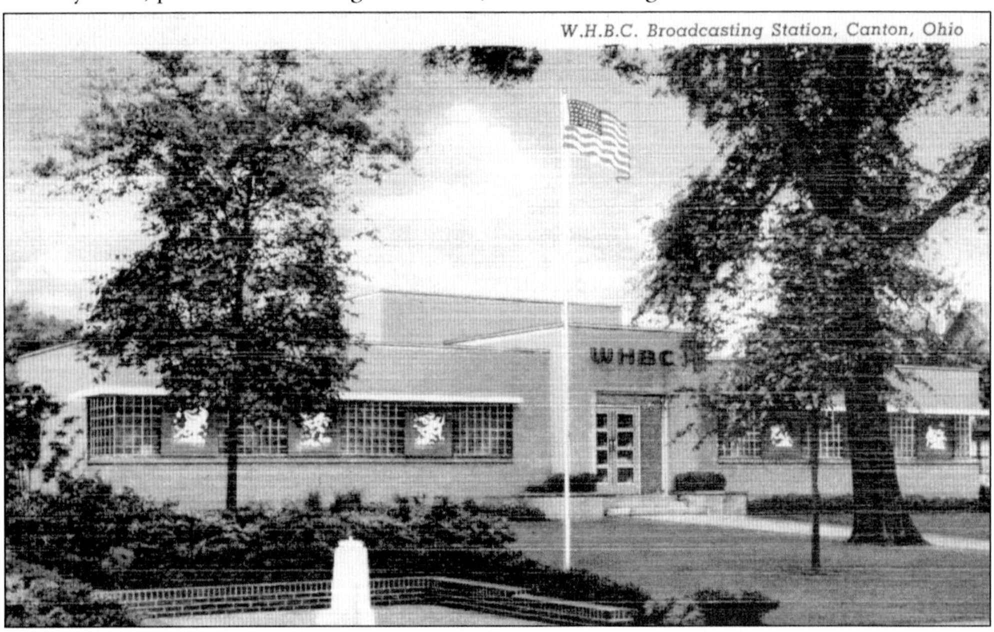

Licensed to St. John's Catholic Church in 1925, WHBC is one of the oldest radio stations in the country. Located on South Market Avenue, the 1939 art deco studio was constructed with locally made Belden bricks. The station features six low relief terra-cotta sculptures depicting the various roles of radio broadcasting. The interior retains many art deco features, including black walnut veneer walls with maple accents.

"Mack" of the John C. Kramer Motor Company at 1703 West Tuscarawas Street sent this postcard announcing the new 1940 Studebakers to prospective customers. The eight-cylinder President, the six-cylinder Commander, and the economical Champion were the "proud products of the matchless craftsmanship of America's Great Independent."

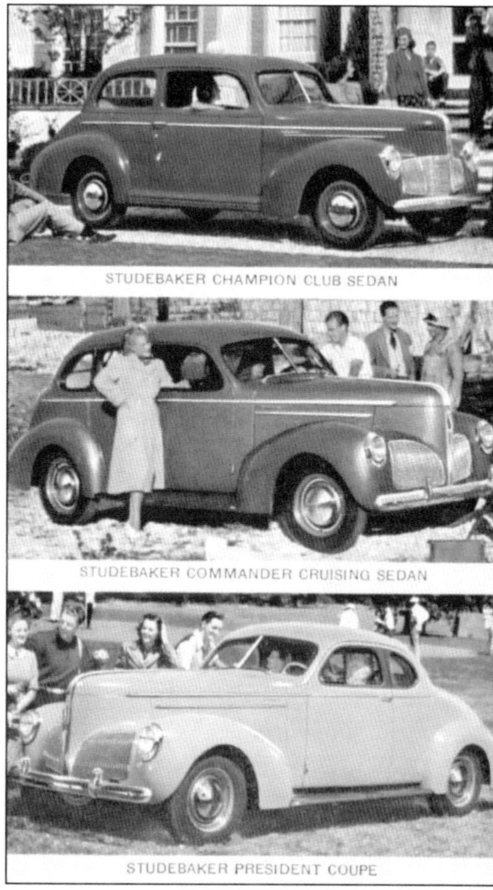

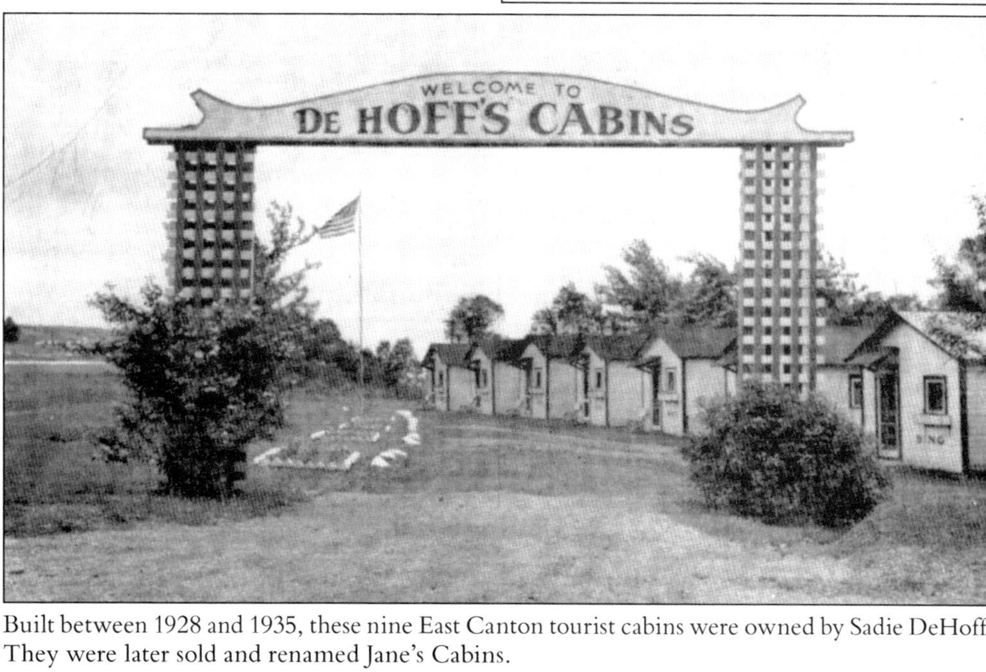

Built between 1928 and 1935, these nine East Canton tourist cabins were owned by Sadie DeHoff. They were later sold and renamed Jane's Cabins.

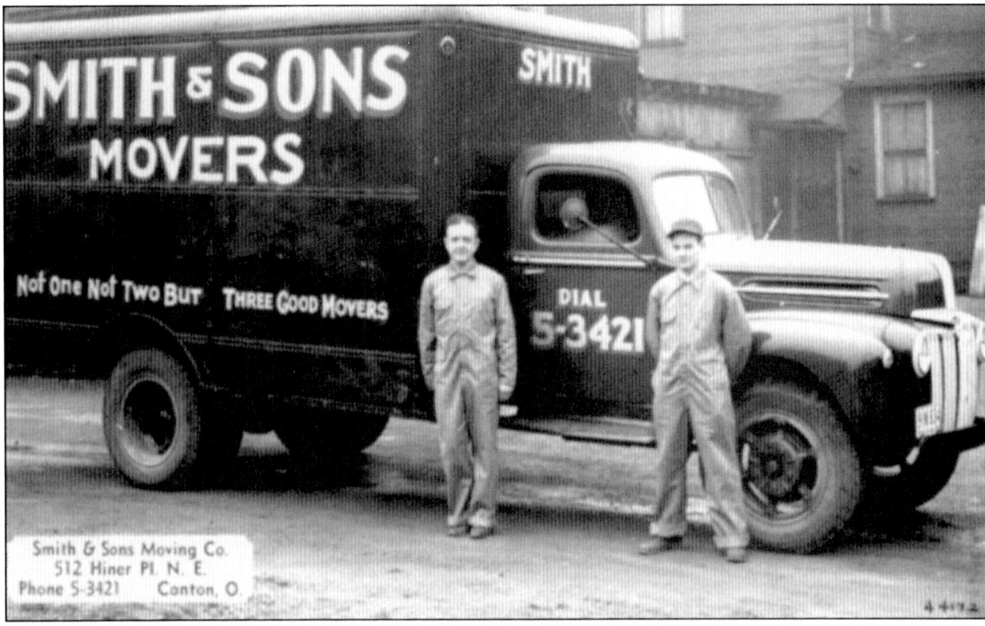

Smith and Sons Movers assured customers that the business was "All in the family—no outside help." Pianos and refrigerators were a specialty.

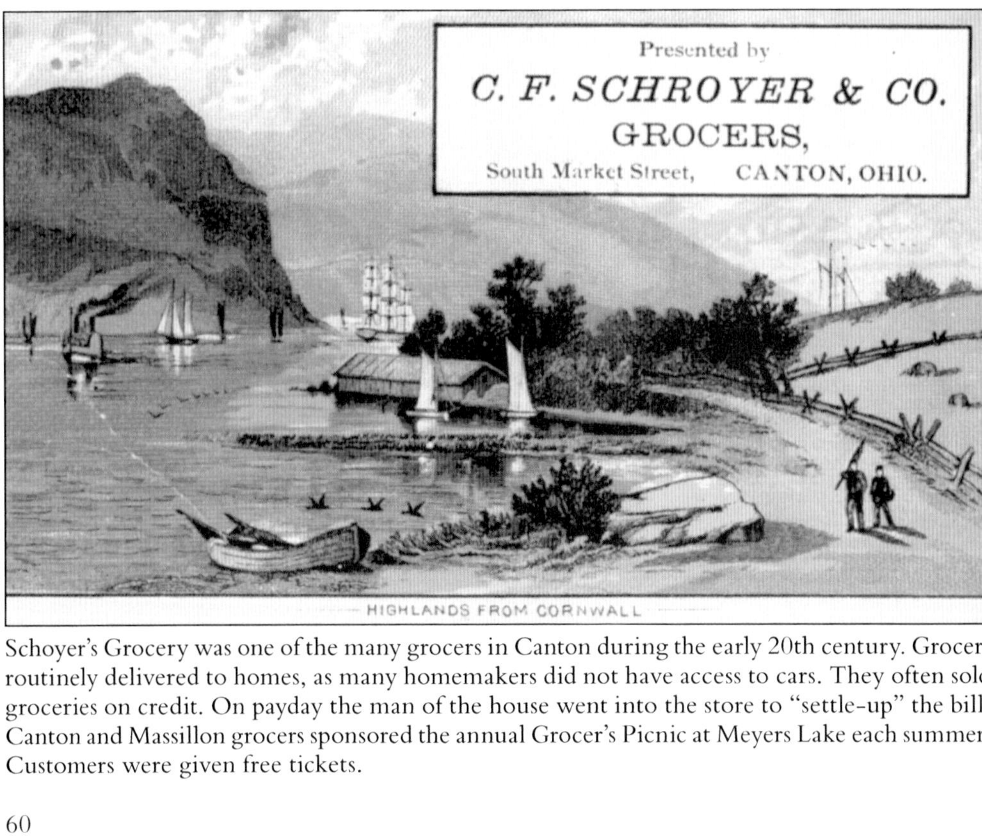

Schoyer's Grocery was one of the many grocers in Canton during the early 20th century. Grocers routinely delivered to homes, as many homemakers did not have access to cars. They often sold groceries on credit. On payday the man of the house went into the store to "settle-up" the bill. Canton and Massillon grocers sponsored the annual Grocer's Picnic at Meyers Lake each summer. Customers were given free tickets.

Five

Hotels, Banks, and the Railroad

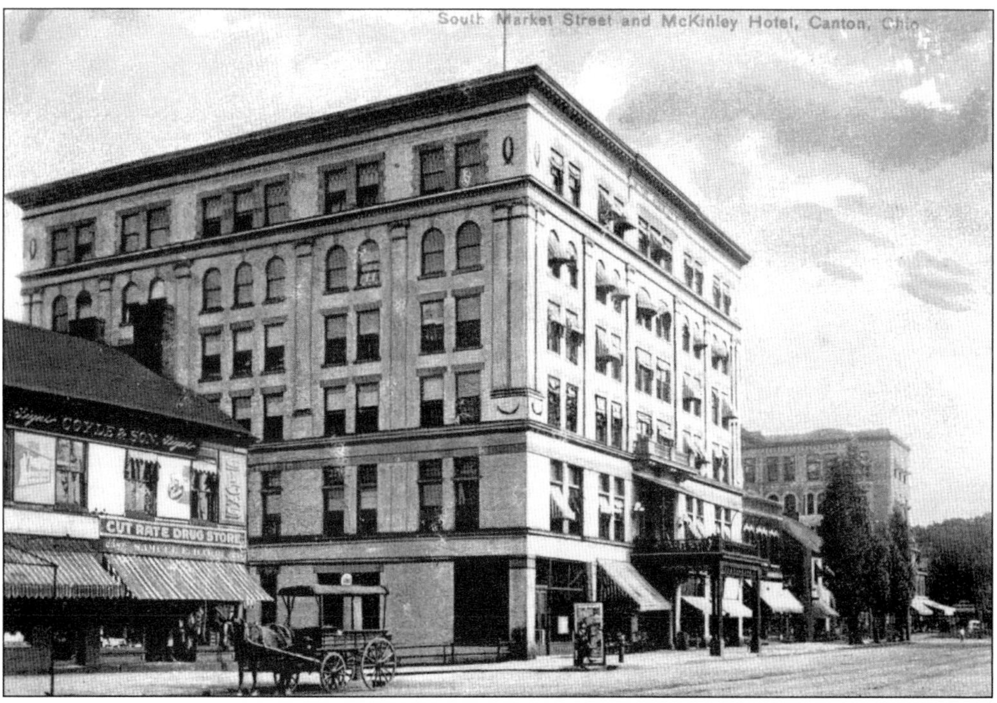

Located on Market Avenue, just south of the square, the McKinley Hotel opened in 1902. The seven-story, 110-room hotel played host not only to performers Rudolph Valentino and Al Jolson but also Pres. Theodore Roosevelt. A 1907 description of the hotel portrays the manager J. D. Lawrence as "a traveling man, he knows the needs and comforts of the American traveling salesman and is in high favor with the man of the grip."

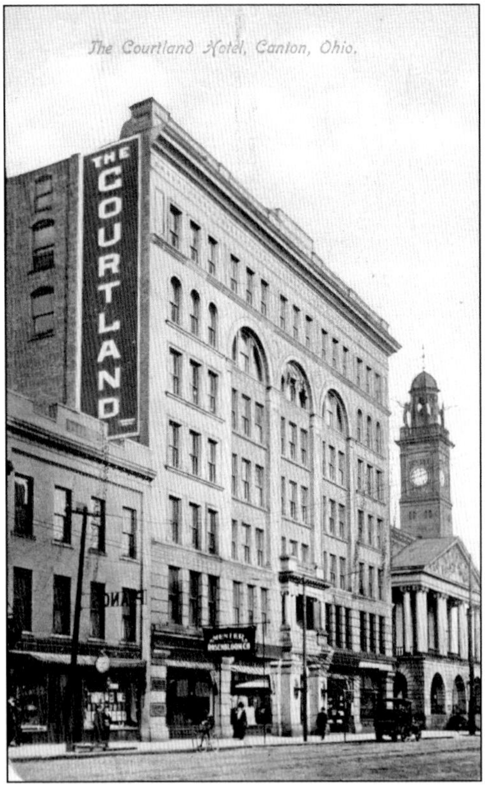

Designed by Guy Tilden, Canton's leading architect at the time, the Courtland Hotel opened in 1905. It was the scene of many social events, including the first charity ball in 1916. It was later the scene in 1921 of the meeting to organize the National League of Football Clubs, which would later become the National Football League.

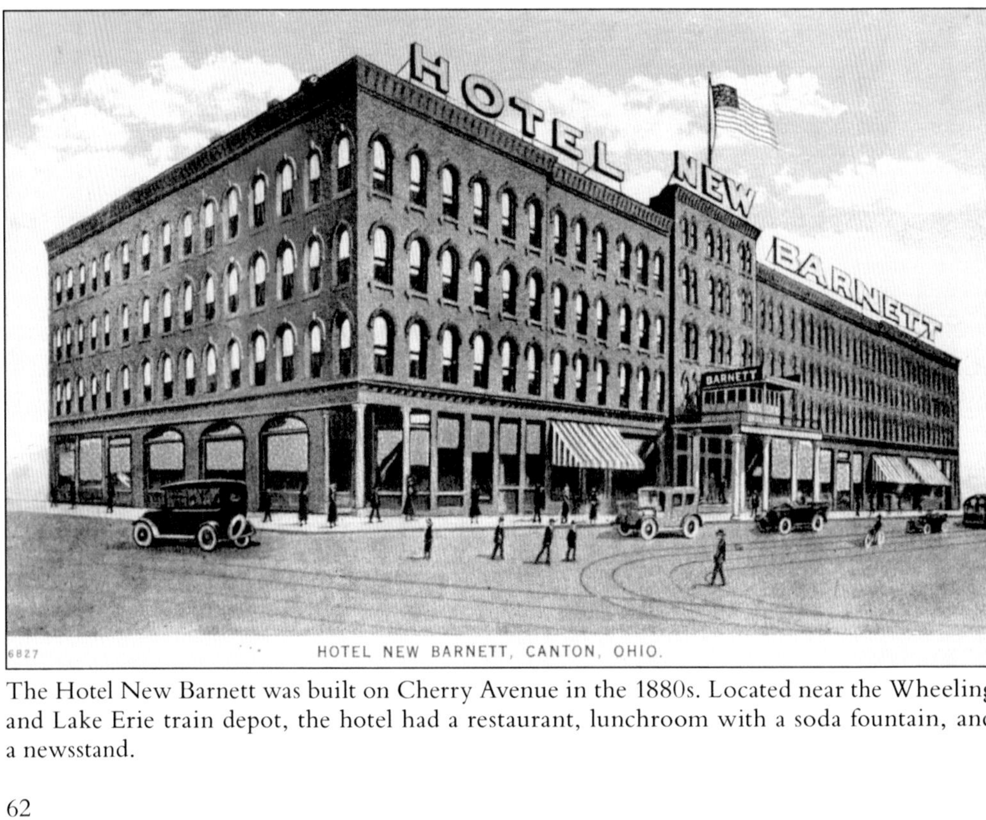

The Hotel New Barnett was built on Cherry Avenue in the 1880s. Located near the Wheeling and Lake Erie train depot, the hotel had a restaurant, lunchroom with a soda fountain, and a newsstand.

Built in 1922 on North Market Avenue by the Knights of Pythias as a hotel and headquarters, by 1926 when "Ben" was in Canton for the Rio Motor Car Company, it was the Hotel Northern. In 1935, it was purchased by Paul Belden and renamed the Belden. The hotel's Viking Restaurant was a popular lunch spot. According to a *Repository* article, the most expensive meal in 1940 was 90¢.

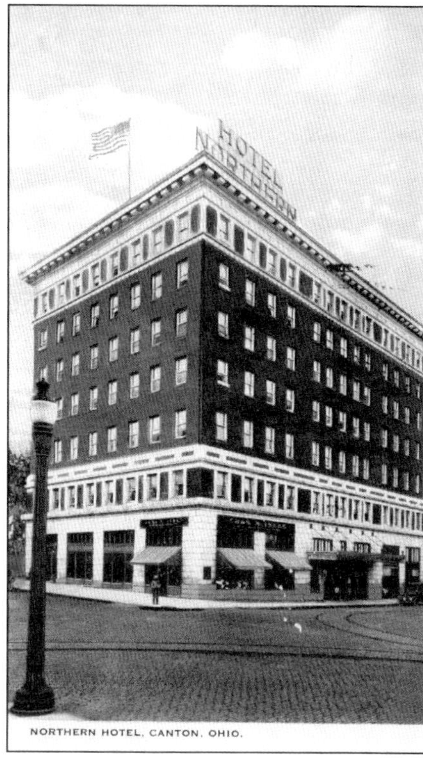

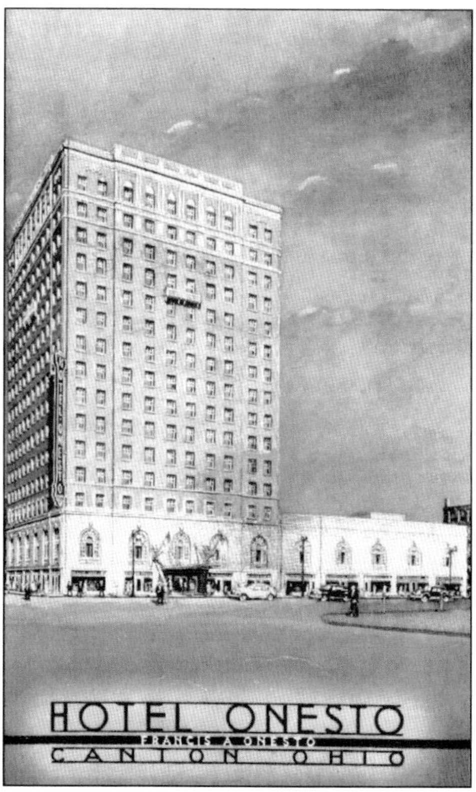

In August 1945, "Tom and Sue" stopped at the Onesto Hotel and wrote to "The Markers" of Lowell, Massachusetts, about their "beautiful trip." Opened by Frank Onesto in 1930, the elegant $1.2 million hotel featured 200 rooms "each with bath, circulating ice water, oscillating fans, and a radio." Suites were air-conditioned. Frank Onesto often greeted the hotel's guests personally and was said to have more friends than anyone in Canton.

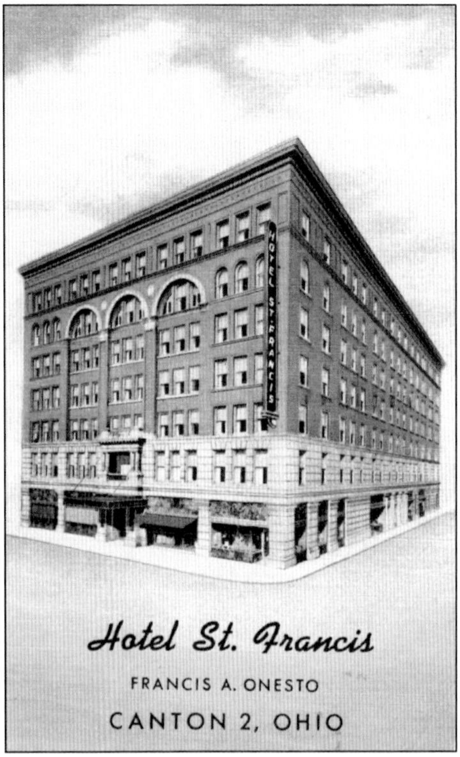

In 1946, Francis "Frank" Onesto purchased the Courtland Hotel, remodeled it, and reopened it as the St. Francis. A tunnel connected it to the Onesto across Second Street. Together the hotels offered over 450 rooms with the most modern accommodations. In 1960, Stark County purchased the hotel for office space, but the building was later demolished. Only the hotel's archway remains as the entrance to the ice rink.

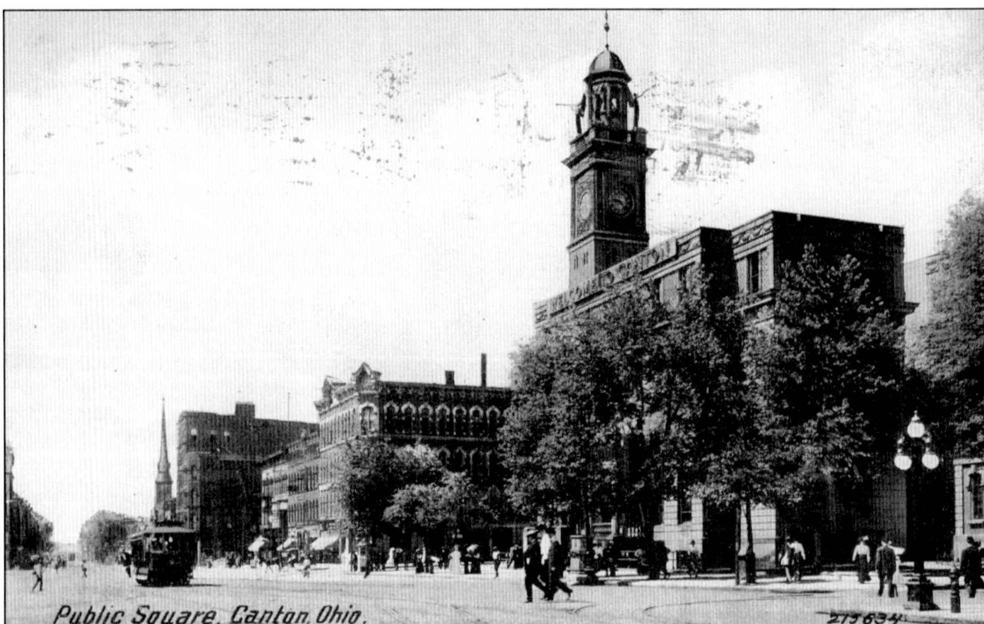

Organized in 1863, the First National Bank received the 76th charter issued by the United States to a national bank. The bank's location at 101 Market Avenue, next to the courthouse, was a prestigious business address. In 1911, Annie Hobbuis of Niles received this card from her "Papa" telling her that "if I am not home tomorrow evening you will know I have got work." Canton's mills and factories attracted many workers from surrounding areas.

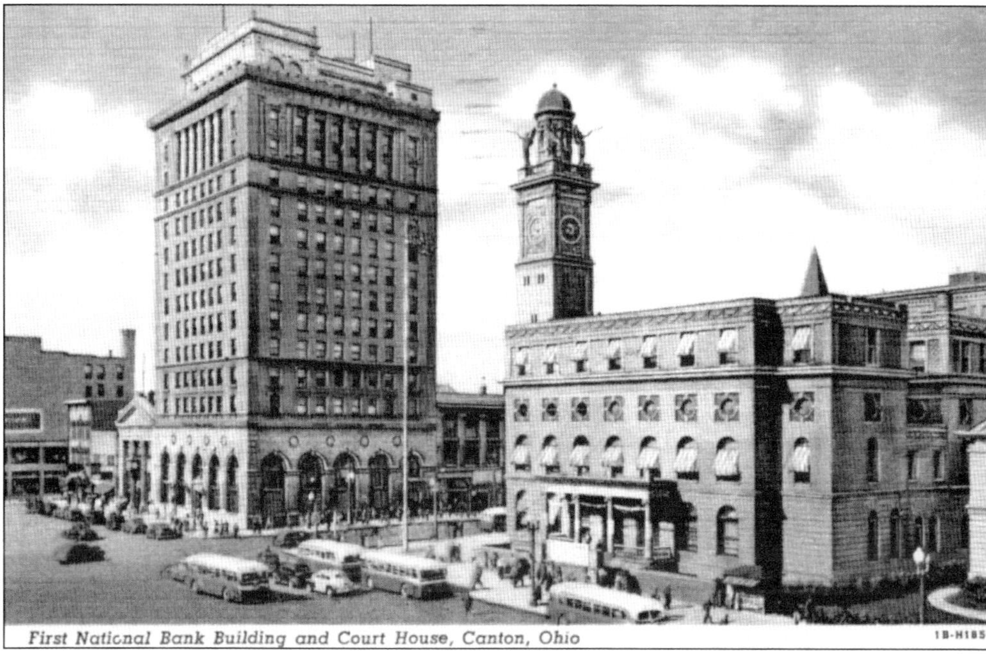

The First National Bank, now Bank One, built this Beaux-Arts classical revival building in 1924. Constructed at a cost of $1.6 million, the first floor retains much of its original finishes. The penthouse level is home to the Canton Club, the social and political center of Canton for over 70 years. Once private, the restaurant is now open to the public.

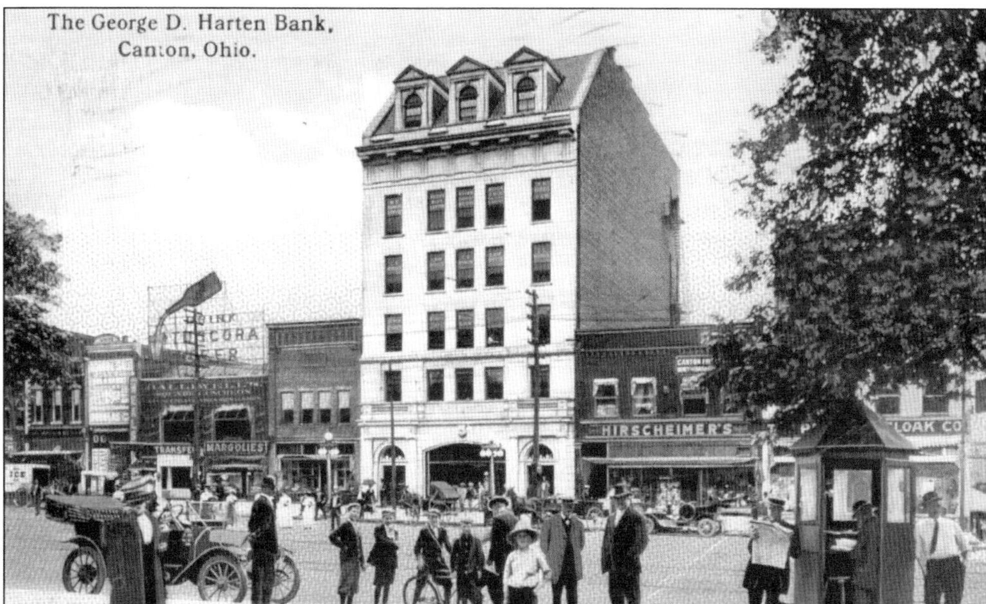

Although the name of the bank is misspelled, the George Harter Bank on the east side of Market Avenue is clearly identifiable. George Harter's father, Isaac, arrived in Canton in 1822 as an indentured servant. By 1854, he and his sons had opened their first bank. In December 1914, Julia Steiner of Sterling received this card from her cousin stating that the "Cashier of this bank received a new auto for Christmas. He asked how you were."

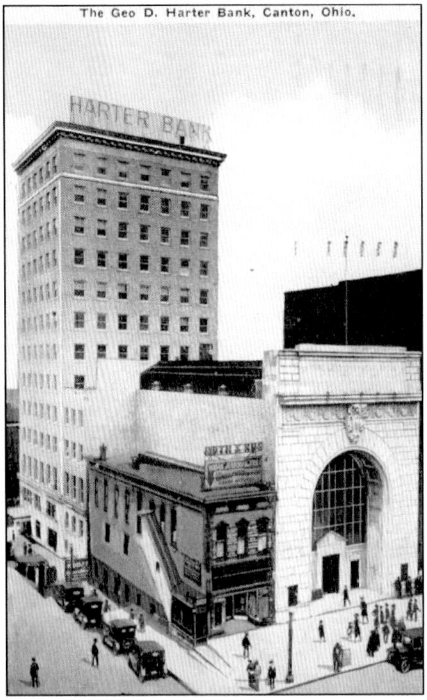

By 1922, when this card was mailed, the Harter Bank was one of the largest banks in northeast Ohio. The three-story building on Market Avenue is an example of bank vault design. The high, windowed arched entryway, dubbed the "Doorway to Opportunity," led to the elaborate skylighted main banking room. The 13-story tower connects to the original building.

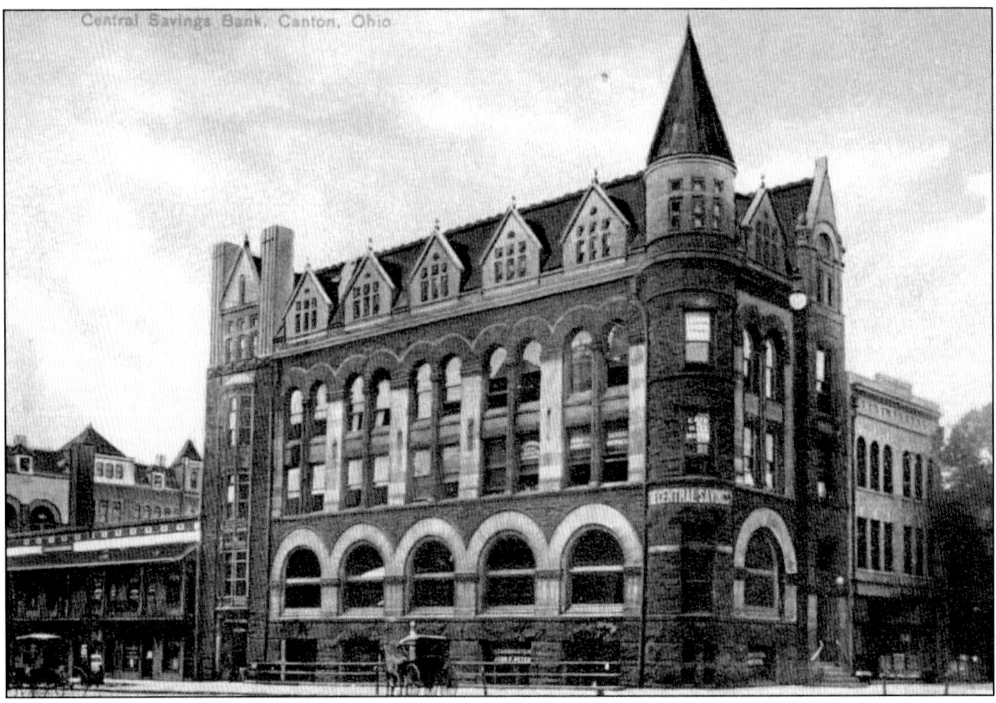

Located on the corner of Tuscarawas Street and Cleveland Avenue, the Central Savings Bank was established in 1887. In 1907, the bank reported nearly $2 million in deposits and a profit of $122,840. The Richardson Romanesque–style building was designed by Guy Tilden, who also designed the county courthouse, public library, Courtland Hotel, Trinity Lutheran Church, and the Frank Case home.

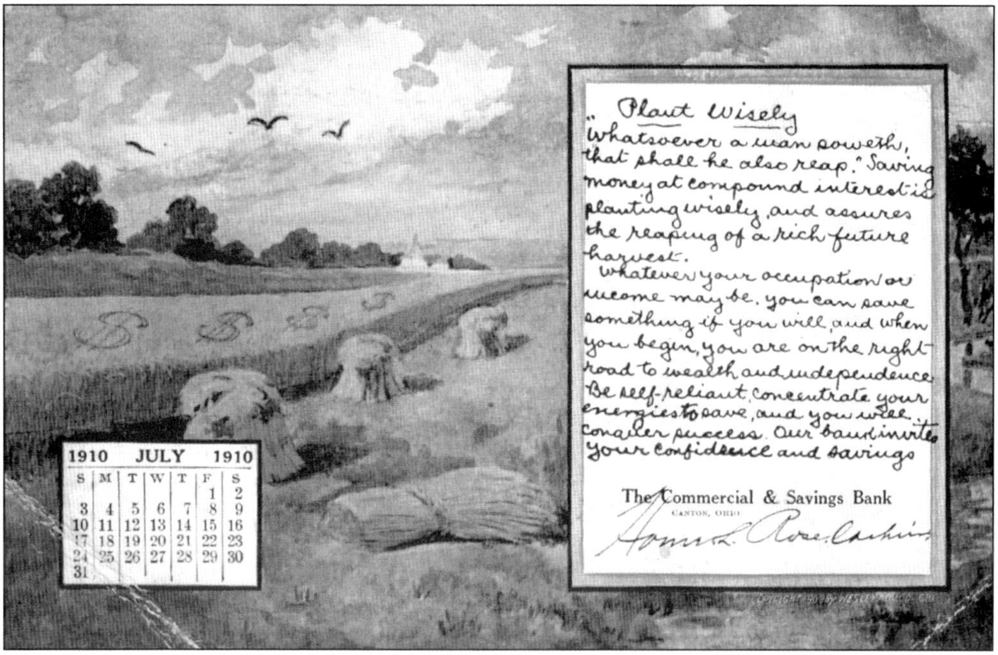

The Commercial and Savings Bank was incorporated in 1909. Located in the Courtland Hotel, during 10 years of operation the bank's assets grew from $500,000 to $1 million. It was absorbed into the City National Bank.

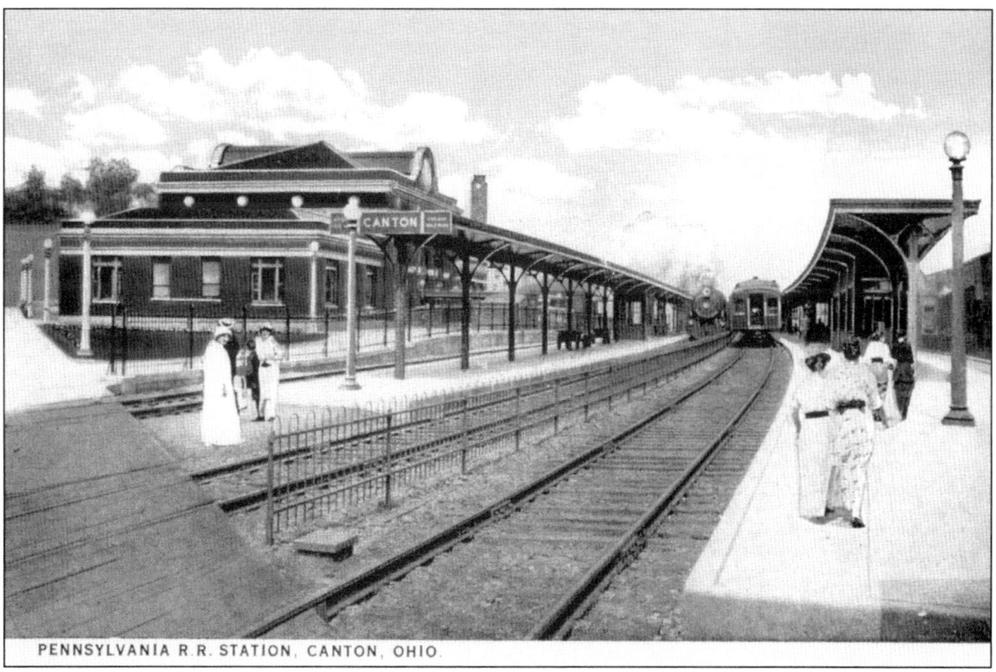

Built in 1909 on Market Avenue South, the Pennsylvania Railroad Station saw many public and personal arrivals and departures. As the heyday of American train travel ended, the station was razed in 1976 despite efforts by preservationists to save it.

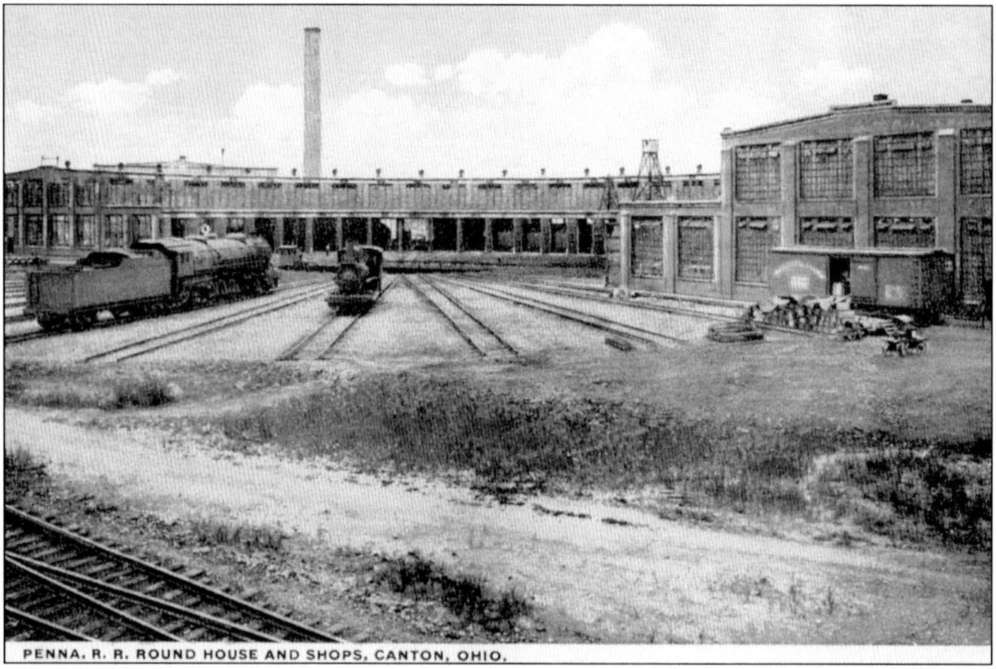

The Pennsylvania Railroad round house and shops were located in the Crystal Park addition on Canton's industrial east side.

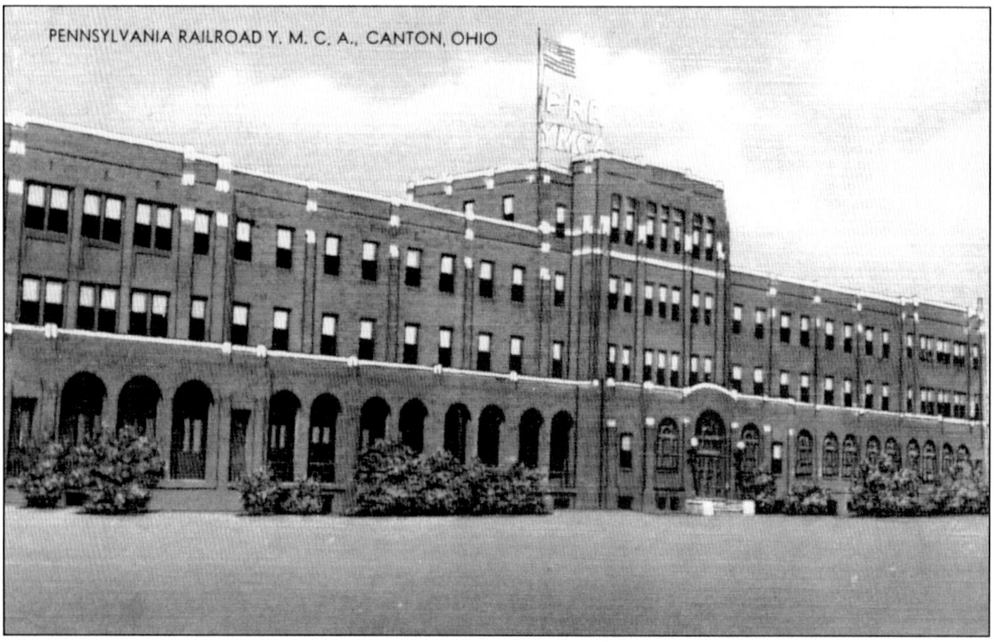

The Pennsylvania Railroad maintained a branch of the YMCA close to the roundhouse and maintenance shops as a "home away from home for P.R.R. men."

Six

Schools and Hospitals

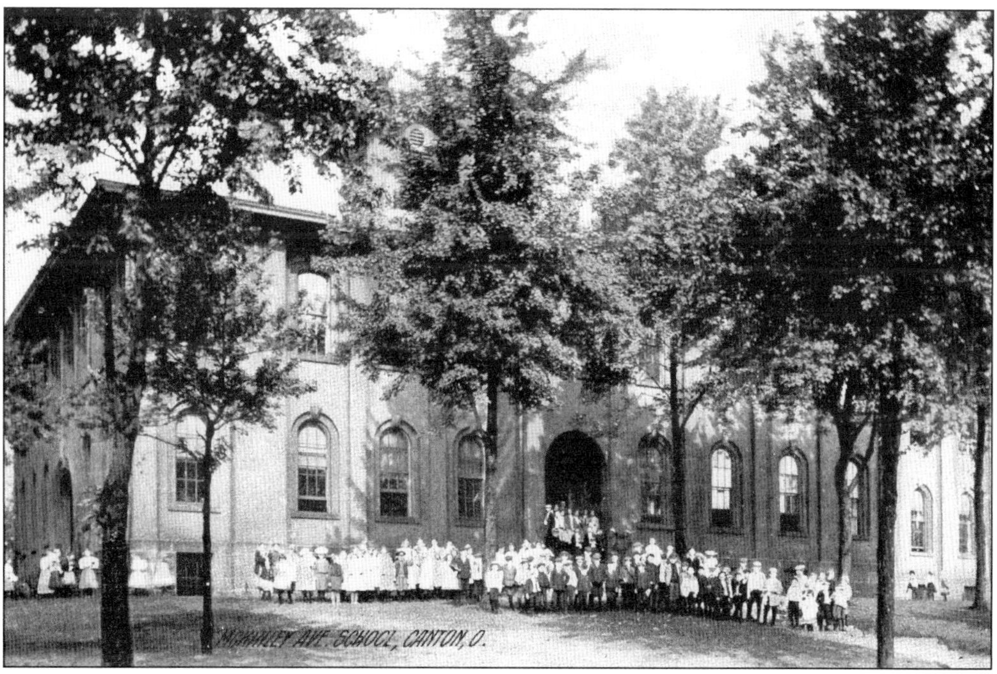

Located on McKinley Avenue, just south of Sixth Street, Wells School was originally Plum Street School. When the street was renamed McKinley Avenue, the school became McKinley Avenue School. When McKinley High School opened in 1918, the school was renamed Wells School after Canton founder Bezaleel Wells. This card predates the 1918 name change. A new Wells School was built on the site in the 1950s.

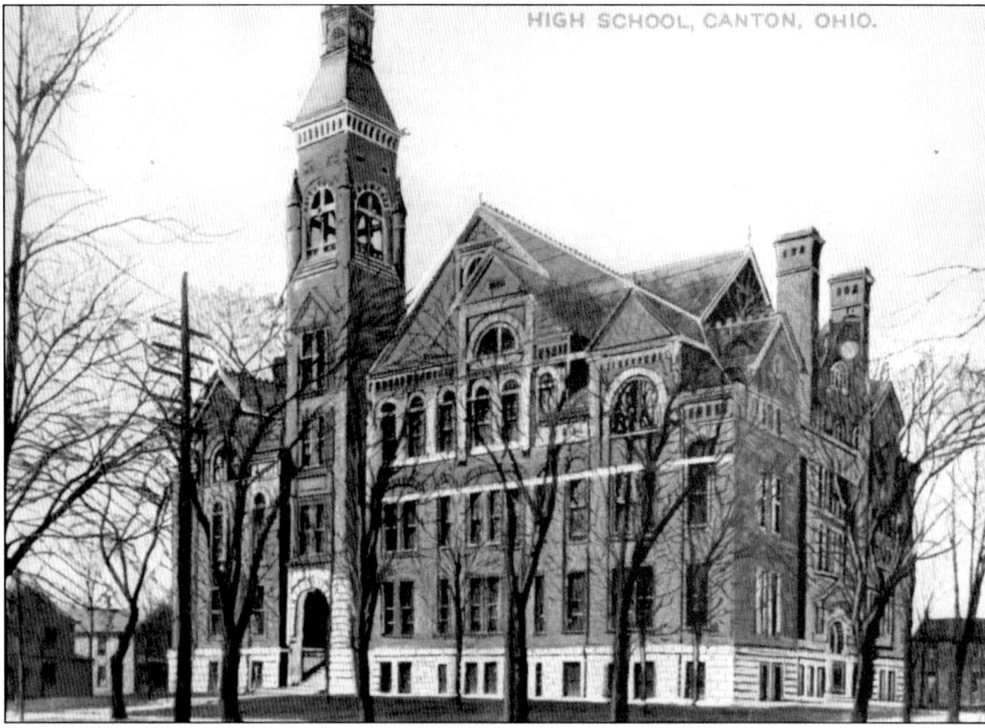

Central High School was Canton's first public high school. Built in 1887 on the current site of the Timken Vocational School, the school occupied the original Bezaleel Wells designated school site. The high school was academically quite successful. By 1905, colleges in the Northwest Ohio Association accepted Central High School graduates without an entrance examination.

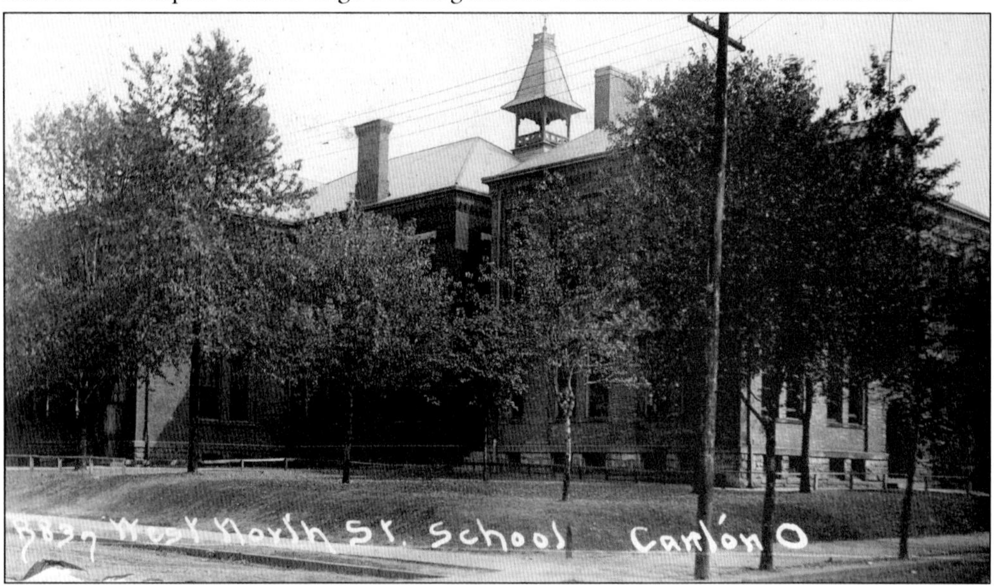

By 1902, the West North Street School, built prior to 1900, needed an addition. Due to Canton's rapid industrial growth between 1900 and 1920, the number of students and teachers increased from 9,221 students and 134 teachers and principals in 1900 to 17,483 students and 432 teachers and principals in 1921.

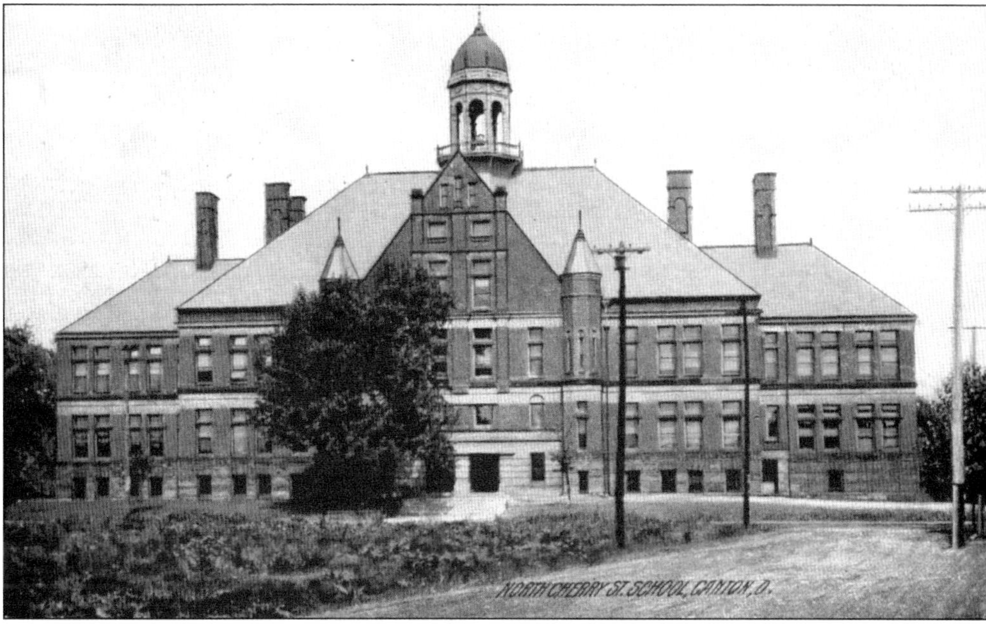

At the time of its construction in 1898 on the corner of Ninth and Cherry Streets, Cherry Street School was one of the finest schools in the state. Special trains ran from Youngstown and East Liverpool for the dedication. The school had 12 classrooms, a domestic science room for the girls, and a workshop for the boys. Two of its early principals, John Lehmann and John Saver, became school superintendents.

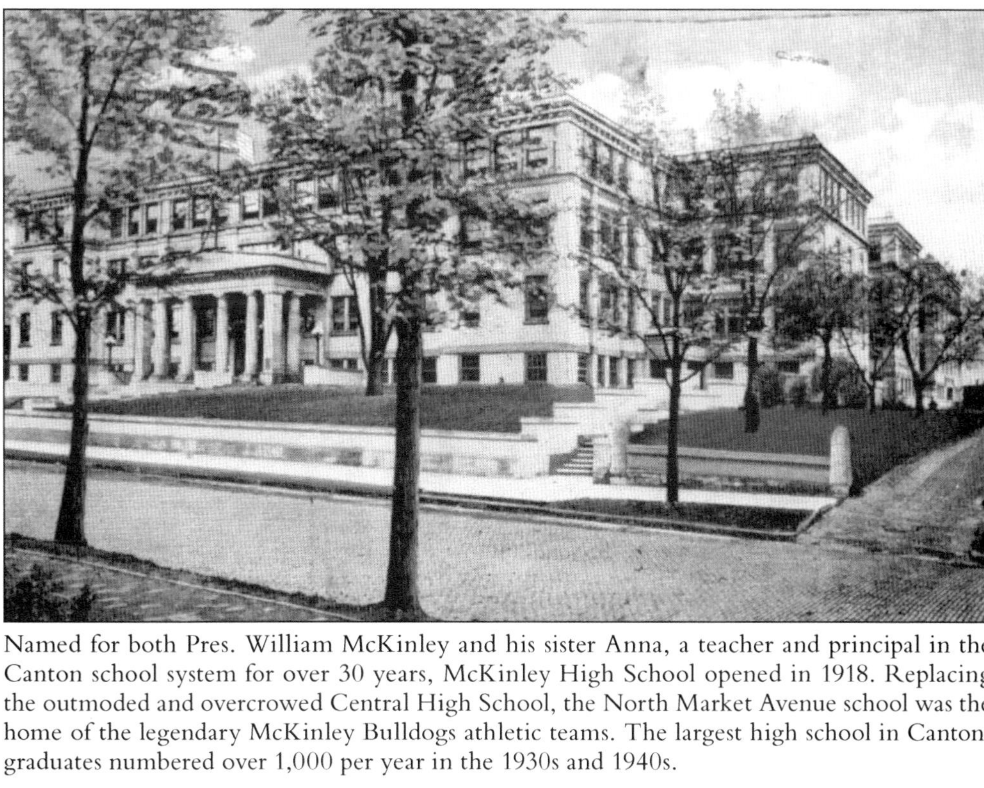

Named for both Pres. William McKinley and his sister Anna, a teacher and principal in the Canton school system for over 30 years, McKinley High School opened in 1918. Replacing the outmoded and overcrowed Central High School, the North Market Avenue school was the home of the legendary McKinley Bulldogs athletic teams. The largest high school in Canton, graduates numbered over 1,000 per year in the 1930s and 1940s.

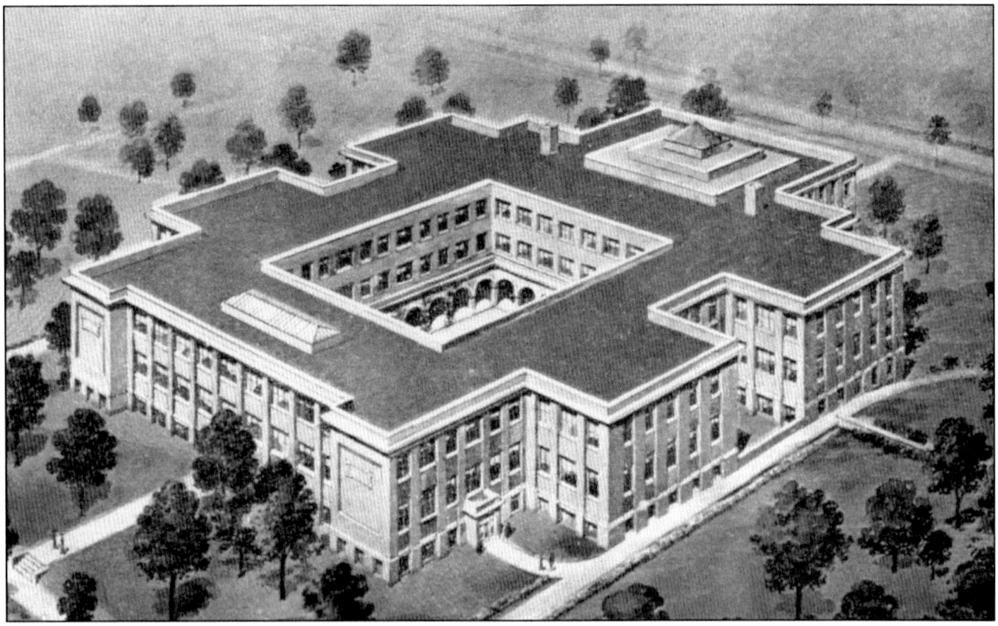

Mistakenly identified as North High School, this aerial view of McKinley High School shows the unique architecture of the 100-room school. When it opened, the school had the largest heating plant in the United States, an auditorium, two gymnasiums, a swimming pool, a cafeteria, a library, printing and machine shops, and a state-of-the-art internal communication system. Today a portion of the building is home to the McKinley Life Care Centre.

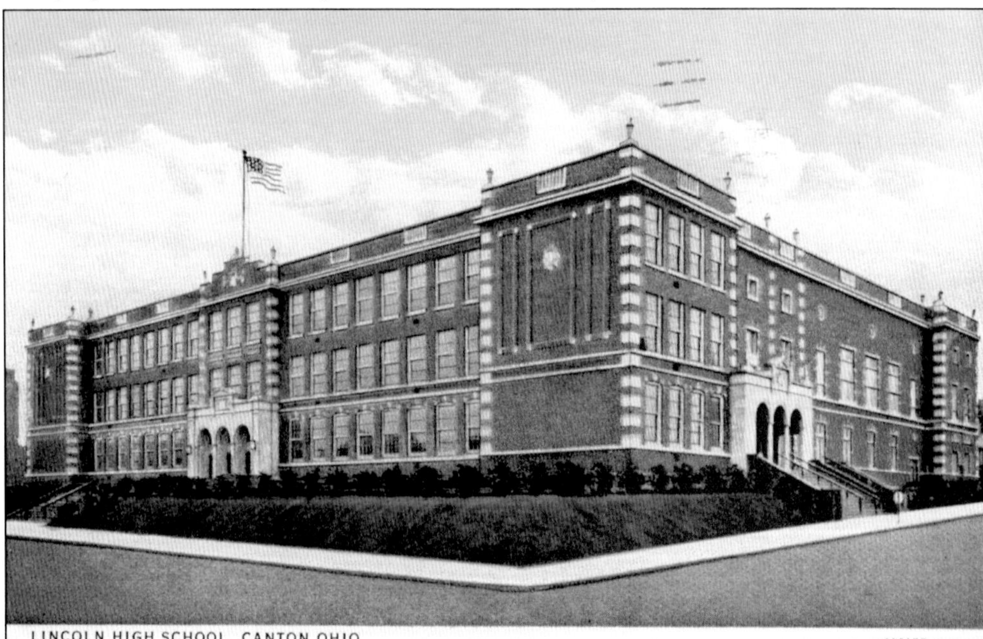

Opened in 1927 as a junior high school, Lincoln became a high school in 1942. Located on Sixth Street NW and built to accommodate 1,200 students in 40 classrooms, it was closed in 1978 due to declining enrollment. It is now Heritage Christian School, a private interdenominational school for students from preschool through 12th grade.

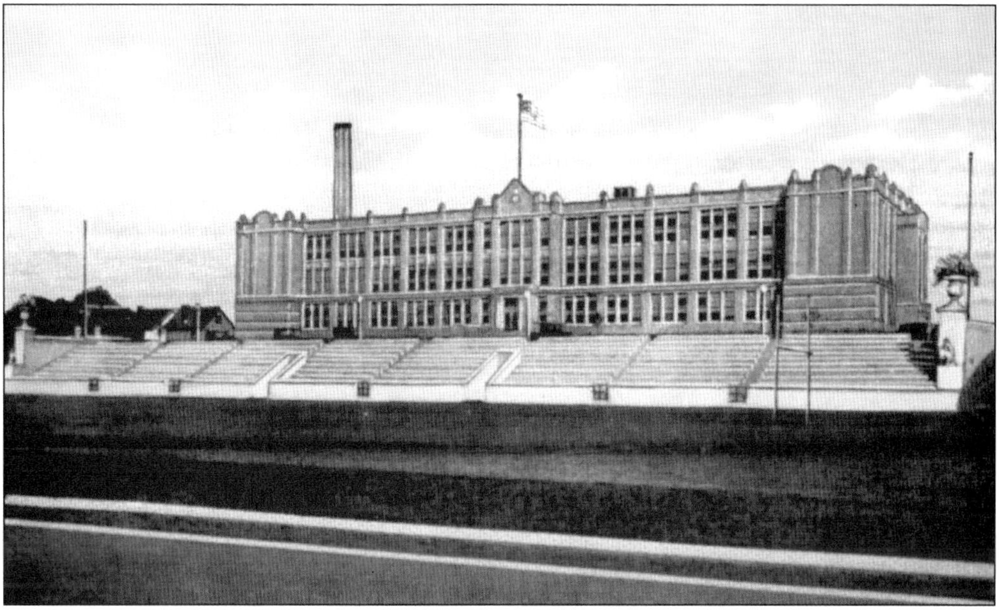

Completed in 1921, Lehman High School was named for school superintendent John Lehman. Opened as a junior high school, it became a high school in 1937. Designed with 80 percent exterior window space, the motto over the doorway quotes a city ordnance: "Schools and the means of education shall be forever encouraged." Lehman returned to use as a middle school in 1993.

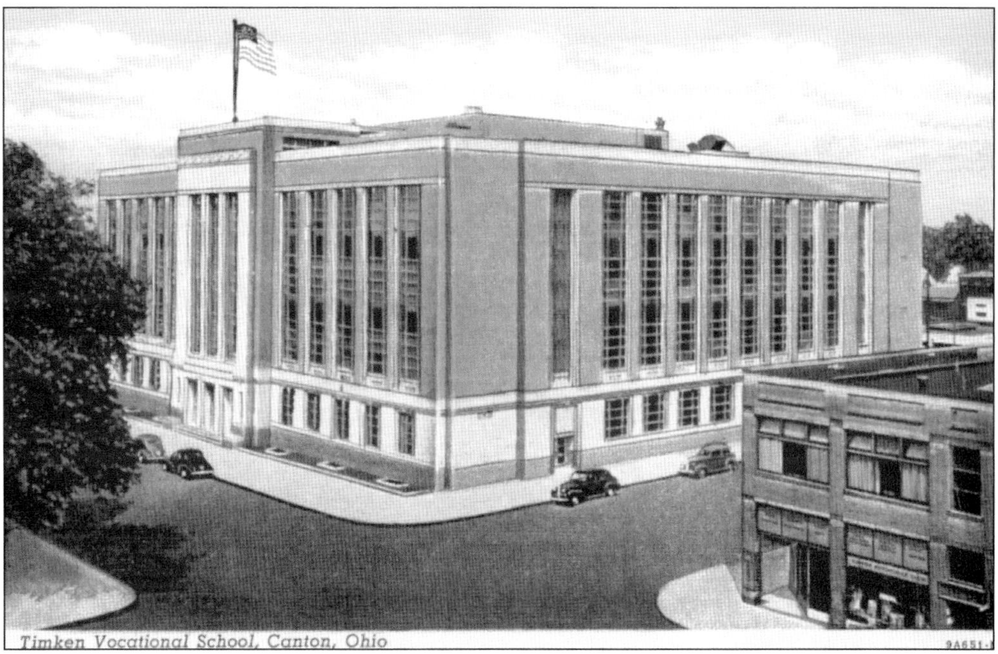

A gift from H. H. Timken, Timken Vocational School was opened in 1939 on the West Tuscarawas Street site of Central High School. The school's curriculum was designed to give vocational training to unemployed high school graduates. Students were required to pass an entrance examination before being accepted into the school's many vocational programs.

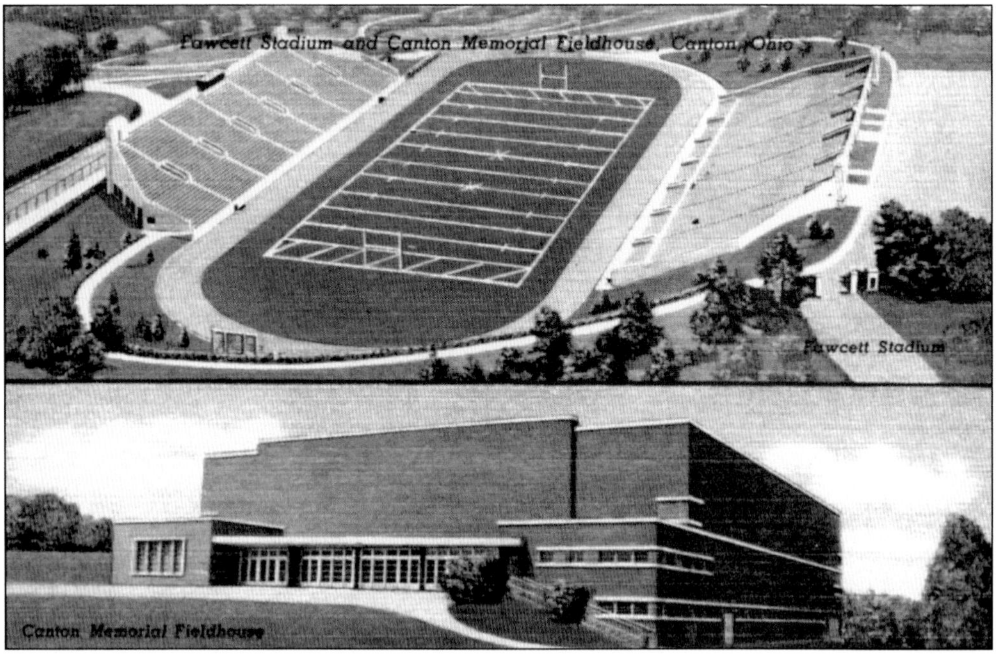

Fawcett Stadium was officially dedicated in 1938. Still considered the number one high school sporting venue in the United States by *Sporting News*, the 22,400-seat stadium hosts the National Football League Pro Football Hall of Fame Game and the Ohio High School Athletic Association State Football Championship each year. The close by Memorial Fieldhouse has a seating capacity of 5,530.

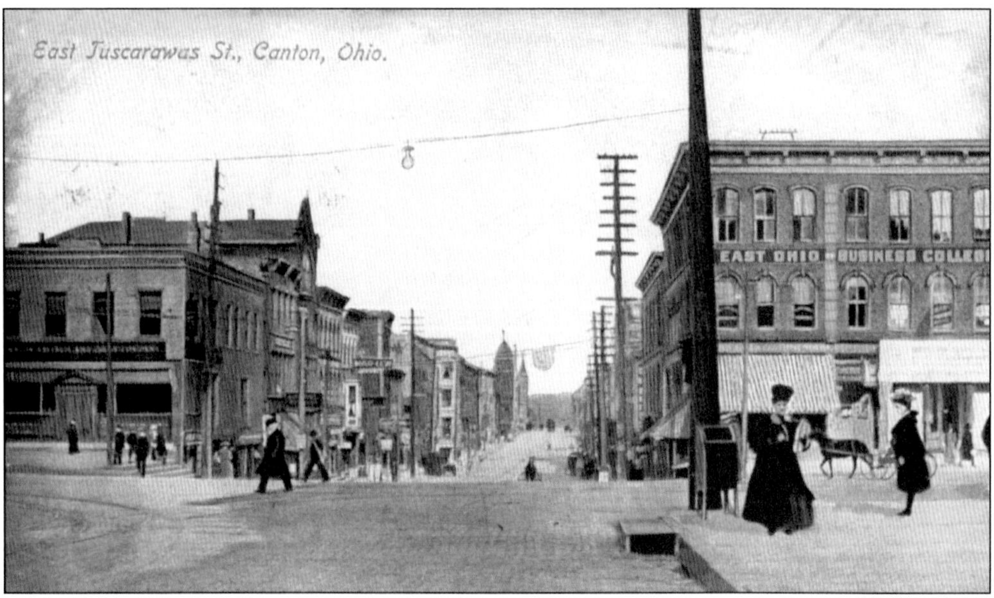

This 1909 card shows the location of the East Ohio Business College on East Tuscarawas Street. A 1907 publication reissued by the Canton Preservation Society states that the college had been a "prestigious school for many years, teaching business, shorthand, and preparatory courses of study." Furthermore, the "students fill important positions all over the United States, which is proof of the thoroughness of the teaching and the loyalty of the faculty."

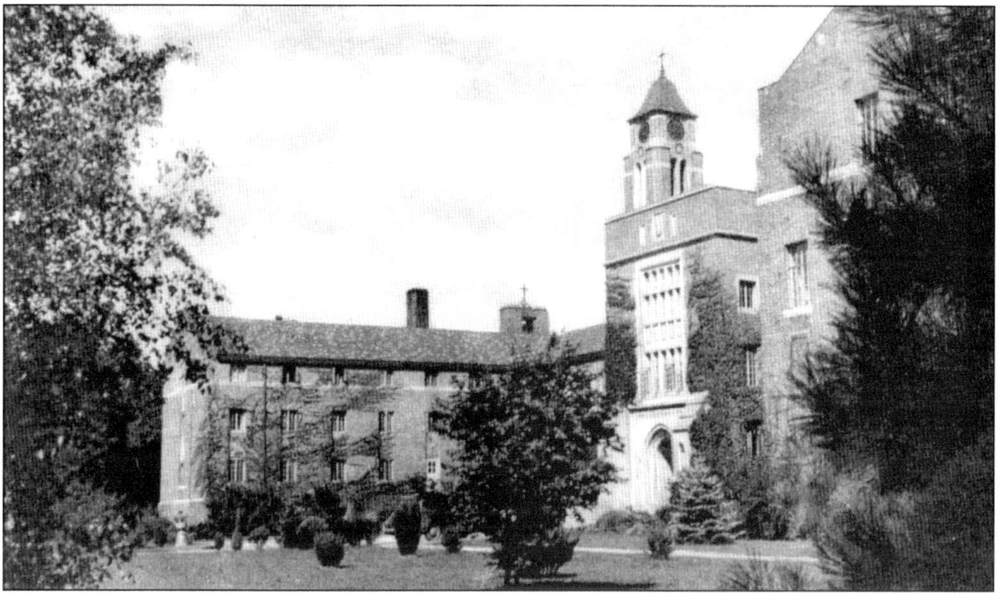

Located on 540 acres, six miles east of Canton in Jackson Township, Bunerdale Seminary was built in 1931 by the Society of the Precious Blood. Dedicated to preparing young men for the Catholic priesthood, the seminary was one of four educational institutions run by the group for students 14 to 27 years of age. The seminary site was sold in 1989. The main school building is now part of the Glenmoor Country Club.

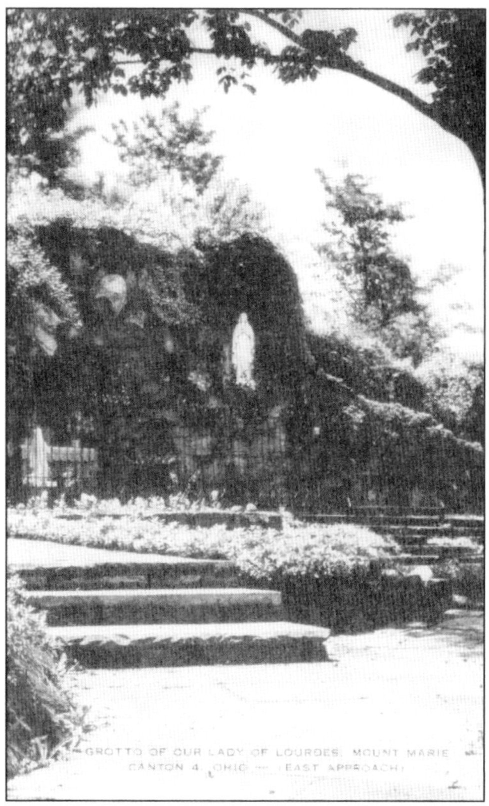

The Sisters of the Holy Humility of Mary fulfilled their dreams of building a girls' boarding school with the opening of Mount Marie Academy in 1908. During the construction of the building, the sisters desperately needed $500. They had nearly given up hope when a man came to their door with a gift of the needed funds. The man was later identified as Edgar Snow, an Ohio Gas Company employee.

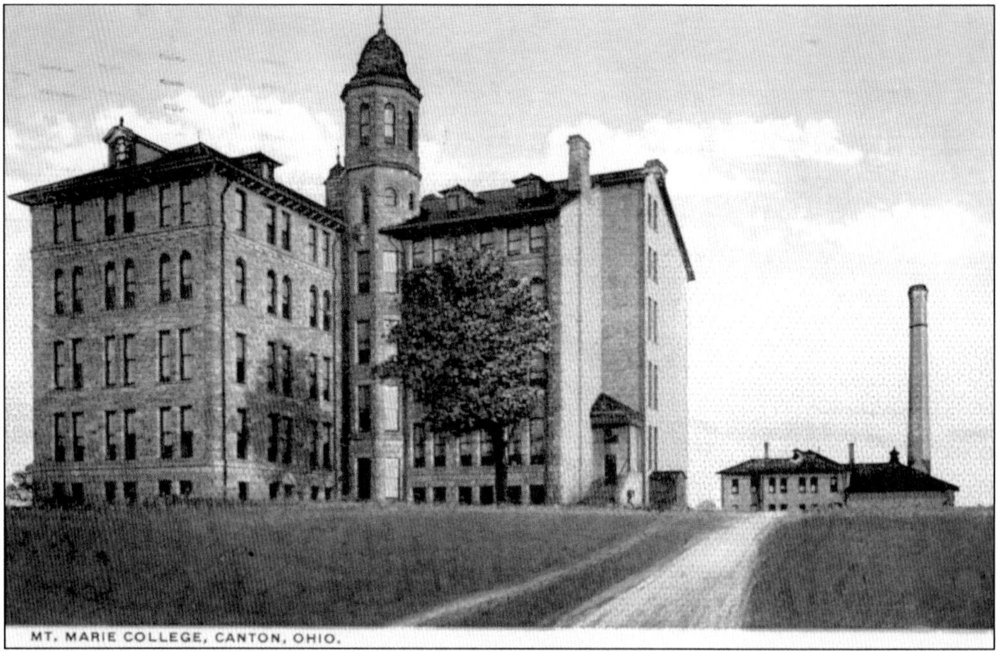

Mount Marie Academy remained a boarding school until 1939 when it became a day school. It was consolidated into St. John's High School in 1944. In 1949, the Diocese of Youngstown took over the school and it became part of Central Catholic High School located on West Tuscarawas Street near Reedurban.

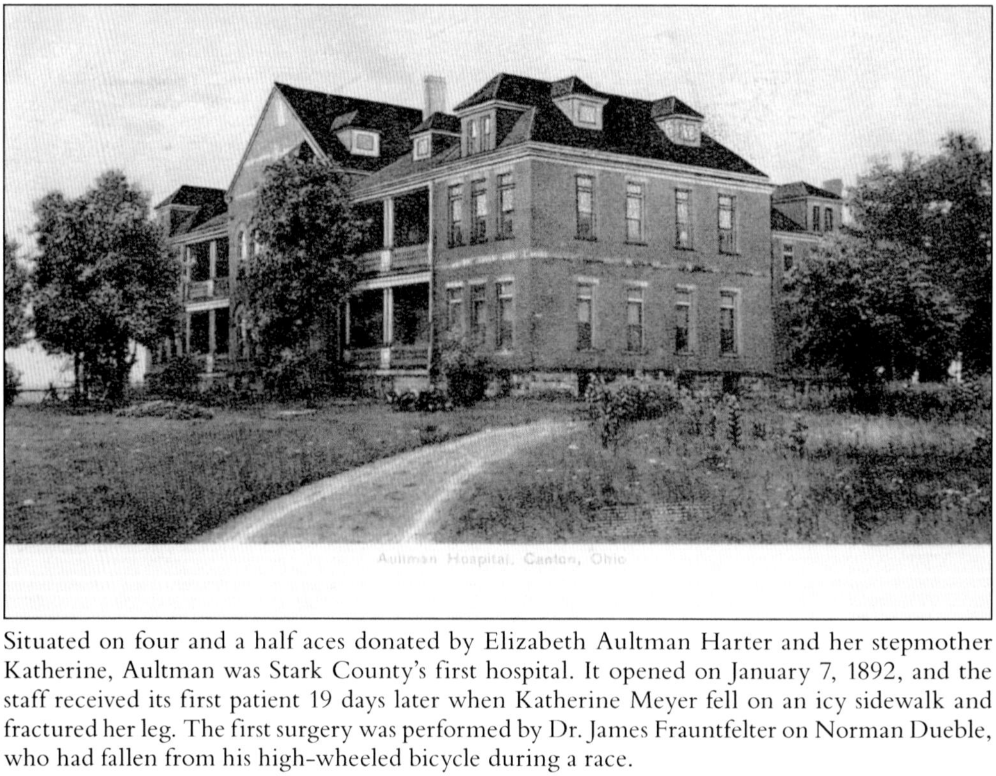

Situated on four and a half aces donated by Elizabeth Aultman Harter and her stepmother Katherine, Aultman was Stark County's first hospital. It opened on January 7, 1892, and the staff received its first patient 19 days later when Katherine Meyer fell on an icy sidewalk and fractured her leg. The first surgery was performed by Dr. James Frauntfelter on Norman Dueble, who had fallen from his high-wheeled bicycle during a race.

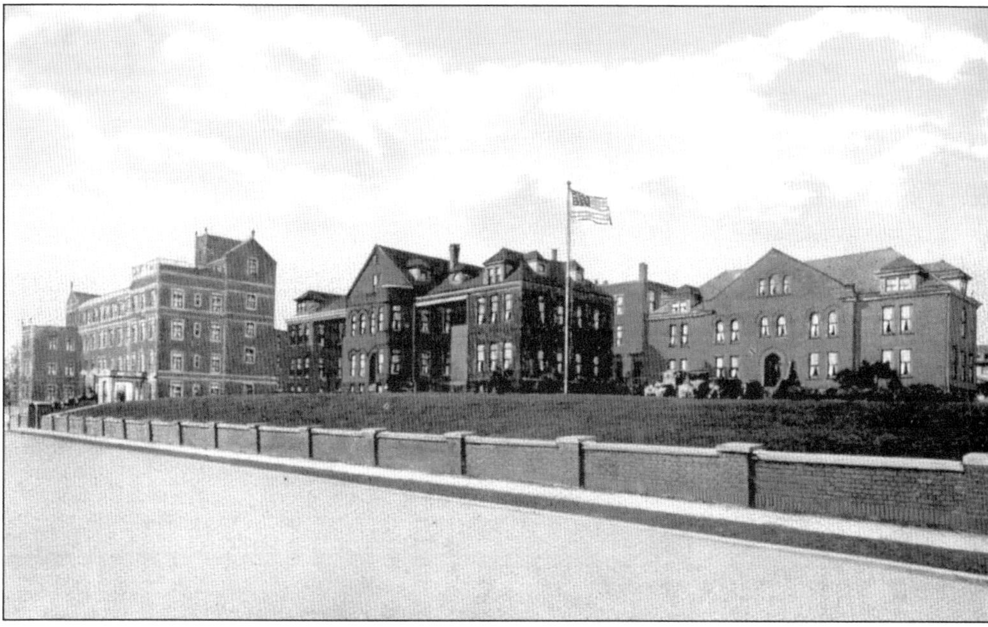

Located on the site of the current Aultman Hospital, the hospital staff often had to push wagons bearing patients up the muddy road. Conditions improved as Canton and the hospital grew. The 100-bed Elizabeth Harter Building was added in 1925. The McKinley Building opened in 1944, adding 106 beds. Three years later the 117-bed Harter annex was built.

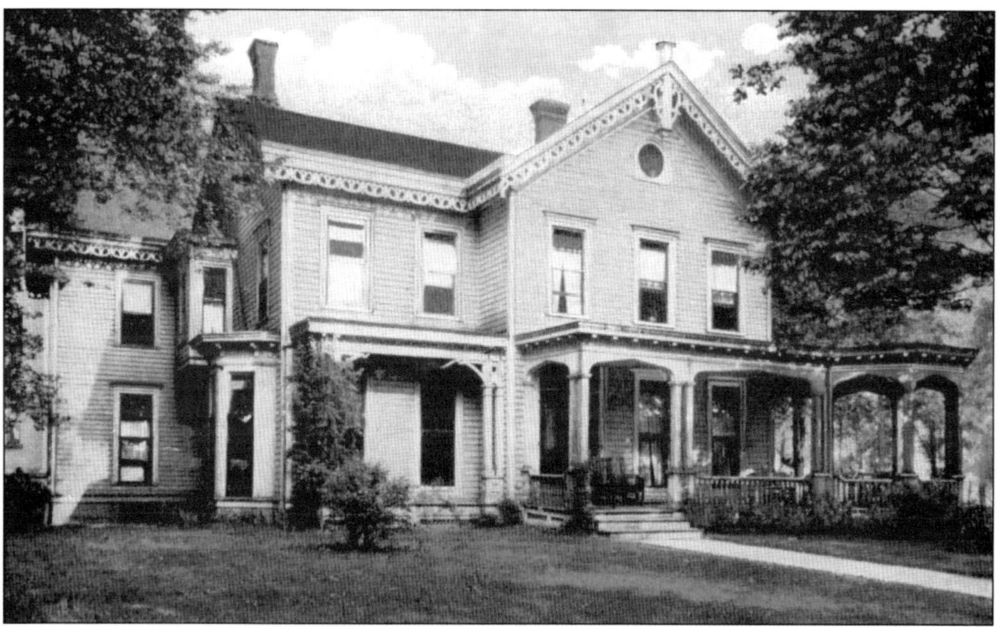

After Ida McKinley's death in May 1907, her home was purchased by Elizabeth Klorer and deeded to the Catholic Diocese of Cleveland for a hospital in memory of her husband Herman, a founder of Berger Manufacturing. Under the direction of the Sisters of Charity of Augustine, the residence was converted to an 18-bed hospital. Fittingly, Ida's suite became the children's ward.

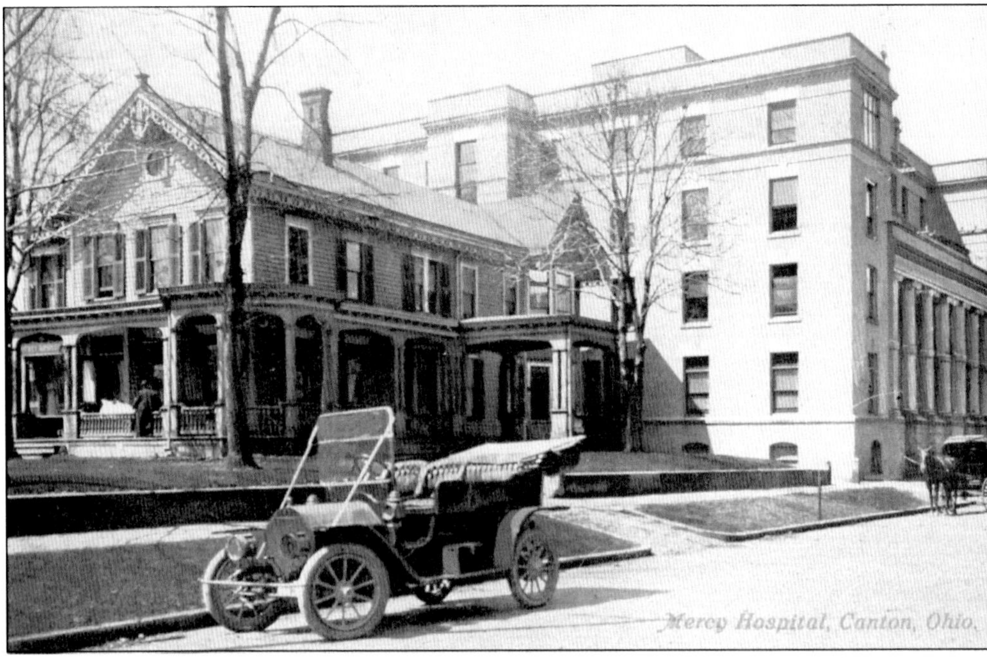

By 1909, Mercy Hospital outgrew the McKinley home and added an adjacent building. Hospital benefactor Rosa Klorer had a suite of three rooms created for her in the new addition and resided there from 1911 until her death in 1936.

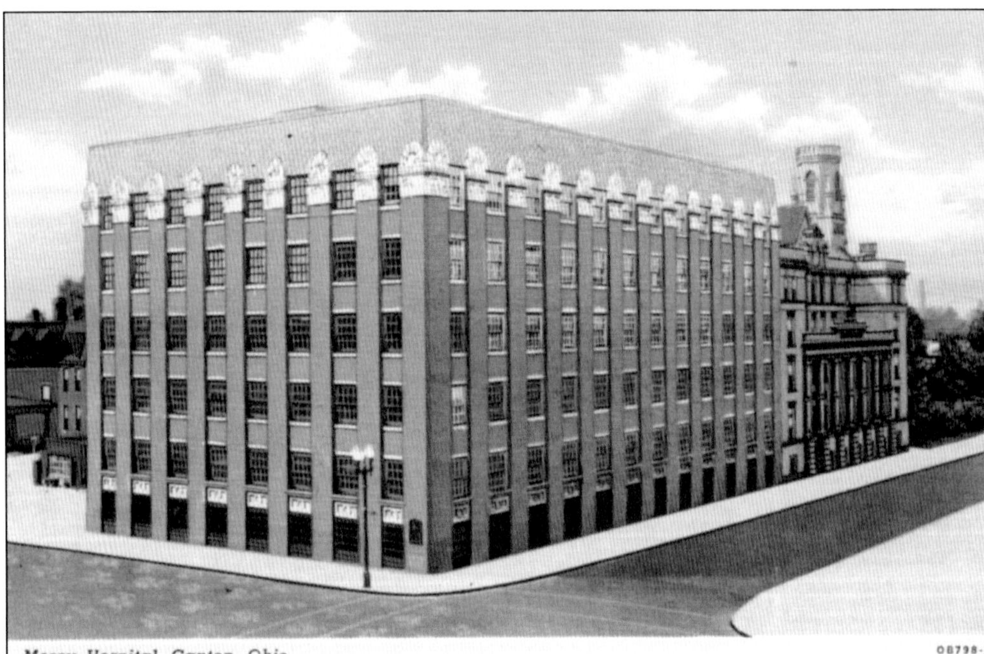

The 1928 Mercy Hospital wing forced the removal of the McKinley home. The home was moved to Meyers Park, a residential area, but the 1929 stock market crash and resulting depression forced cancelation of plans to preserve the house. It was demolished in 1935 as a fire hazard.

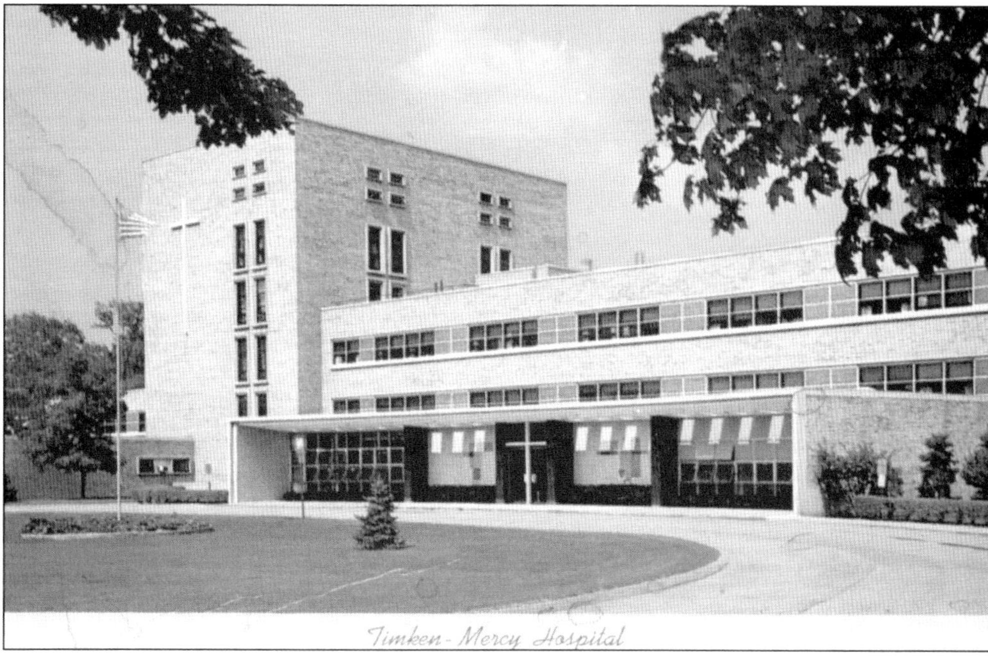

By the late 1940s, Mercy Hospital was badly overcrowed. The need for additional beds led the Timken family to offer the H. H. Timken home and surrounding 32 acres to the hospital. The modern hospital was built around the mansion. By 1970, all hospital facilities were moved from the downtown location to the current Timken Mercy Medical Center site.

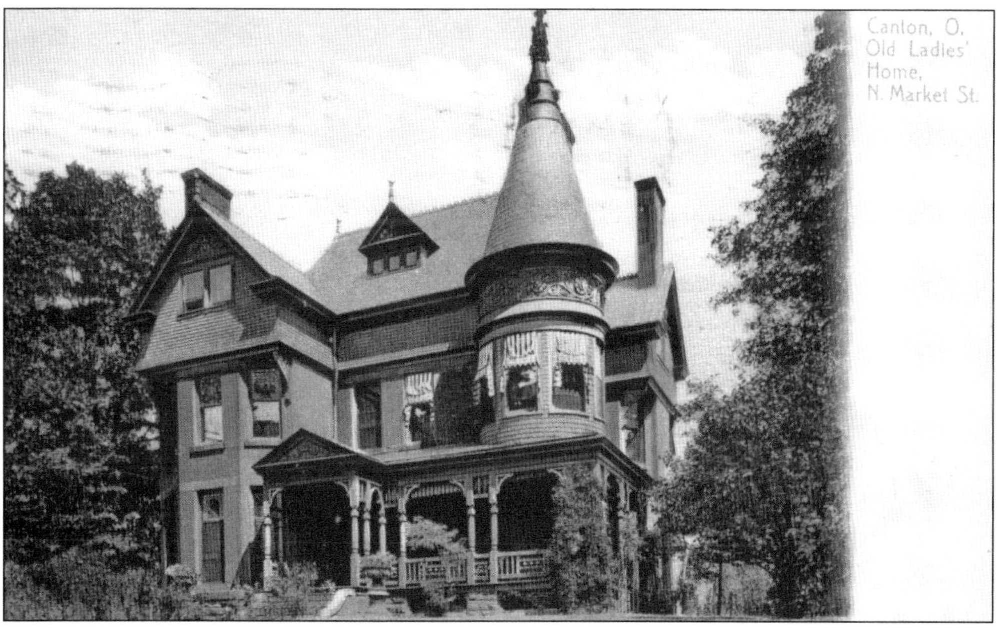

Established in 1903 in the former Aultman residence on North Market Avenue, the Aultman Home for Aged Women served the needs of elderly women until 1959 when a new residence was built. In 1909, "Master Everett Jones" of Salt Lake City, Utah, received this card from his grandmother thanking him for the beautiful cards and telling him of her wish to see him just once more.

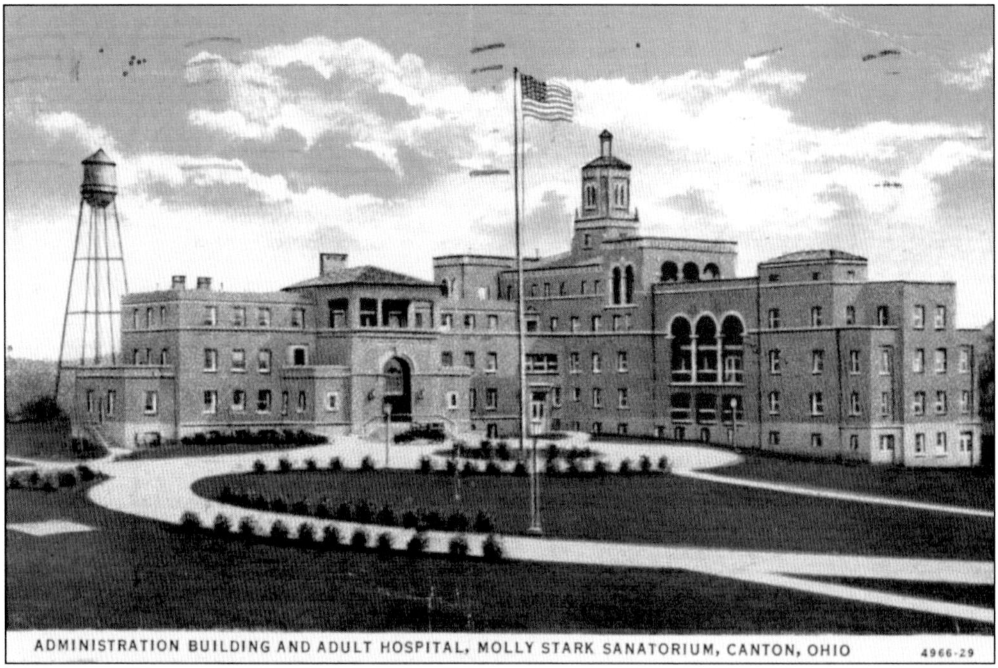

Named for the wife of Revolutionary War general John Stark, Molly Stark Sanatorium opened in 1929 on 43 acres south of Canton. Before the development of effective antibiotic treatment for tuberculosis, children and adults remained at the facility for extended periods of time. Treatment consisted mainly of good nutrition and prolonged rest. The hospital had a library, canteen, movies, beauty shops and barbershops, and a patient-run newspaper.

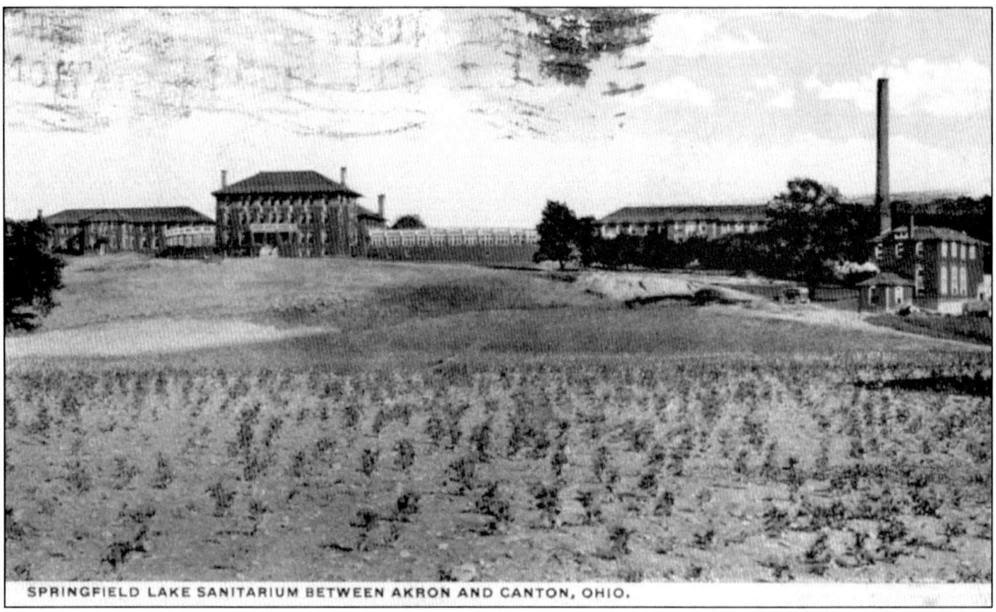

Founded in 1915, the Springfield Lake Sanatorium treated tuberculosis patients from the counties surrounding Akron and Canton. Part of a system of tuberculosis hospitals set up in the United States in the early 20th century, the hospital is now a part of the Edwin Shaw Hospital for Rehabilitation.

Seven

Churches and Worship

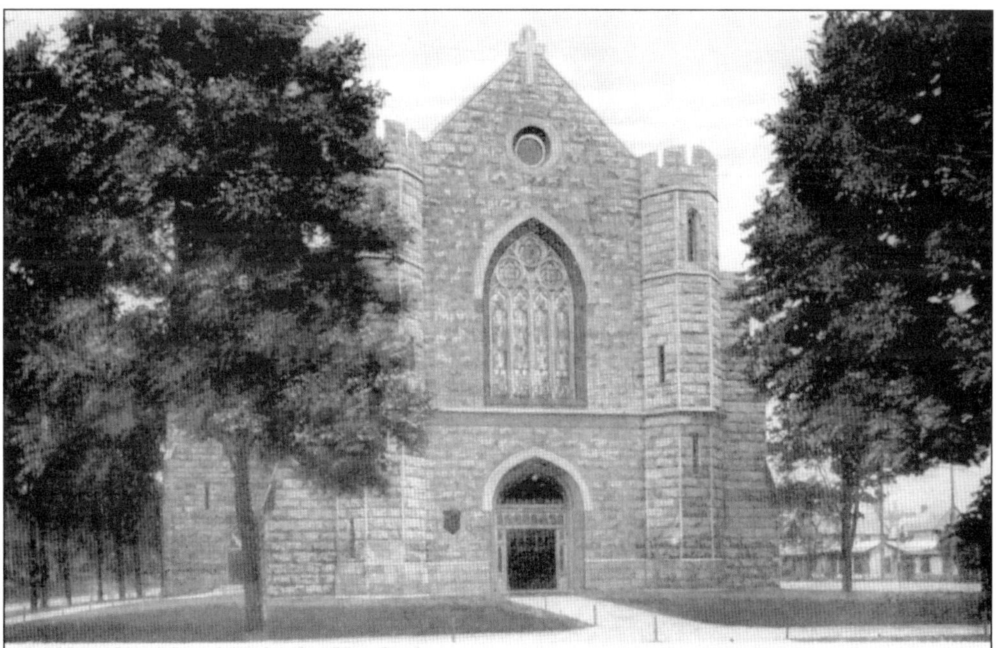

First Presbyterian Church, now Christ Presbyterian, occupies the lot on West Tuscarawas Street set aside for a house of worship by Bezaleel Wells. Originally the site of a combined Reformed and Lutheran congregation, the current church was built in 1871. Although construction was not complete, the church was the site of the wedding of Ida Saxton and William McKinley on January 25, 1871.

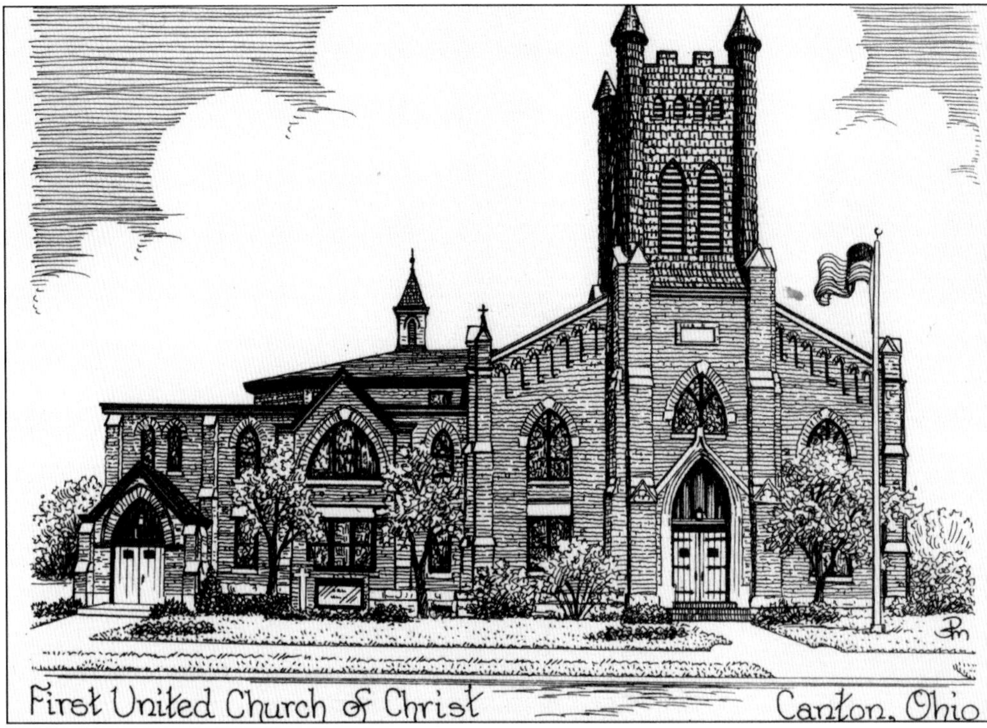

Established in 1810 to serve the German immigrant population, First Lutheran and First Reformed congregations once occupied the West Tuscarawas site designated for a house of worship. The congregations moved in 1822 to the site of the First Lutheran Church on East Tuscarawas Street. When the congregations split, the First Reformed congregation, now the First United Church of Christ, built the present church in 1862.

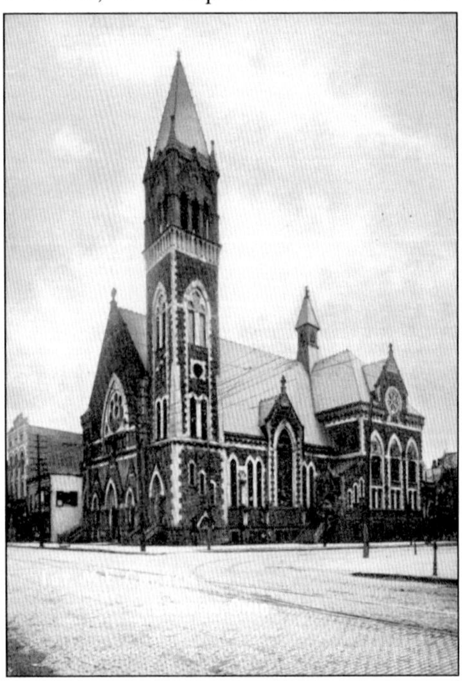

In 1906, Violet Woolston of Garfield Avenue in Canton sent this card to Minnie Summers of St. Elmo, Tennessee, telling her, "This was the church where President McKinley used to go." The High Victorian Gothic First United Methodist Episcopal Church, now Church of the Savior, was built on the corner of West Tuscarawas Street and Cleveland Avenue in 1883 after a fire destroyed an earlier church in 1881.

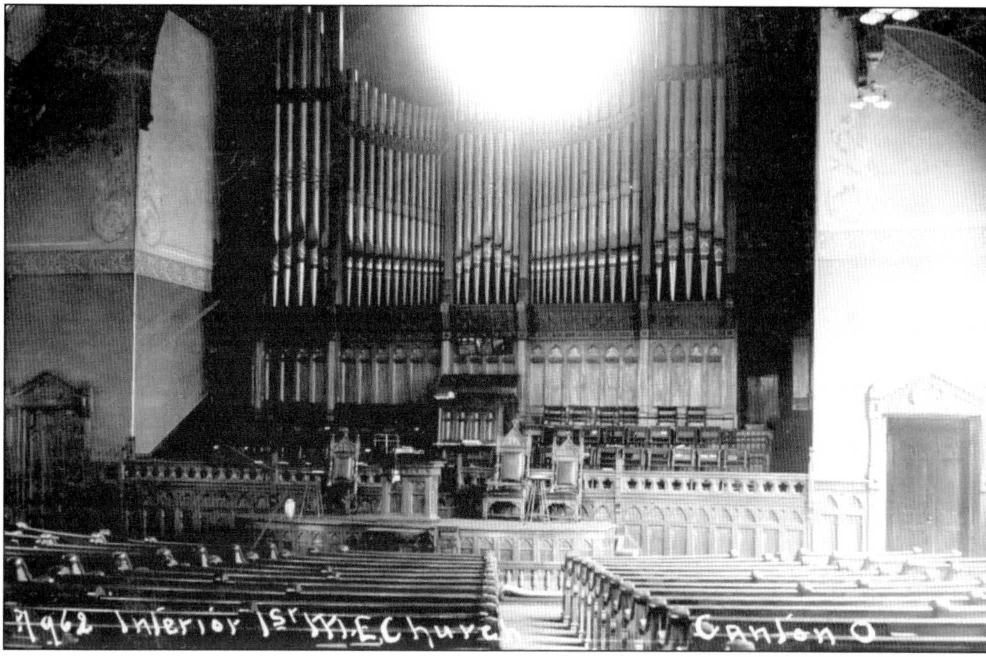

This real-photo card shows the interior of the First Methodist Episcopal Church as it looked when William McKinley attended. His funeral was held here on September 19, 1901. The fifth pew from the front was designated the McKinley pew and was marked with a silver plate in 1903. McKinley's mother was an active member of the church, and he served as a Sunday school teacher and superintendent and member of the board of trustees.

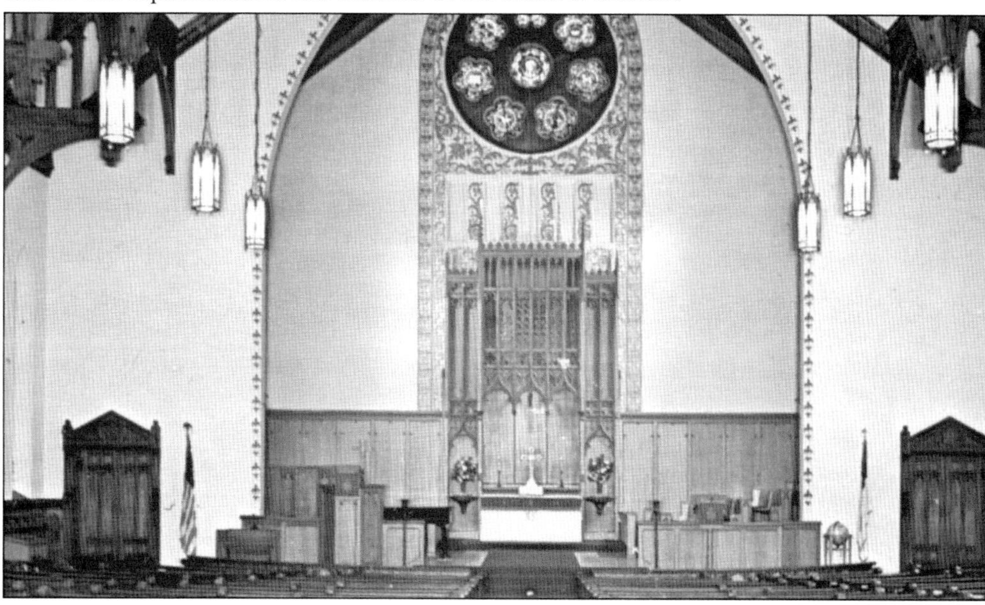

This is the interior of the Church of the Savior as it looks today following a major renovation in 1950. Known for its exceptional European stained-glass windows, the church also has four McKinley memorial windows. A gift from Ida McKinley in 1907, each window represents an aspect of McKinley's life and character: Gideon the soldier; Moses the law giver; John the humanitarian; and Cornelius the man of God.

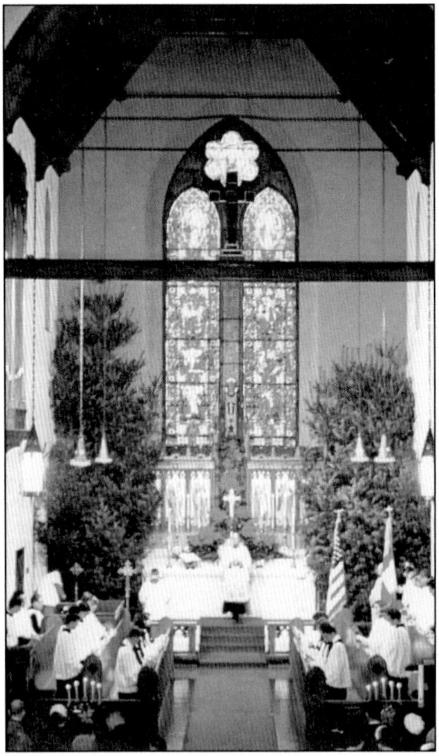

The 15th-century English Gothic style St. Paul's Episcopal Church is located on South Cleveland Avenue. Constructed in 1923 in just eight months, the Indiana limestone church has over 40 stained-glass windows, including the lancet windows over the altar patterned after those in the Chartres Cathedral in France. Italian marble and carved oak adorn the altar.

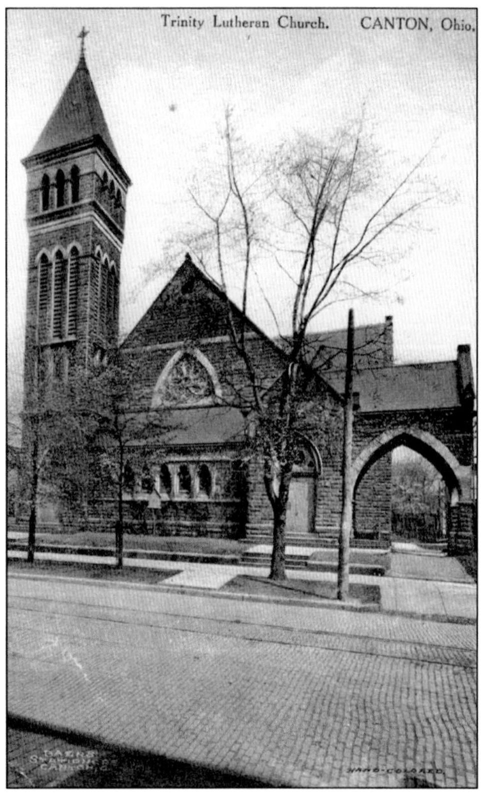

Trinity Lutheran was founded in 1838 by members of the German Lutheran Church who preferred services in English. It was one of the first buildings designed by Guy Tilden in 1886, and the title of Martin Luther's hymn "A Mighty Fortress Is Our God" is inscribed on the facade. This 1919 card shows the church before the front doors were painted red. The red doors are said to discourage the devil from entering.

Jennie Buffenmeyer of Canton received this card with the photograph in August 1908. A month later "Viola" wrote her sister, "Mrs. S.A. Wilkerson" of Norwalk, telling her that she had "heard a good sermon last night" at the First Baptist Church. The subject was "The Danger of Hesitation—I will follow the Lord, but——." This 1849 building was replaced by a much larger church in 1913.

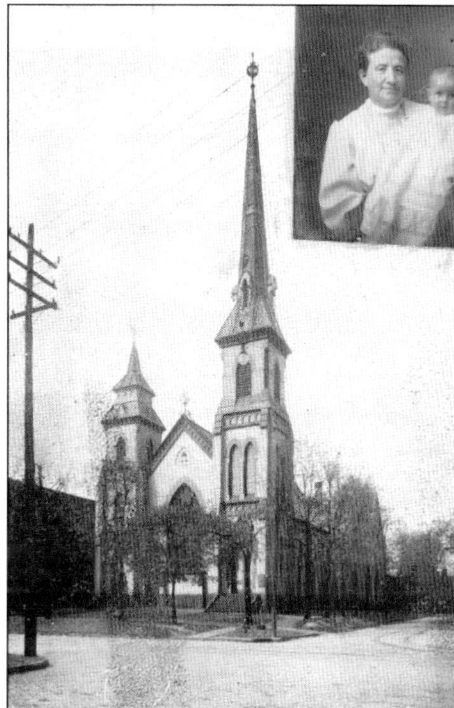

First Baptist Church, Canton, Ohio

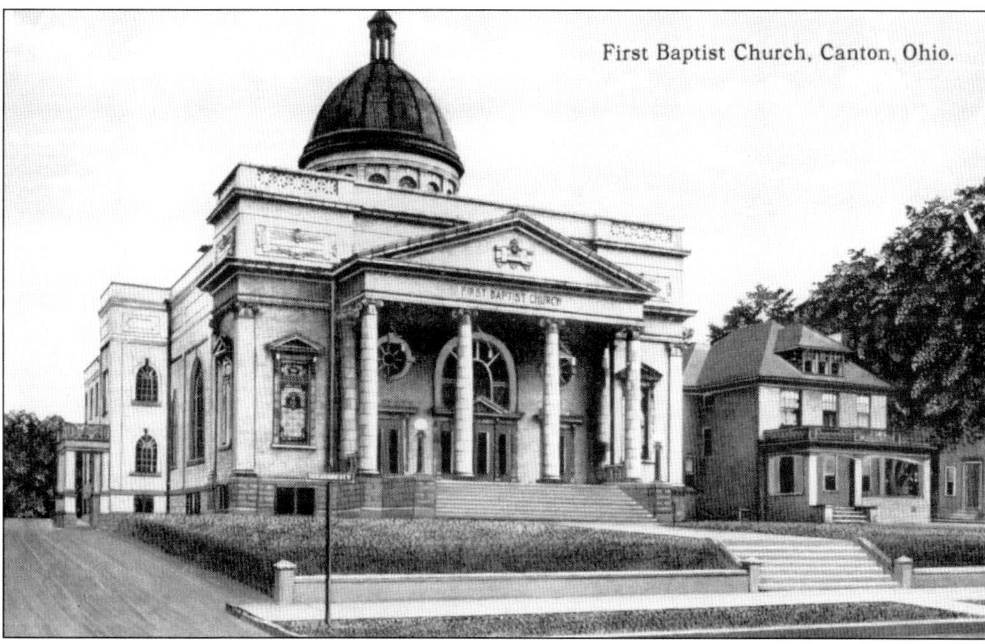

Located on West Tuscarawas Street, the Renaissance Revival–style First Baptist Church was completed in 1913. The church was known for its numerous Tiffany windows, including those in a 32-foot basilica-style dome. The congregation moved to a suburban church in the early 1990s, and although efforts were made to sell the building for alternative uses, it was destroyed by fire in 1991.

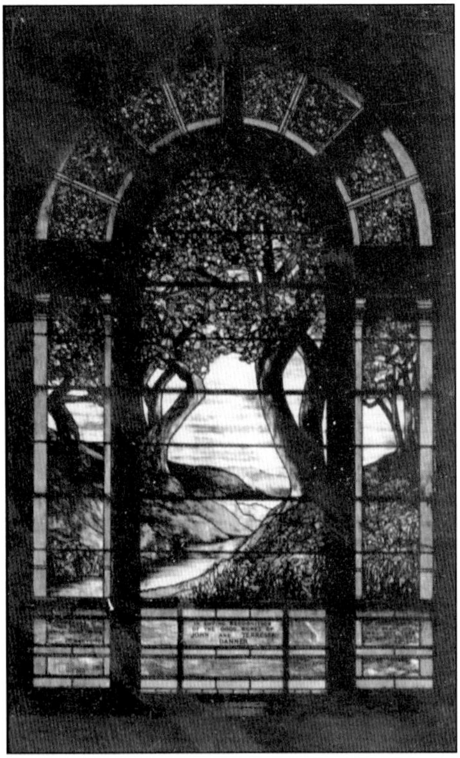

The most outstanding of the Tiffany windows in the First Baptist Church was the Danner window, given by John and Teressa Danner. One of the first natives of Canton, John owned the John Danner Revolving Bookcase Company. A wealthy and influential man, he was a staunch prohibitionist. When the church closed in 1990, the window was removed and sold at auction in 2000 for $1.9 million.

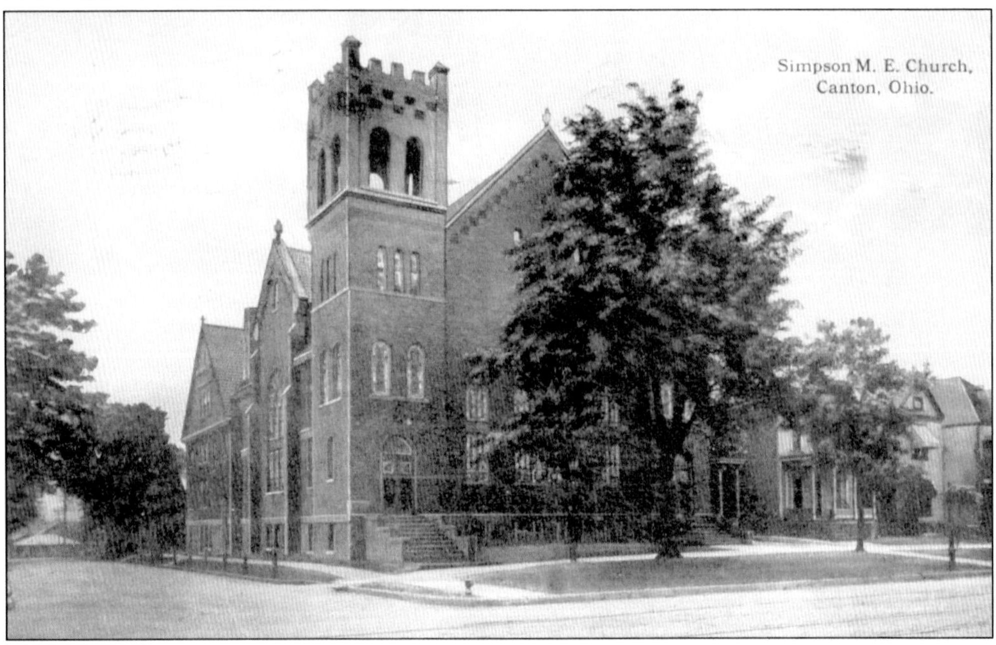

Established in 1871, with the assistance of the First Methodist Episcopal Church, Simpson Methodist Church met for a time in an unused Pennsylvania Railroad building. Originally called Second Methodist, the church was renamed in honor of Bishop Matthew Simpson. Located on South Market Avenue, this 1908 building is the current home of the Shiloh Missionary Baptist Church.

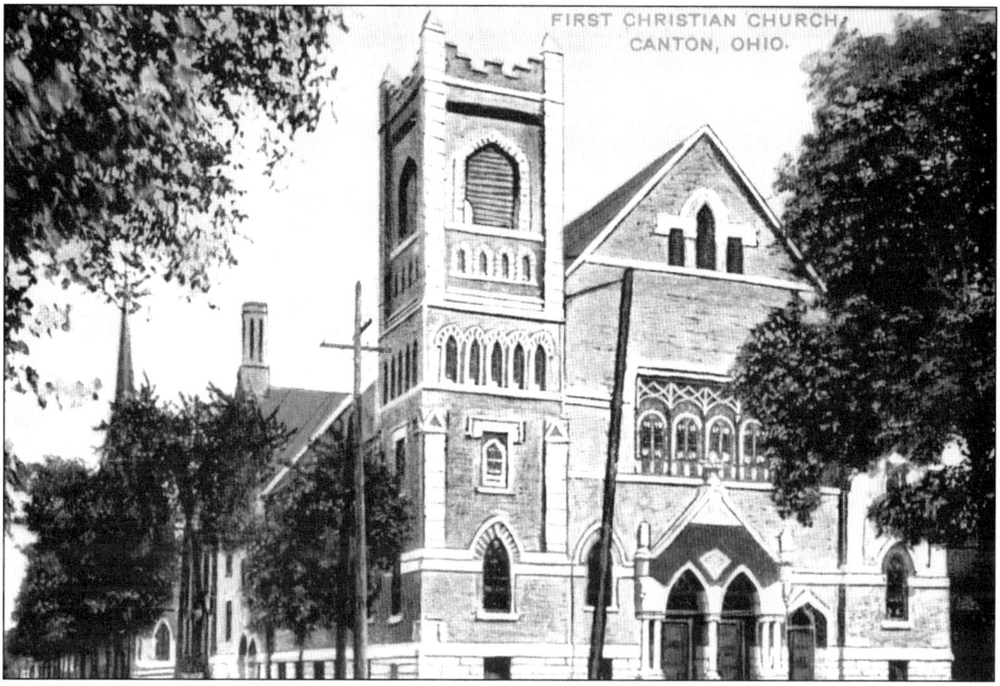

Organized in 1855 with 35 members, the First Christian Church was located on the site of the current city hall. In 1880, the congregation sold the 300-seat building to the city and built the 450-seat church shown in this card. Located on Dewalt and Fourth Streets, the church was sold in 1903, and a 1,000-seat church was erected on Cleveland Avenue. P. H. Welshiemer led the church from 1902 until 1959.

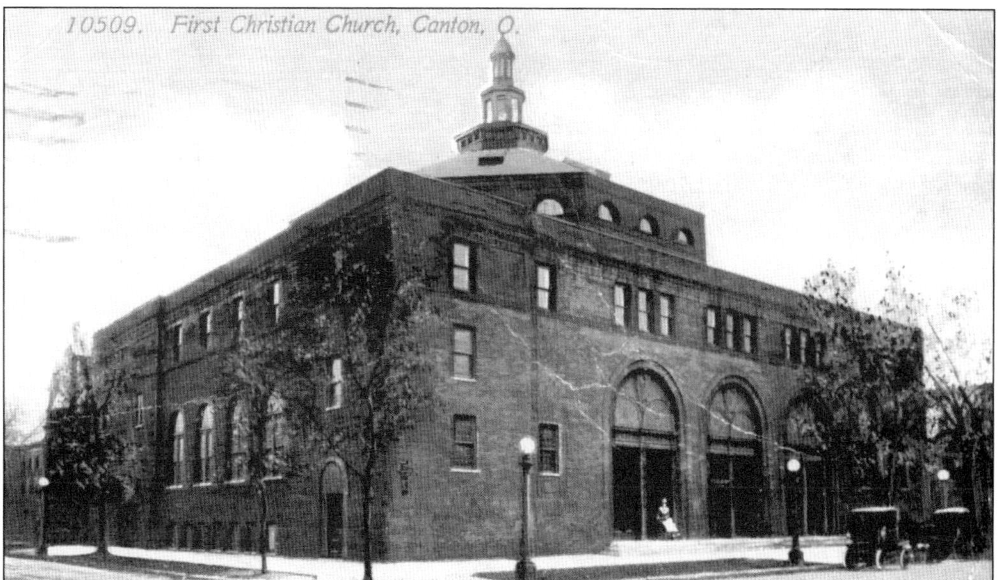

Located at the corner of Cleveland Avenue and Fourth Street, the First Christian Church was dedicated in 1912. In 1916, "Ida Mae" wrote to her mother in Fort Recovery that "the church has 56 rooms, but their meeting on Sunday will be held at the City Auditorium." The church also established the Phillips Bible Institute, which had an enrollment of over 500 in 1913.

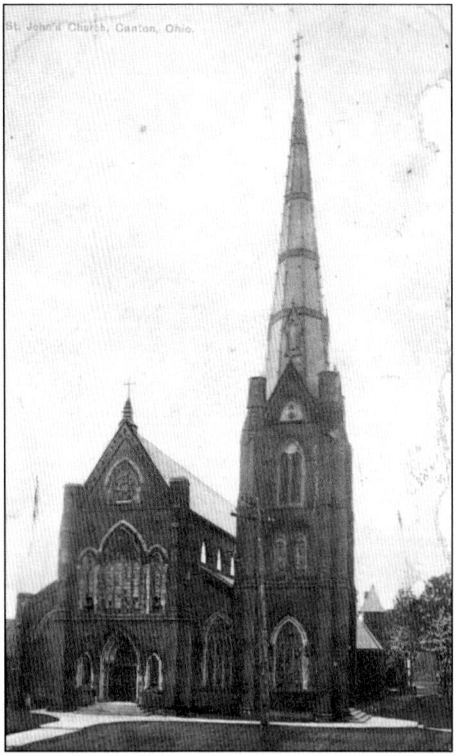

Officially established in 1823, St. John's is the oldest Catholic parish in northeast Ohio. John Schorb, said to be Canton's first Roman Catholic, donated the land for the 1872 building on McKinley Avenue and Sixth Street. The church was designed by Renwick and Kiely, architects of Manhattan's St. Patrick's Cathedral. In 1924, St. John's pastor, Msgr. Edward P. Graham, established radio station WHBC in order to broadcast his sermons.

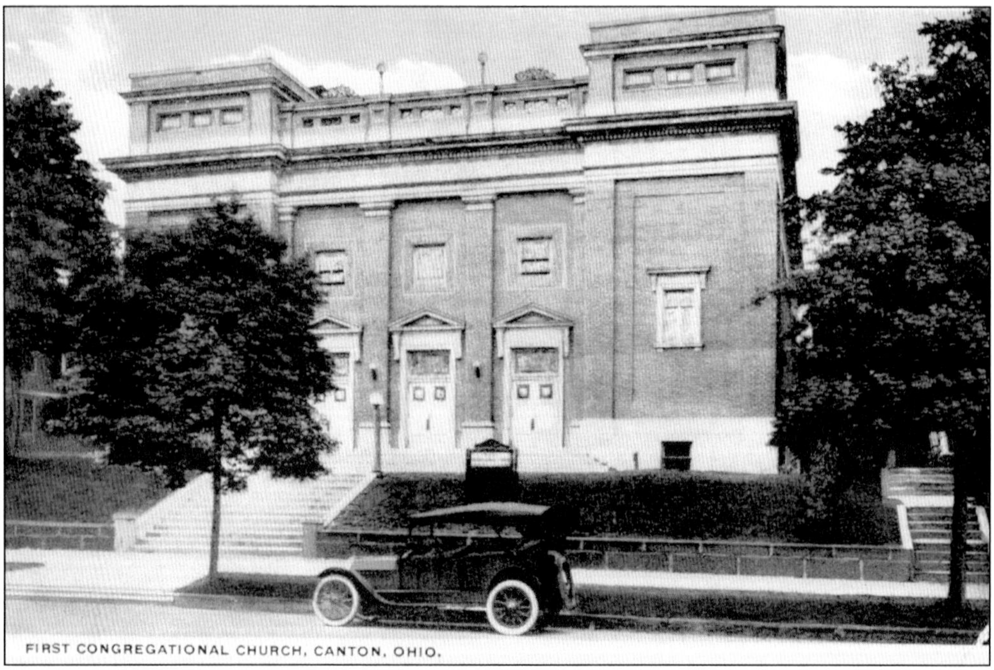

The First Congregational Church on West Tuscarawas Street was founded in 1914 following a split from the First Evangelical United Brethren Church. Meeting in a garage and later a tabernacle on this site, the 800 members laid the cornerstone for the church in 1915. At the time of its dedication it was one of the largest churches in Canton, with a seating capacity of 1,800.

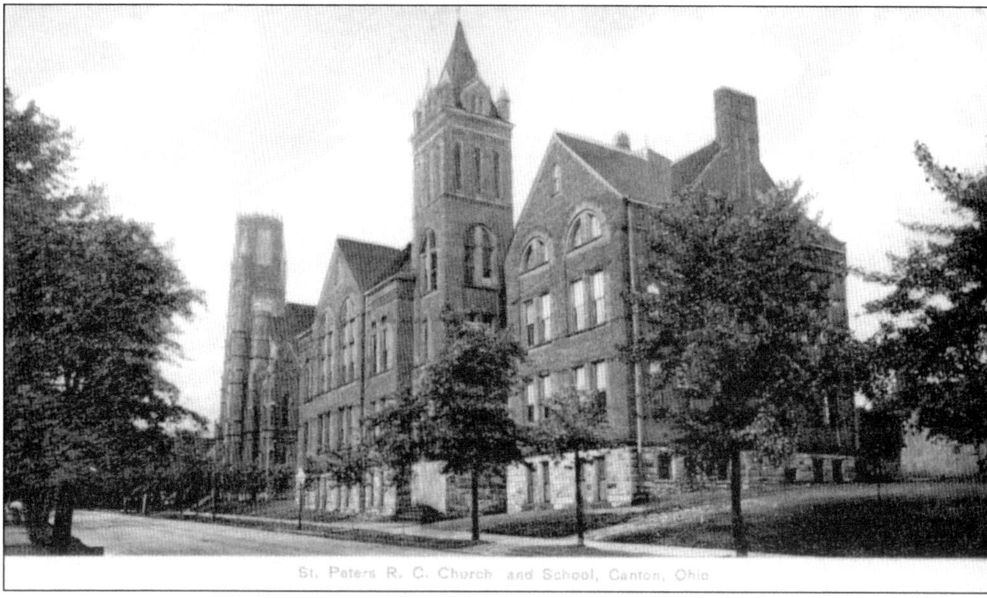

St. Peter's Catholic Church was organized in 1845 for members of St. John's parish who wished to attend German-language services. For many years, St. John's was the English-Irish church, while St. Peter's was the German church. Located on Cleveland Avenue, this card shows the Gothic Revival church and school with the original brick facade.

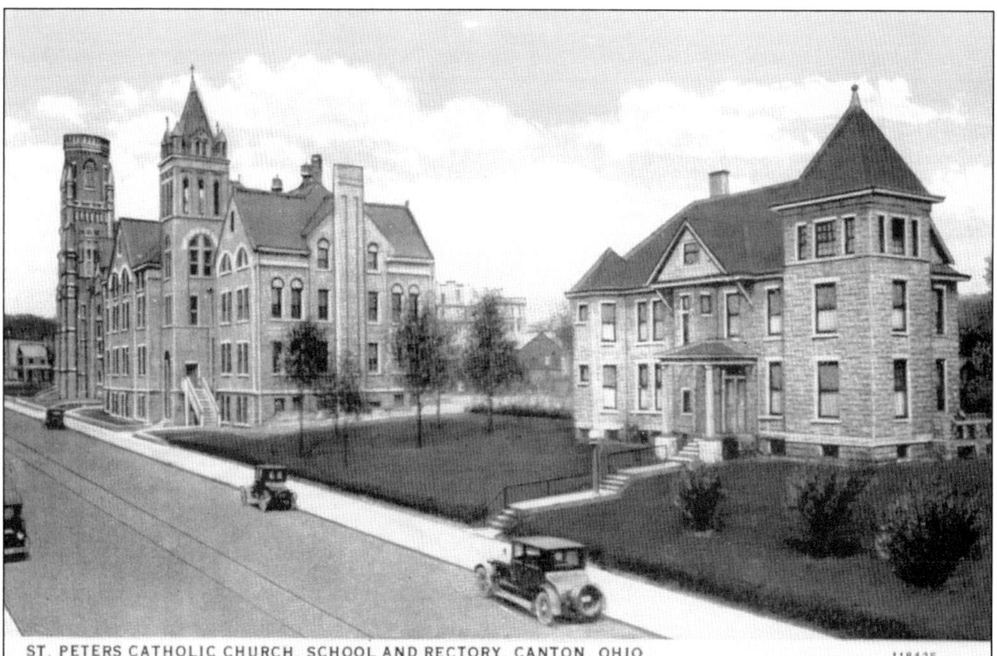

Completed in 1879 after four years of construction, the Gothic Revival interior of St. Peter's Catholic Church focuses worshipers' attention on the marble altar and statuary created by Meyer of Munich. The exterior of the church was covered in 1919 with a stucco surface resembling stone in preparation for its diamond anniversary celebration.

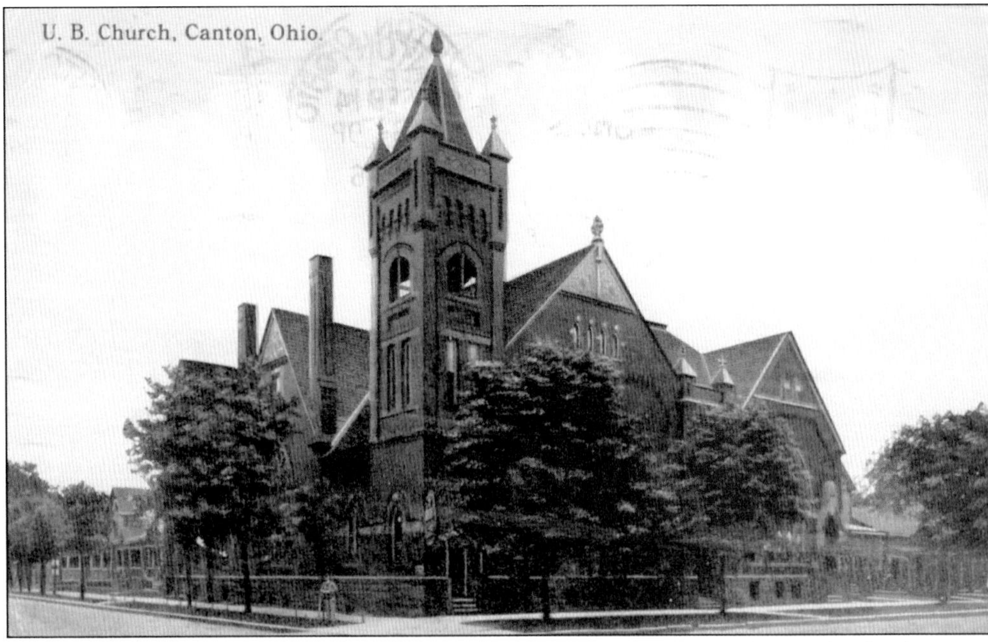

Established in 1867, the United Brethren congregation built this church on Cleveland Avenue and Fifth Street in 1893. The ladies of the church paid much of the building debt by selling bread and pies at the Little Dutch Oven, a stall in the city market from 1896 to 1906. This 1916 card shows the 1907 addition. By 1913, there were 2,400 members.

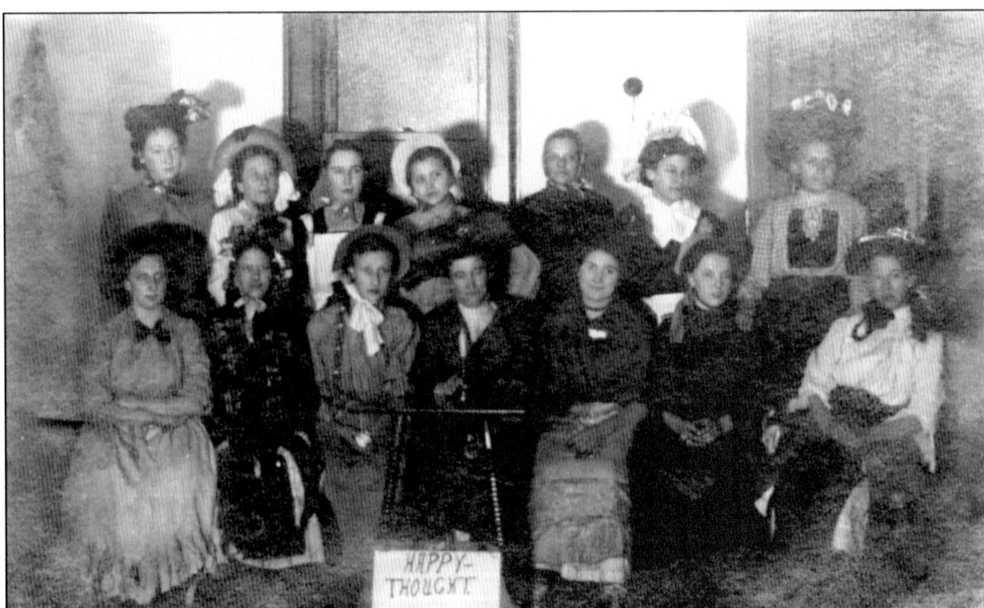

"Julia" of Canton sent this card to her grandmother Elizabeth Shafer of Canal Fulton on April 14, 1909. Julia wrote, "This is my S. S. class taken in our class room by flashlight, it was a fancy dress affair as you can see. The name of the class is on the grip." The church is not identified.

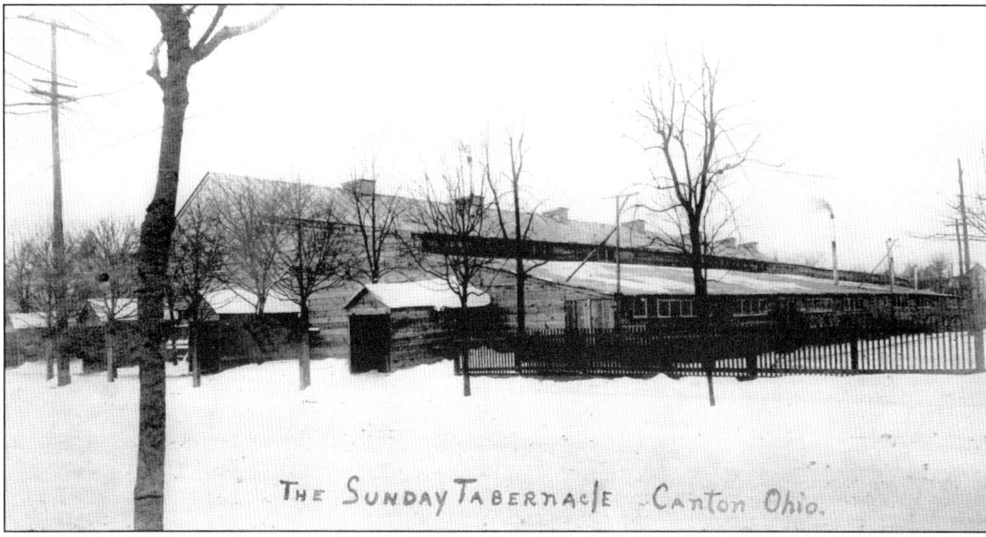

Evangelist Billy Sunday came to Canton for a six-week crusade on December 31, 1911. Erected on the current Market Avenue site of the Memorial Civic Center, the wooden Sunday tabernacle held 8,000. Thousands came to hear him. On January 12, 1912, 10,000 women attended a "ladies only" service despite the minus-24-degree weather. Preaching on the evils of sin and lust, Sunday reportedly had the shocked crowd on the edge of their seats.

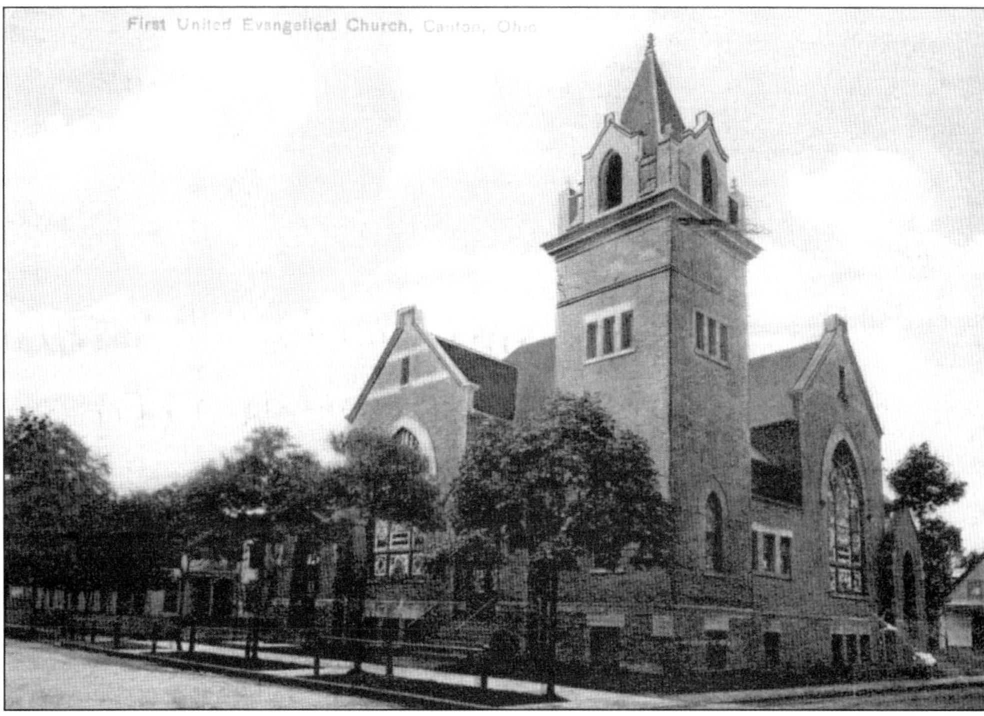

The United Evangelical Church, led by Rev. P. S. Smoke, was one of the 21 Protestant churches that assisted with the Billy Sunday campaign. The wooden tabernacle had a sawdust floor and a stage for a 600-voice choir of local singers led by Homer Rodehaver. At the end of the campaign, Sunday reported 5,654 converts had walked "the sawdust trail." He received a parting gift of $13,000 from grateful worshipers.

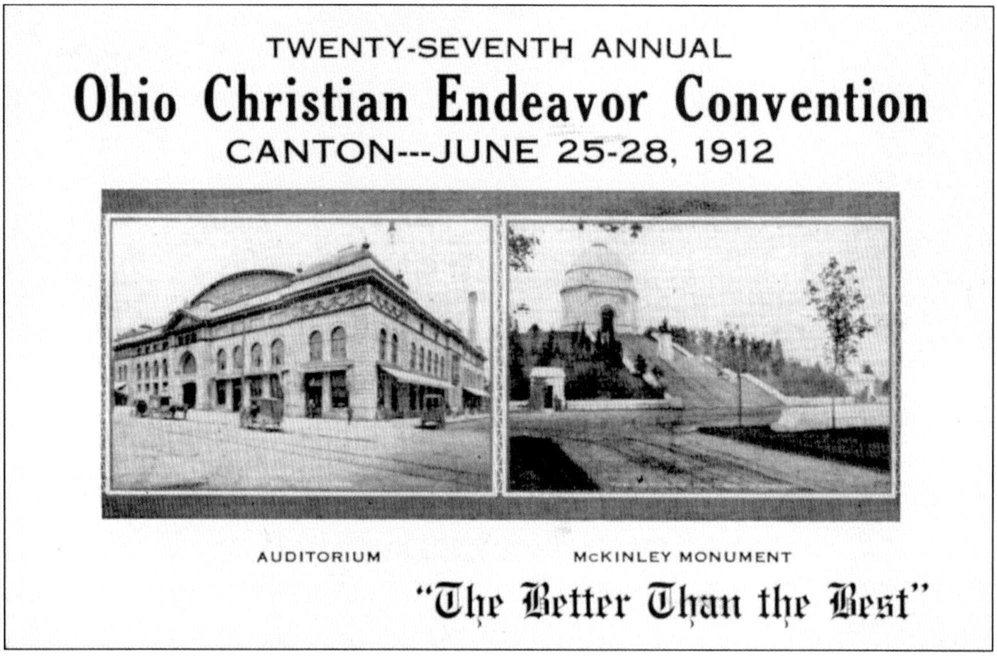

The Christian Endeavor Association was founded in 1881 by Dr. Francis Clark of Portland, Maine. By 1895, the interdenominational association had become an international movement. Among one of the early Christian Endeavor supporters was E. O. Ezell. Born in Uniontown in 1851, Ezell was a music publisher, composer, and Sunday school song leader whose stanza arrangement of "Amazing Grace" remains in use today.

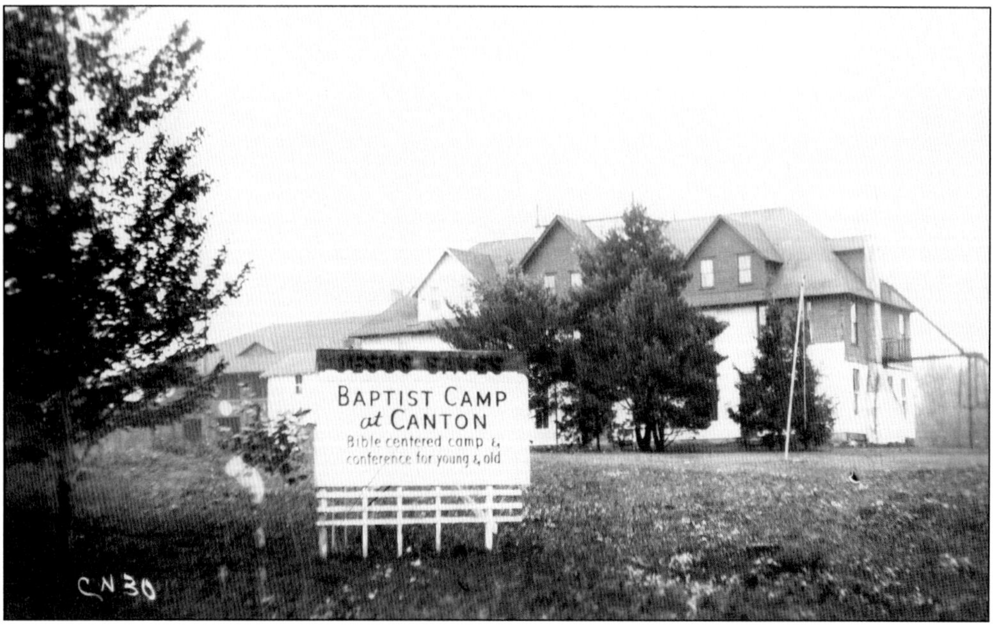

This real-photo postcard shows the "Baptist Camp at Canton Bible centered camp & conference for young & old."

Eight

Parks, Recreation, and West Lawn Cemetery

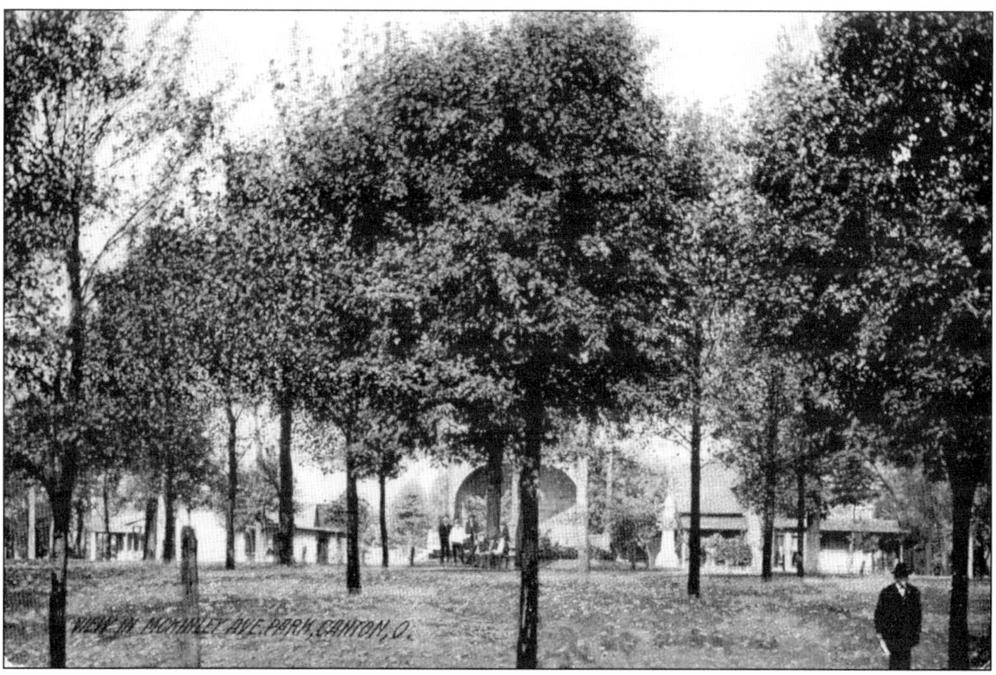

McKinley Park, on McKinley Avenue and Sixth Street, was originally Plum Street Cemetery. Set aside by Bezaleel Wells, it is estimated that 128 people were buried there before 1884. In 1887, the city created the park, hauling in loads of dirt and covering all but two of the grave markers. These markers were left visible to ensure that Wells's heirs could not claim the property was no longer used as intended.

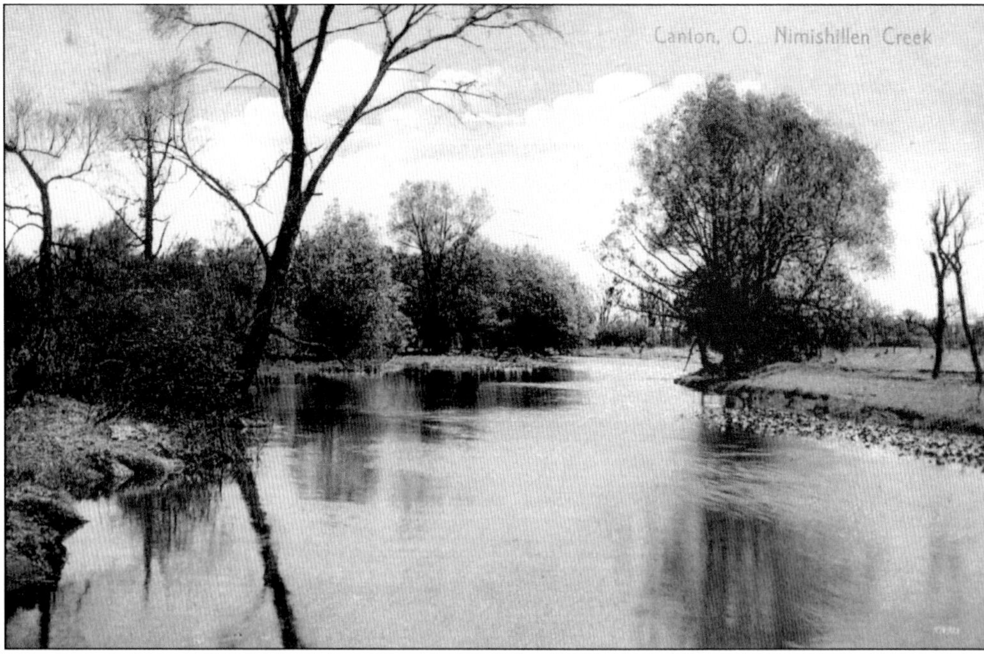

This 1911 card shows Nimishillen Creek. In 1873, Canton began drawing water supplies from the creek. Treatment of surface water supplies was not yet in use, and typhoid cases were numerous, especially during warm months.

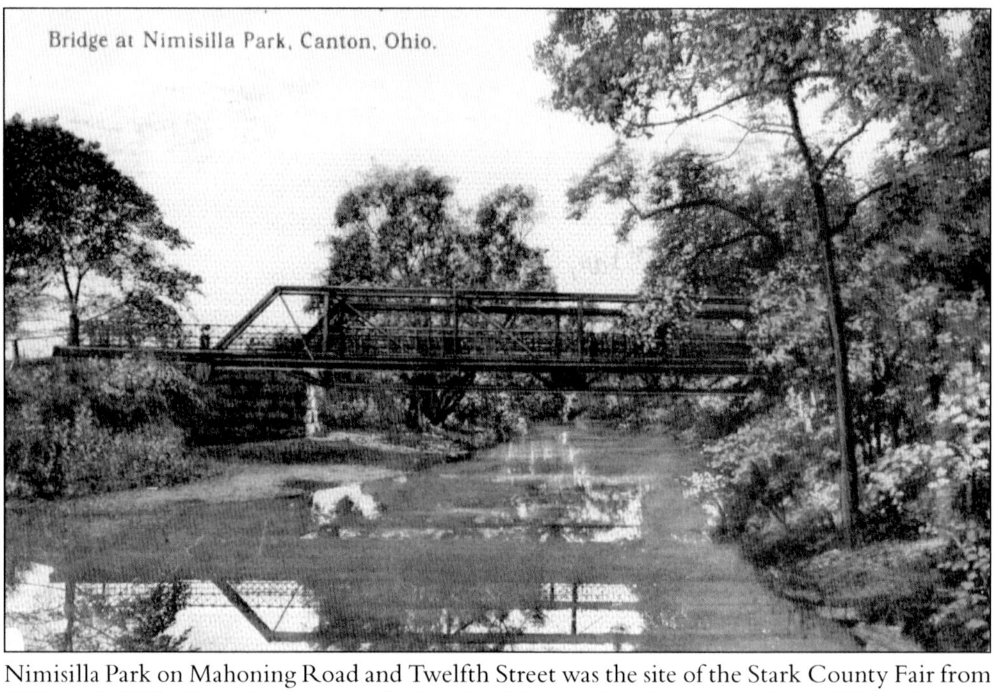

Nimisilla Park on Mahoning Road and Twelfth Street was the site of the Stark County Fair from 1859 until 1894. The park was created when the fair moved to the current site on Wertz Avenue. Originally over 20 acres, the park included a horse racetrack and a zoo with over 200 animals.

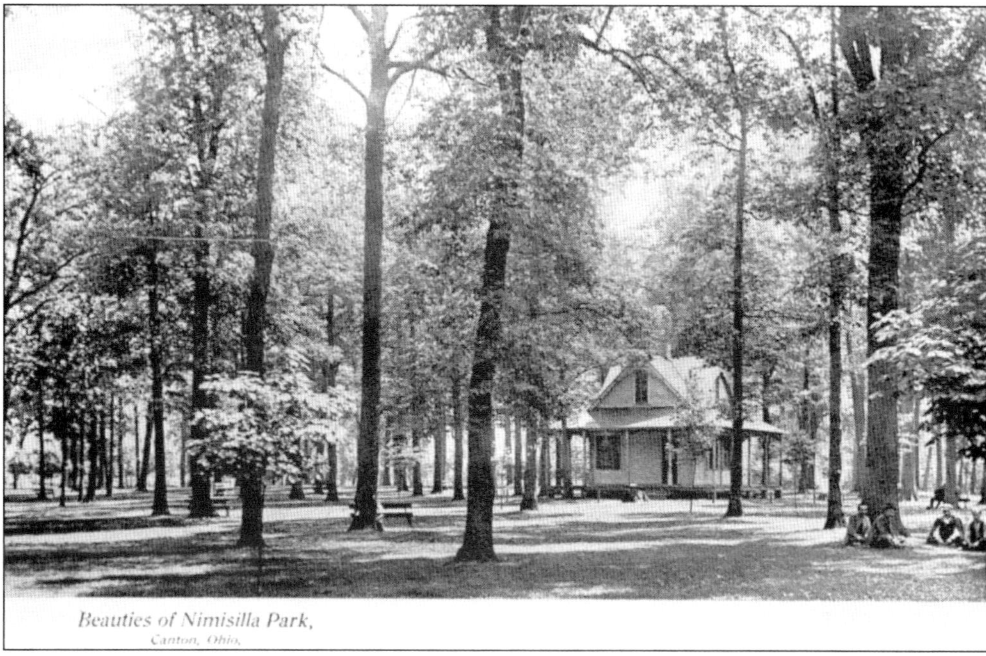

When this card was sent in 1907, most workers had only one full day off a week. It was common practice in warm months for families to go to church on Sunday, go home, pack a lunch, and head to the park for the day. In addition to fishing and canoeing, Nimisilla Park had a fenced meadowland deer run where city residents could see many deer.

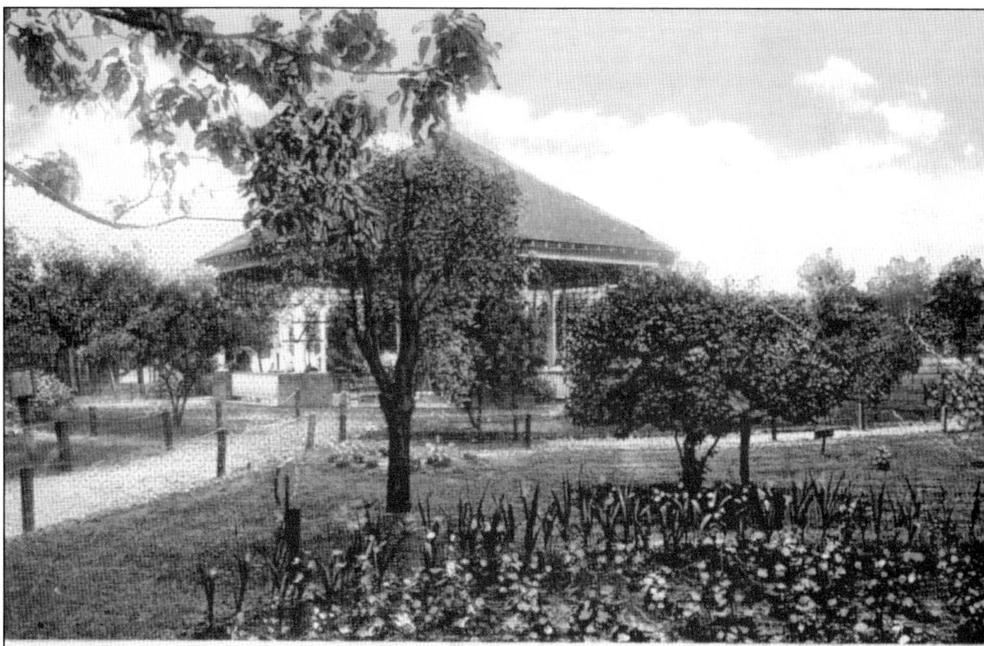

In addition to a park hall, Nimisilla Park had an open-air bandstand. People came for many years to hear concerts by the Thayers Military Band, American Legion Band, and Grand Army Band. Concerts were held there until the 1940s.

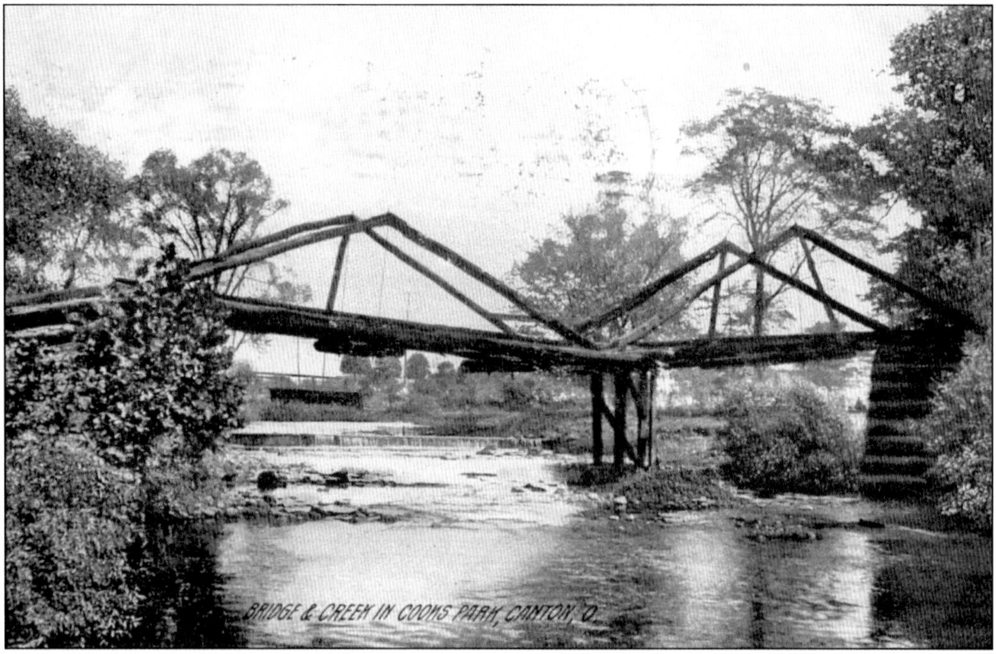

Located on Canton's east side, Cook Park was established in 1891. It was named for George Cook, one of the five young men who had joined Cornelius Aultman to form the Aultman Company in 1851. Like many Canton parks, it was located around an early water source for the city. The bridge is not damaged. This rather odd-angled footbridge was built this way.

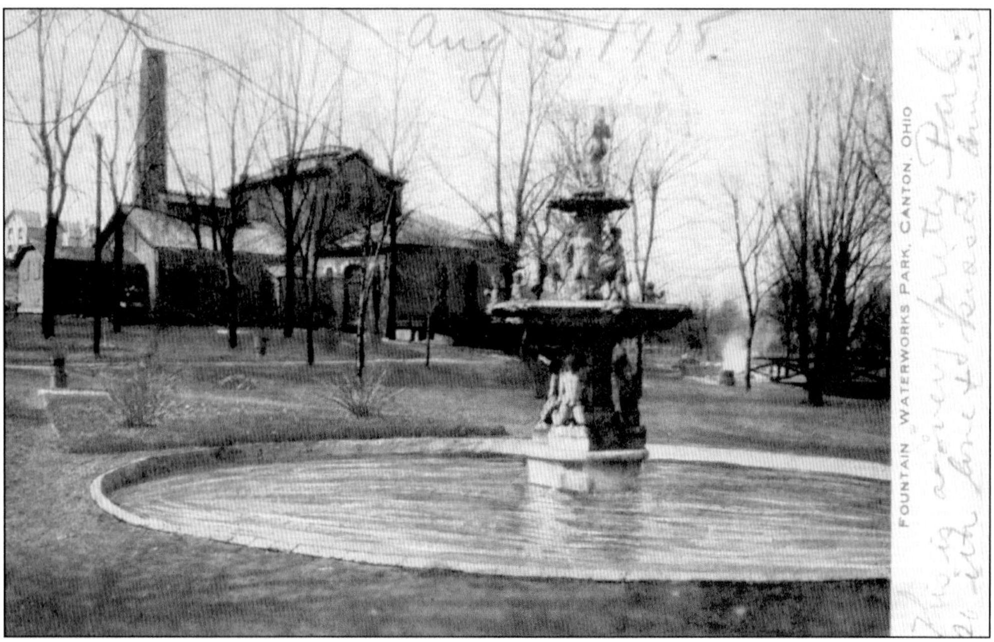

By 1886, the city had begun taking steps to assure an adequate water supply. Water was pumped from Meyers Lake to this pumping station on Elgin Avenue. Water Works Park was developed in 1889 on the property surrounding the pumping station. This 1908 card shows the pumping station and the elaborate park fountain.

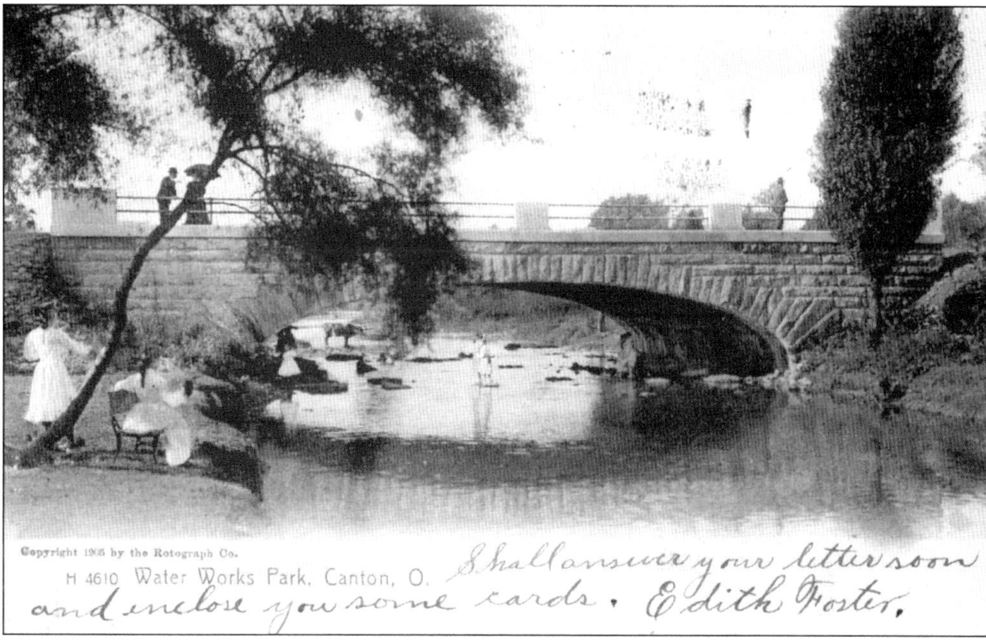

Two bridges crossed Nimishillen Creek in this long, narrow park. This 1906 card shows the main stone bridge.

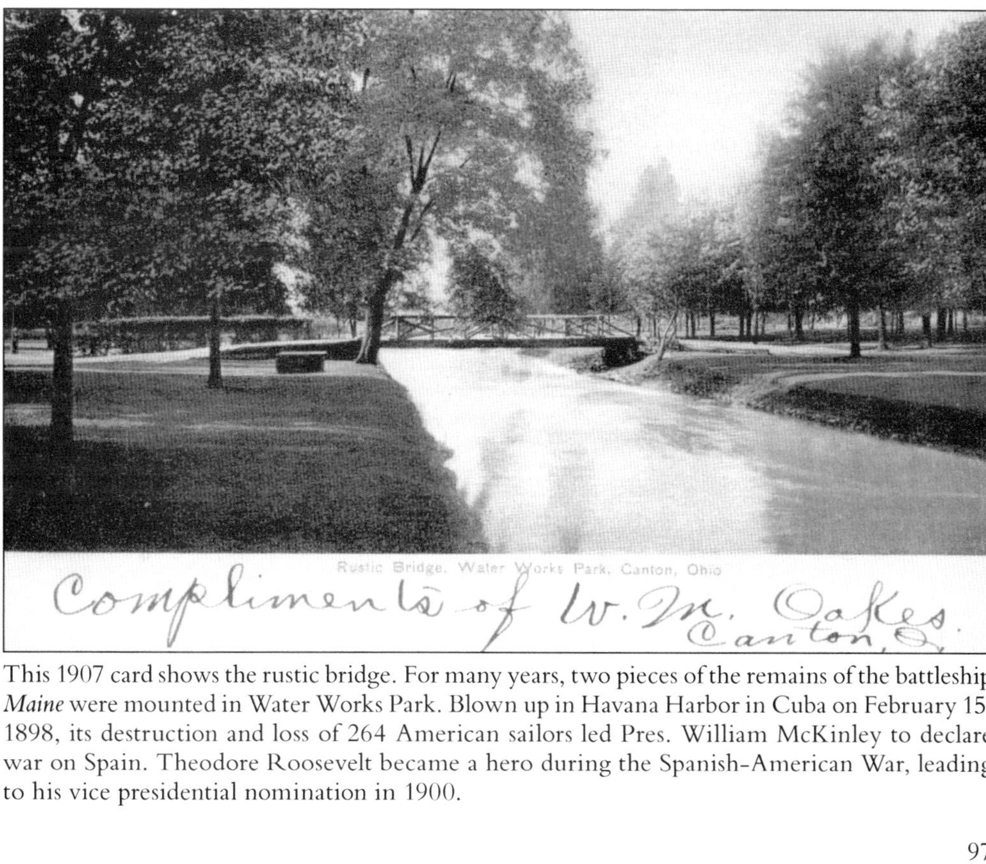

This 1907 card shows the rustic bridge. For many years, two pieces of the remains of the battleship *Maine* were mounted in Water Works Park. Blown up in Havana Harbor in Cuba on February 15, 1898, its destruction and loss of 264 American sailors led Pres. William McKinley to declare war on Spain. Theodore Roosevelt became a hero during the Spanish-American War, leading to his vice presidential nomination in 1900.

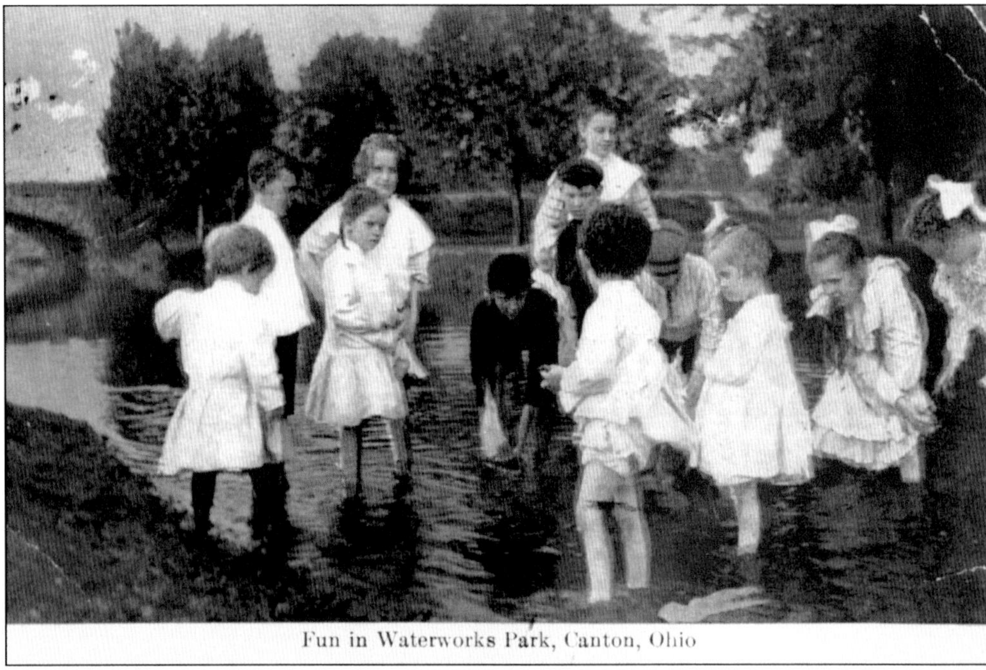

Children have always been attracted to the Water Works Park creek, as this 1910 card illustrates.

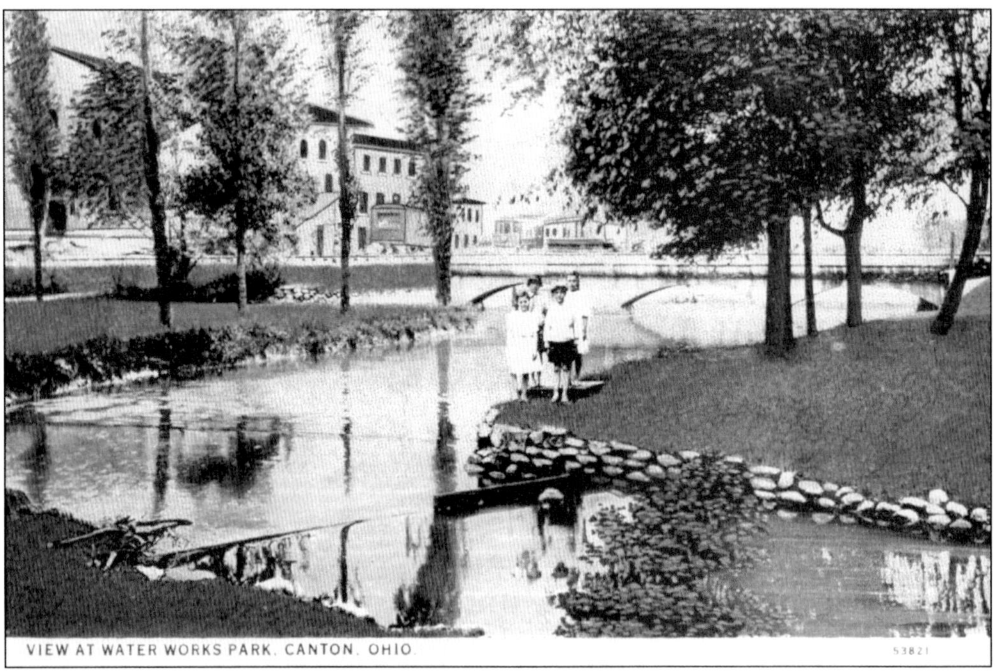

Mailed in 1938, this later card shows children along the edge of the creek near the pumping station. The station was torn down in 1938.

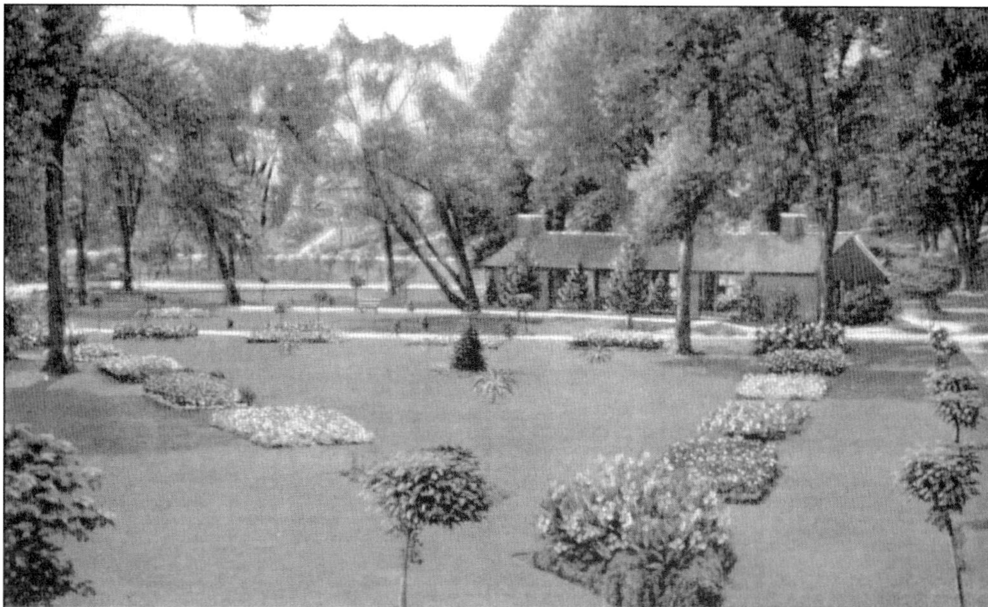

Water Works Park and Shelter House, Canton, Ohio 9A813-N

Although the lovely fountain is gone, Water Works Park remains a wonderful place to walk or have a family picnic. This 1940s card shows the flower gardens and the shelter house. In the early 1930s, Carl Weiss became Canton's park superintendent. Serving for over 25 years, Weiss was able to not only maintain the parks but also improve them, even during the Depression and World War II.

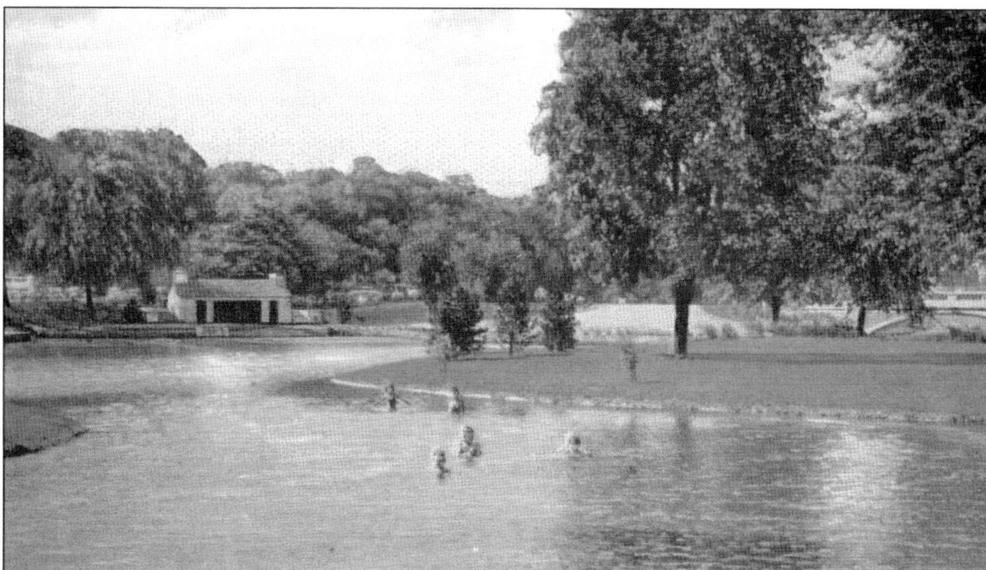

Shelter House and Lagoon in West Creek Park, Canton, Ohio 7A354

West Creek Park opened south of Ninth Street in 1934. Notice the people swimming in the lagoon in this 1938 view. According to historian J. G. Heald, superintendent Weiss acted as "administrator, landscaper, bookkeeper, horticulturalist, archaeologist, brick layer, and personnel director. . . . He personally laid 100,000 bricks and 20,000 stones . . . [and] supervised the planting of virtually every shrub, tree, and flower."

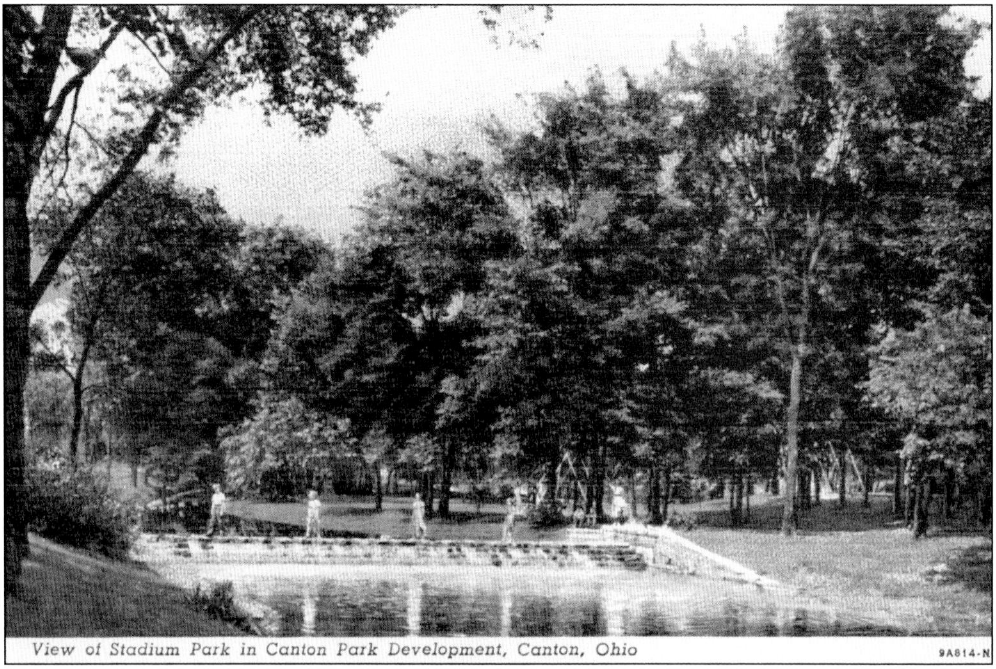

Stadium Park was added in 1935 to the string of parks east of the McKinley Monument. The small dam provided a great place for children to play in the water. The playground is through the trees in the center of the picture.

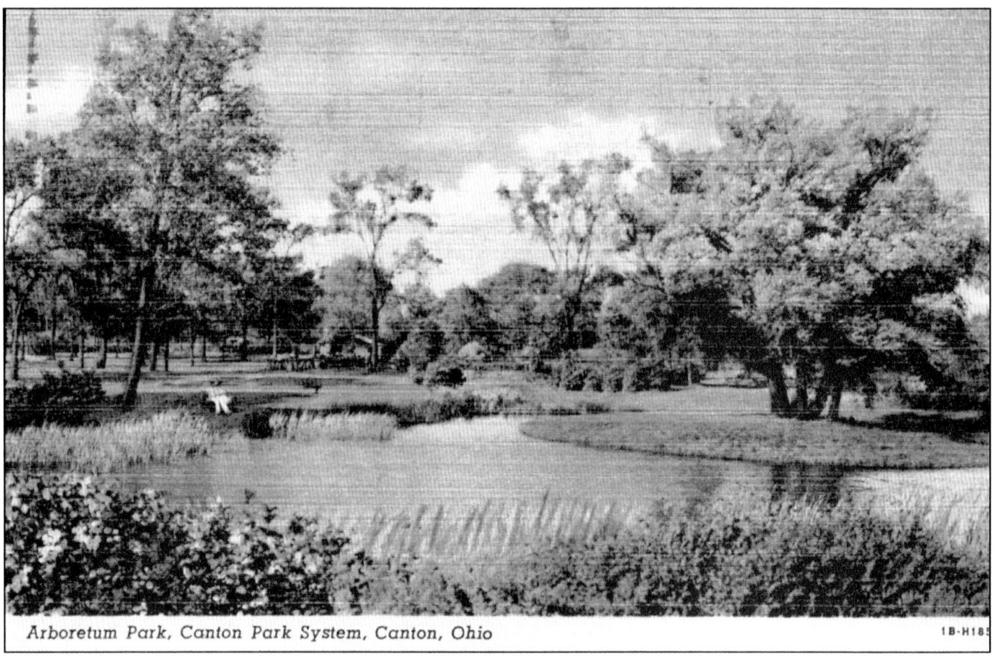

Arboretum Park was the northernmost Canton park. By the mid-20th century, the 600-acre park system ran the entire length of the city from north to south.

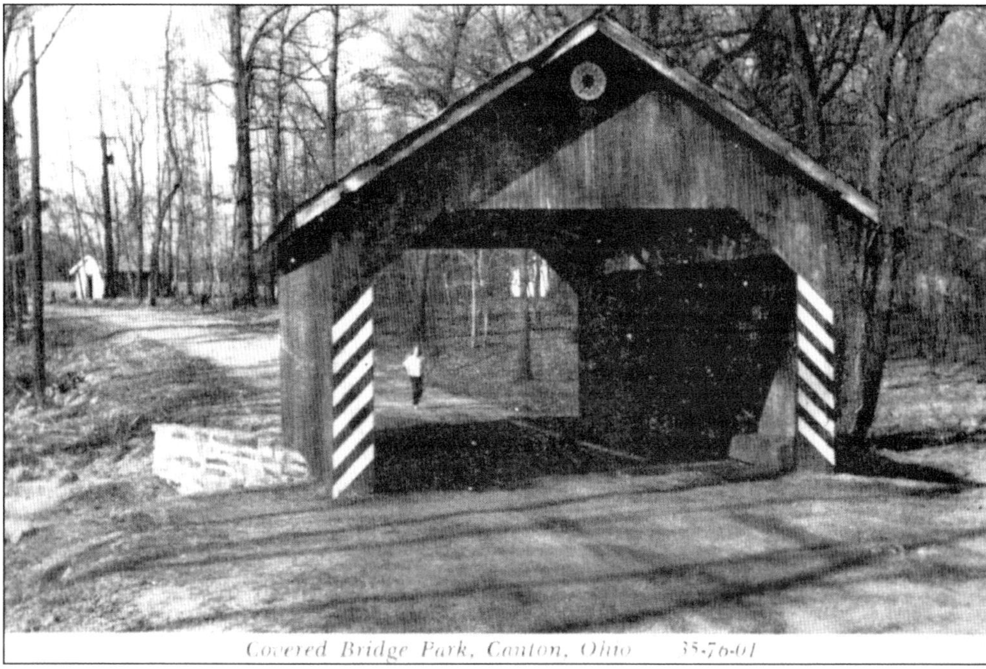

Located at Forty-fifth Street, Covered Bridge Park features a bridge spanning a branch of Nimishillen Creek. The covered bridge was built in 1961.

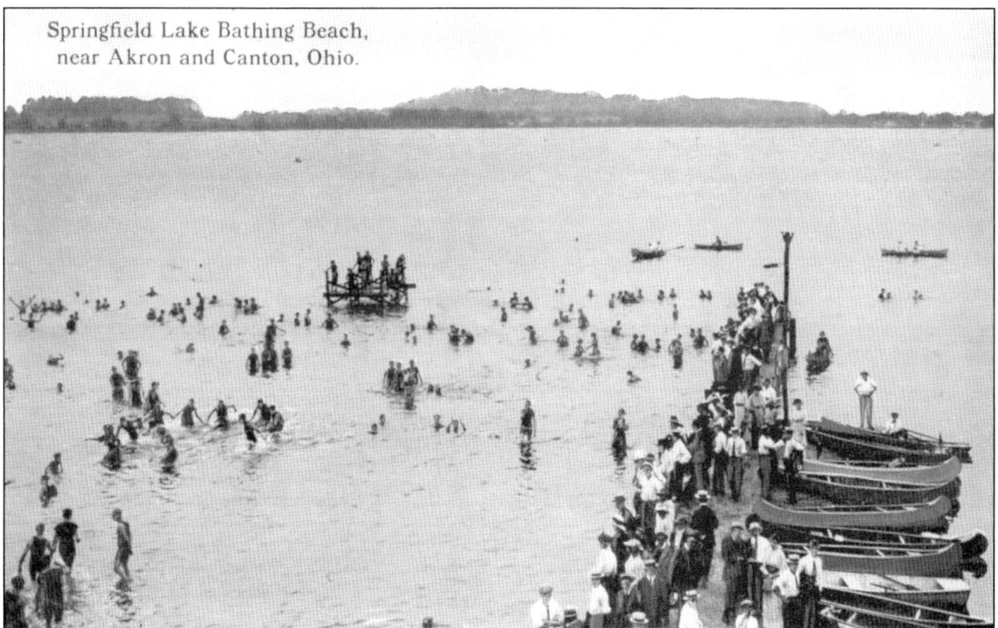

Springfield Lake, between Akron and Canton, is one of the few natural spring-fed lakes in Ohio. This pre-1920s card shows boaters and swimmers at the popular recreation area.

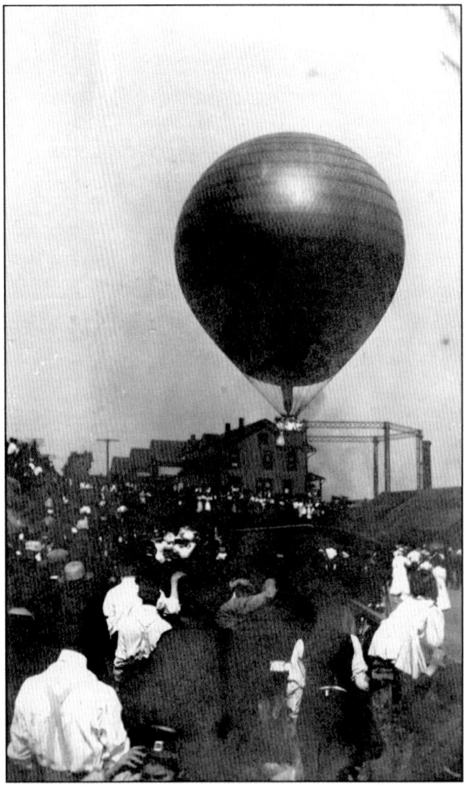

Organized in 1907 by Frank Lahm and several other flight enthusiasts, the Canton Aero Club lasted only three years. Its balloon, the *Ohio*, joined others that flew out of Canton, including the *Sky Pilot* and the *Buckeye*. The 1909 Stark County centennial celebration featured a race between the *Ohio* and the *Sky Pilot*. The *Sky Pilot* won, but fascination with airplanes diminished interest in ballooning.

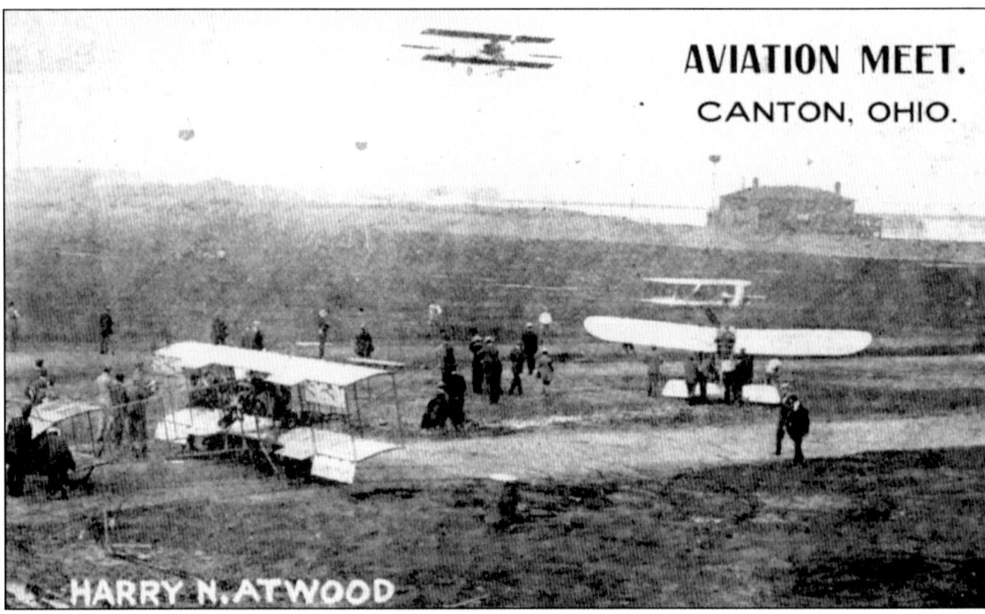

Formed in 1907 to sponsor balloon ascensions, the Canton Aero Club and the Ohio Aero Club sponsored an aviation meet at the Canton Fairgrounds on September 26–29, 1911. Aviator Harry Atwood flew his Burgess Wright biplane. The average speed of the planes was 40 miles an hour. Many local dignitaries flew with the aviators, including real estate developer Garfield Laiblin's 15-year-old daughter, Mildred, who flew with Atwood.

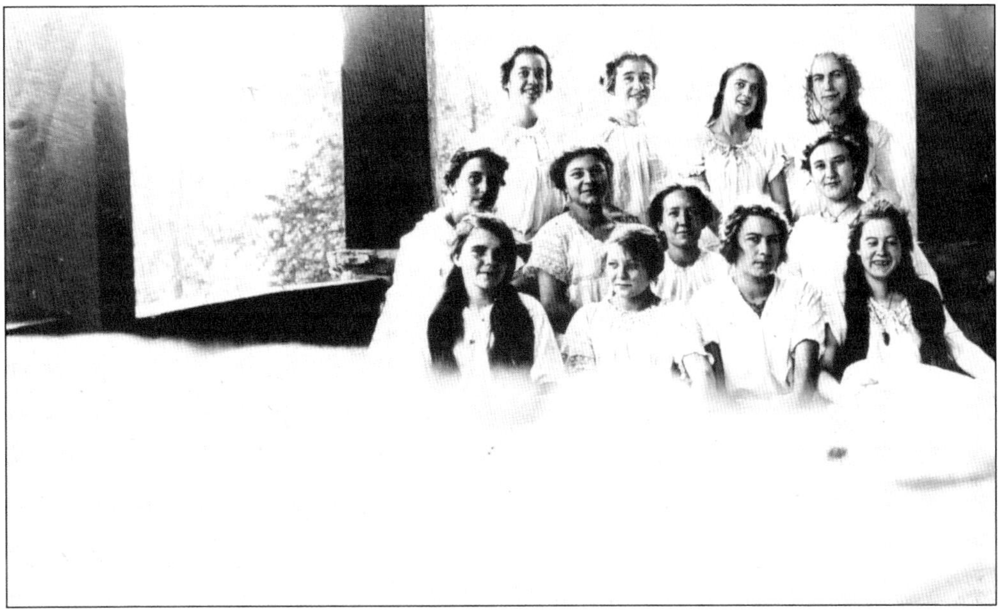

This undated real-photo postcard reads, "Y.W.C.A. gals Canton group at Kurtz Cottage, Congress Lake Ohio." Located close to Hartville in northern Stark County, Congress Lake was the home of the private Congress Lake Club. It was reached by the Connotton Valley Railroad, and the first board of directors included William McKinley when he was governor of Ohio in 1893.

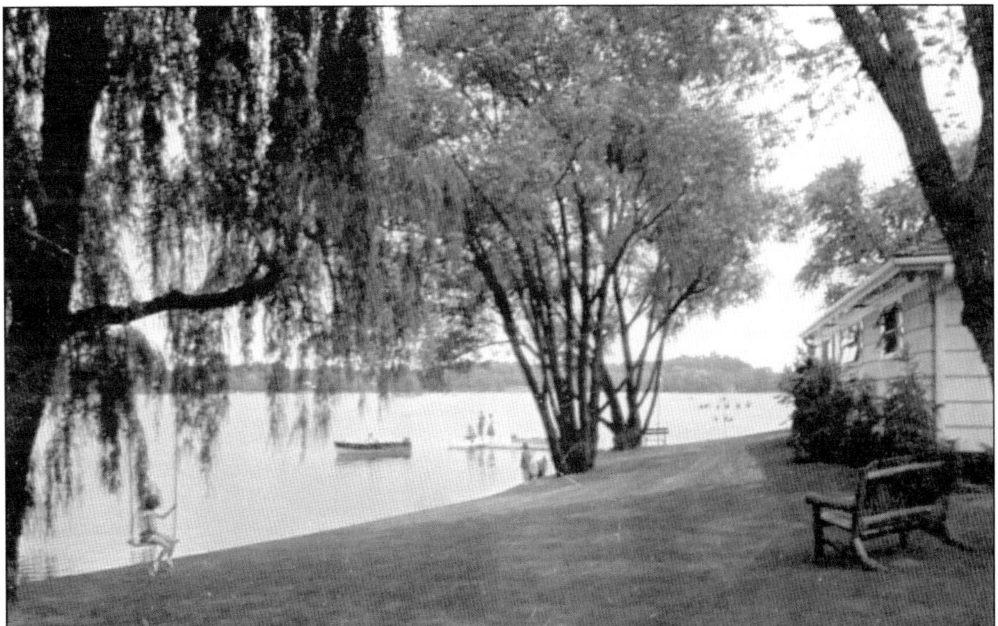

Located five miles west of Canton, Lake Cable is a 265-acre man-made lake. Fed by over 50 springs, the lake with its 10-mile shoreline, beach, and excellent fishing remains a recreational area and community.

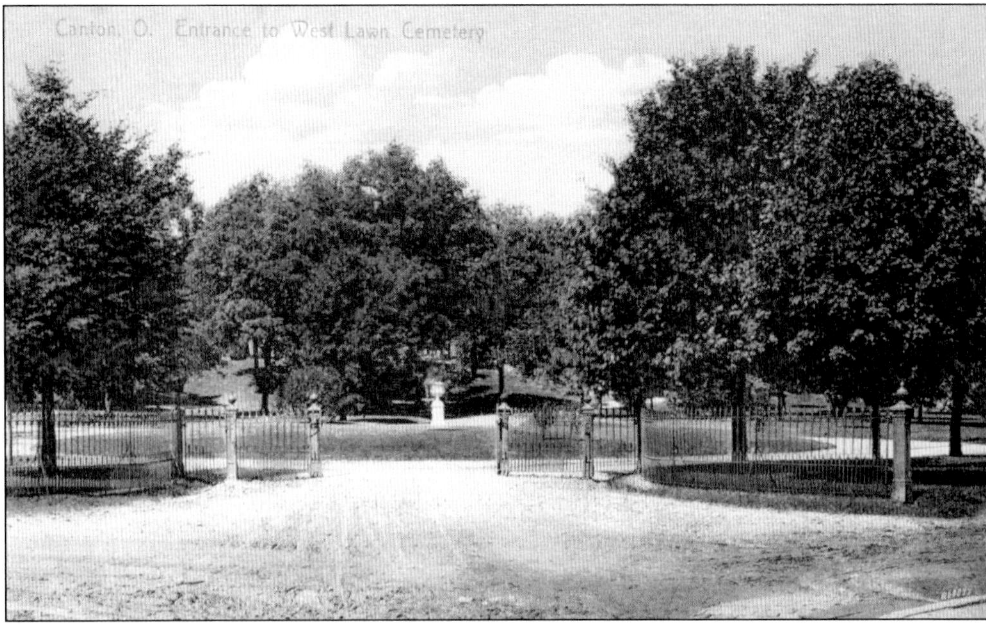

West Lawn Cemetery, opened in 1859, is currently bordered by Interstate 77, McKinley Monument Park, Fourth Street, and Twelfth Street. This card shows the Fourth Street entrance. Among the 44,000 graves of this still active cemetery are the final resting places of industrialists, politicians, soldiers, and inventors, as well as ordinary citizens.

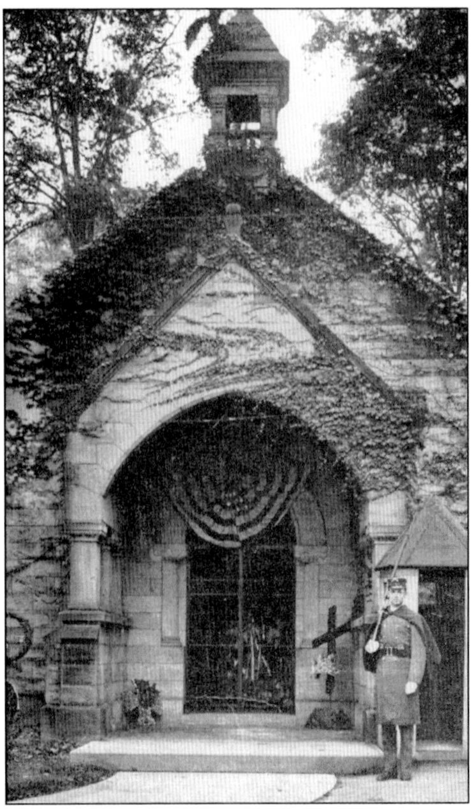

The Wertz vault near the Fourth Street entrance to the West Lawn Cemetery was the temporary resting place of Pres. William McKinley and later his wife, Ida. According to a 2006 episode of the PBS series *History Detectives*, one of the soldiers who guarded the vault was Sgt. Charles Kennedy. Sergeant Kennedy became a sexton in the cemetery and is buried in view of the McKinley Monument.

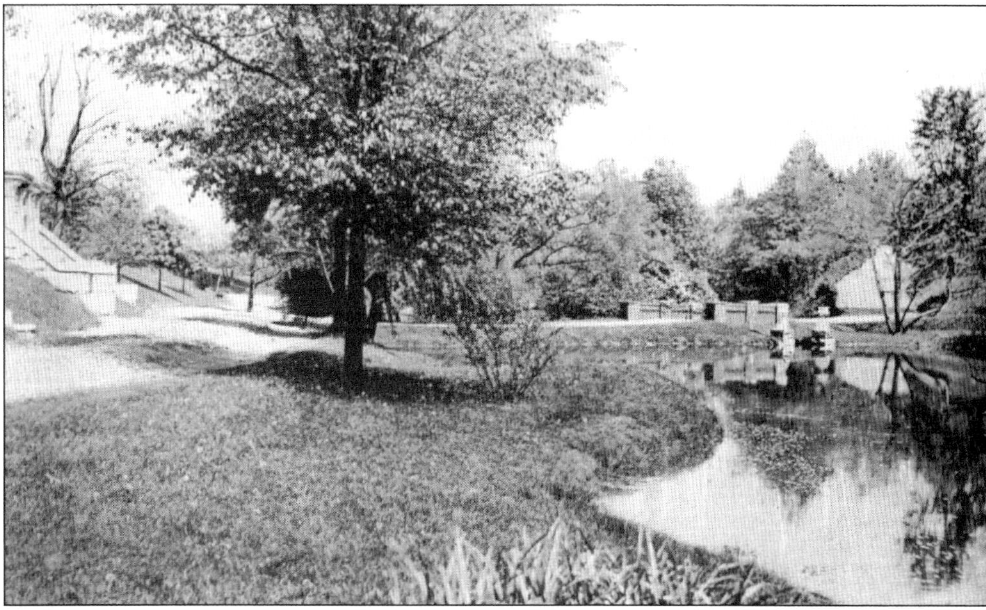

Most of the mausoleums in the West Lawn Cemetery are built into the hillside, like the ones shown here, located near Mirror Lake. The exception is the large freestanding Timken family mausoleum, located at the top of a wooded hill. The number of elaborate mausoleums and grave markers in the cemetery is testimony to the wealth and power of the city as an industrial center in the late 19th and early 20th centuries.

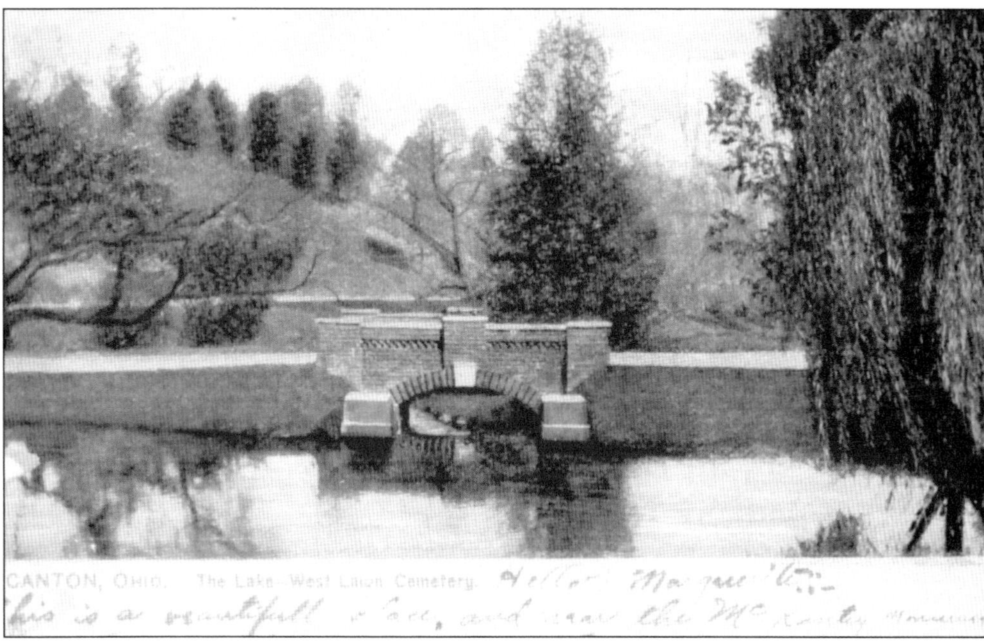

In 1907, "Emma" wrote to Marguerite Rickett in Akron that the West Lawn Cemetery was "a beautiful place near the McKinley Monument." McKinley, who had risen to the rank of brevet major in the Union army during the Civil War, wished to see soldiers from that war honored. He felt that the hill where his monument stands would be a fitting place. An ornate gilded monument in the cemetery honors Civil War soldiers.

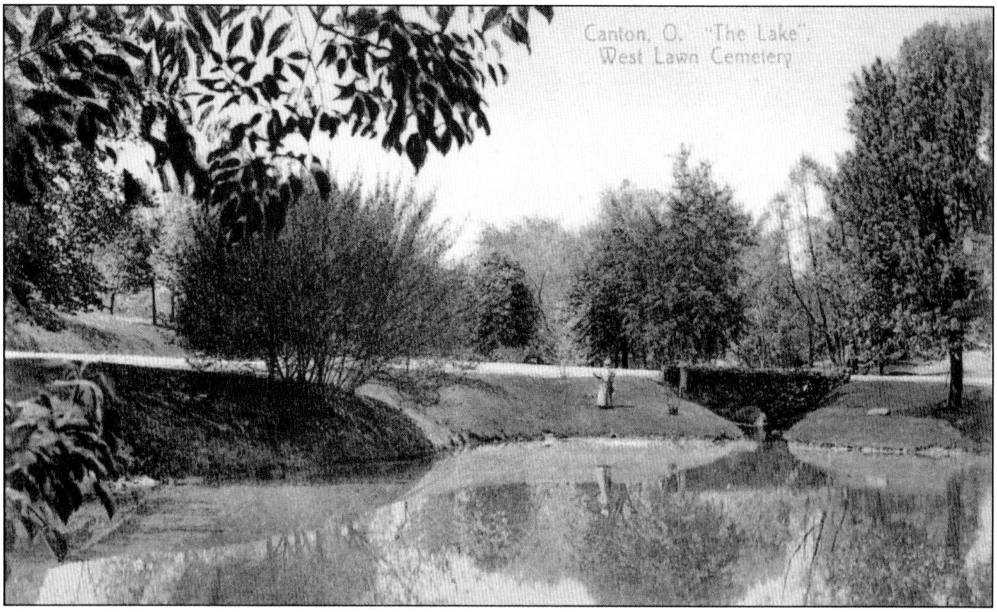

Mirror Lake in West Lawn Cemetery is 540 feet long and 50 feet wide. The lake is lined with marble walls and surrounded by two tree-lined driveways.

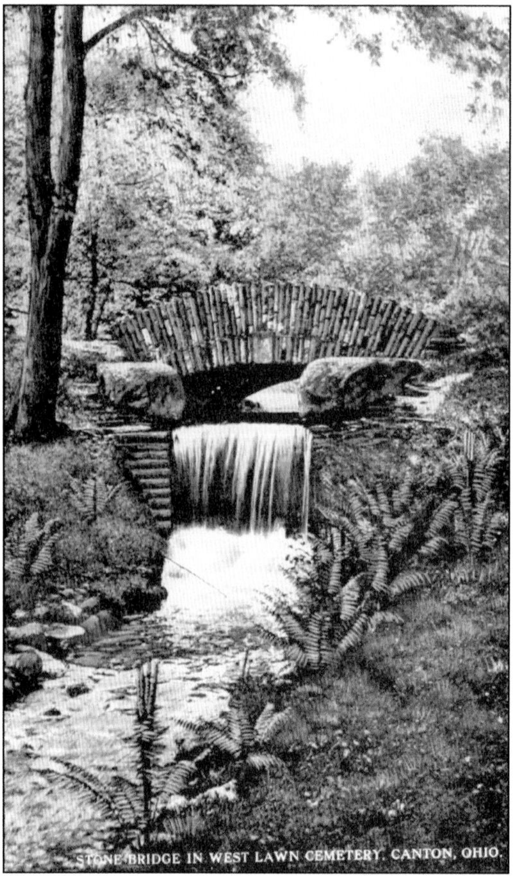

STONE BRIDGE IN WEST LAWN CEMETERY, CANTON, OHIO.

West Lawn Cemetery is the resting place for many nationally and locally prominent people, including William R. Day, William McKinley's secretary of state and later Supreme Court justice. Others buried there include members of the Saxton-McKinley, Timken, Aultman, and Belden families. John Danner, inventor of the revolving bookcase, and John McTammany, inventor of the player piano, are also buried there.

Nine

MEYERS LAKE

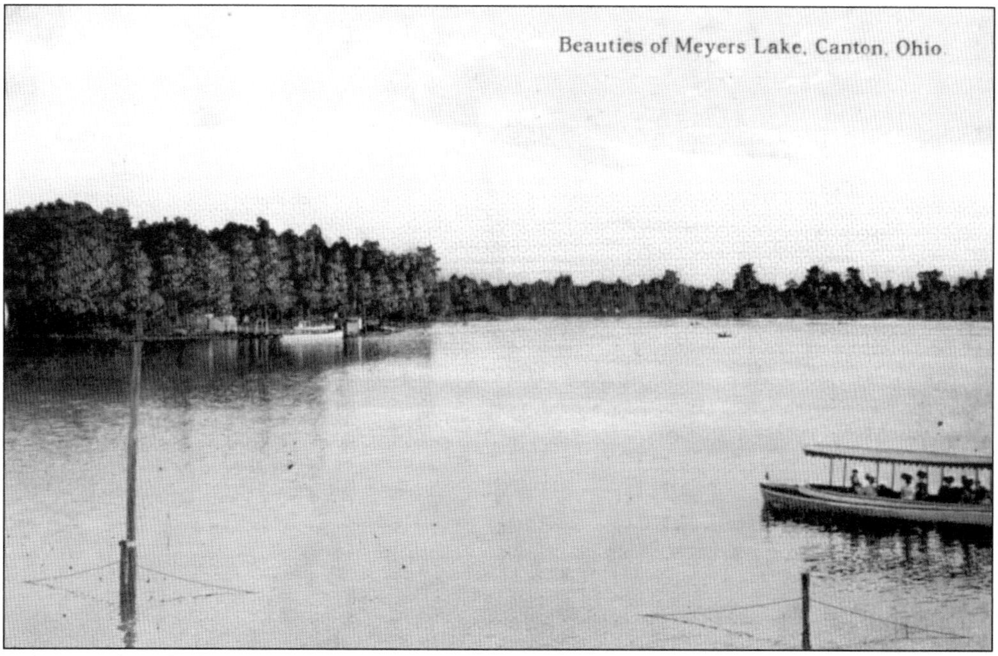

Often misidentified as Myers Lake, Meyers Lake was originally owned by Canton founder Bezaleel Wells. Wells sold the lake and surrounding property to Andrew Meyer in 1817. Meyer, who had been granted additional land surrounding the lake by the U.S. government as compensation for his losses during the War of 1812, developed a large wheat farm on the property.

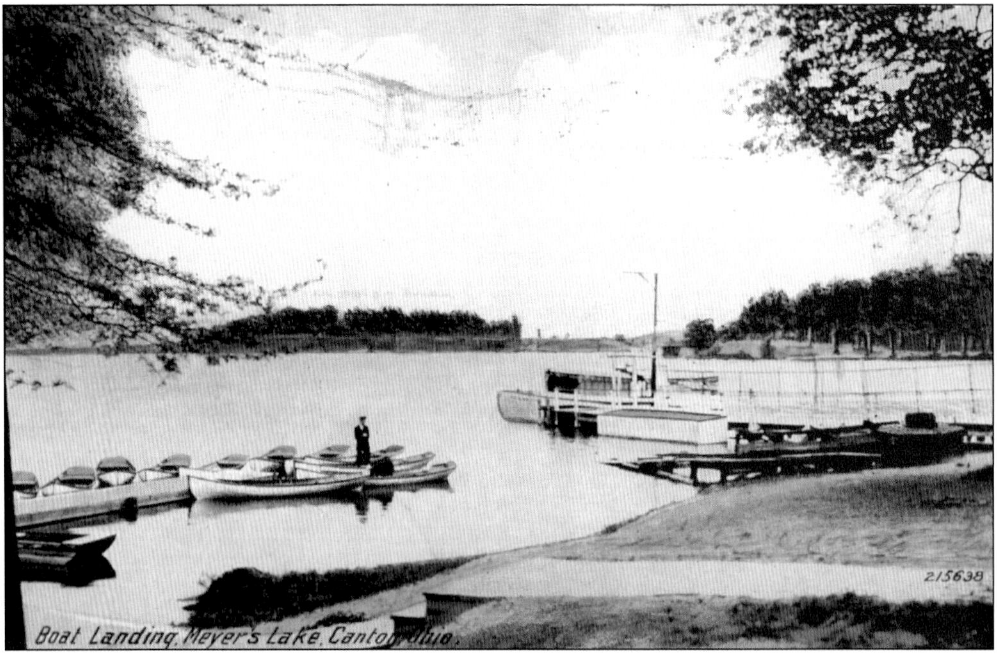

The Lake Park was the first hotel built on Meyers Lake. Located on the north shore, it was built in 1879 by Joseph Meyer, grandson of Andrew Meyer. The two-story wooden structure burned in 1892 but was rebuilt and reopened as the North Park Hotel and Casino. This postcard is an early view of the south shore boat landing.

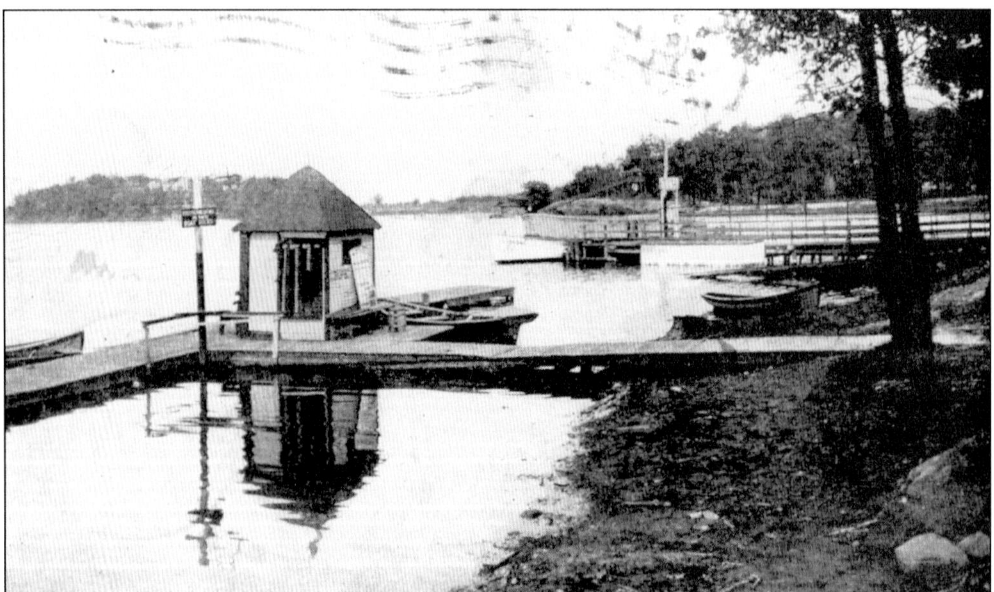

This 1907 card shows the boat landing on the south end of the lake. Recreational activity on the lake began in 1869 with the formation of the Eclipse Boat Club. The club held regattas using double and single racing sculls until an 1886 fire destroyed the boathouse and 15 racing sculls.

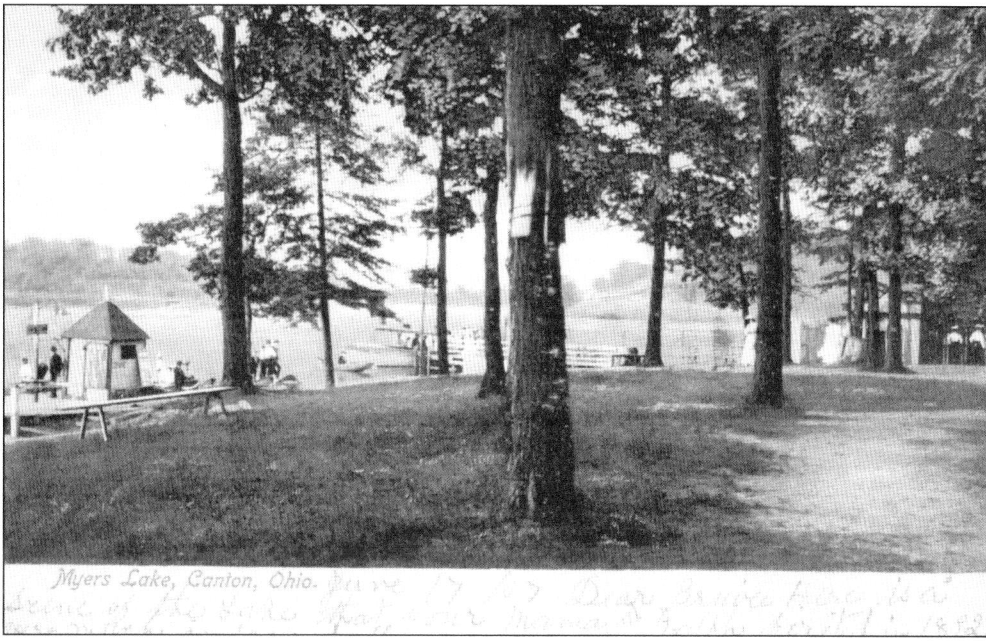

Bruce Reller of Ottivea received this postcard from his grandmother in 1907, telling him that the park his mother had visited in 1892 was "very much improved." Launches took visitors from the south shore of Meyers Lake, pictured here, to the Lakeside Country Club and golf course on the north shore. The country club was a center of social life in Canton for many years, hosting dinners, dances, and golf tournaments.

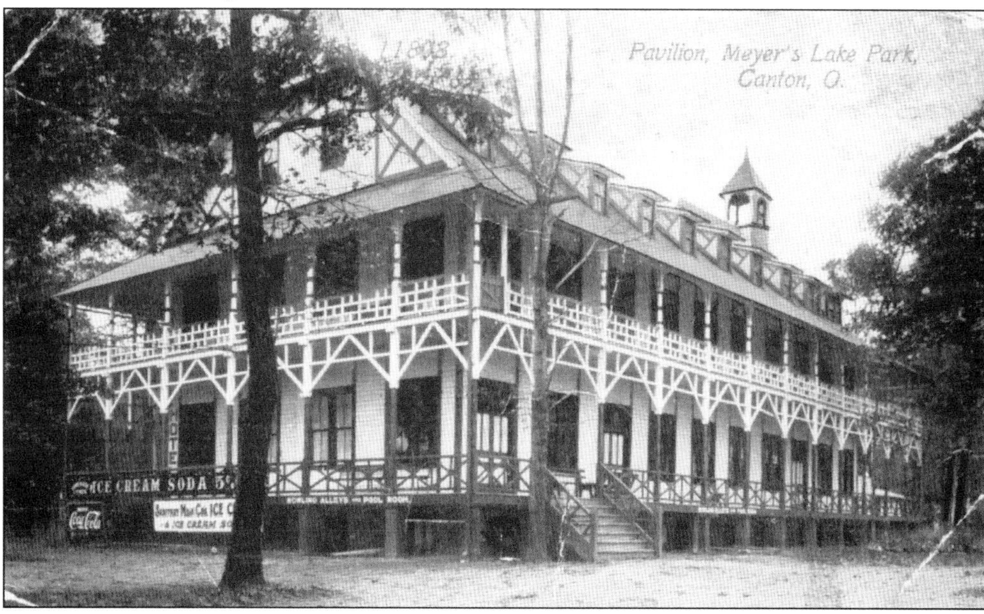

Built in the 1880s, the wooden two-and-one-half-story Lake View Hotel was located on the south shore of Meyers Lake. The first floor included a bar, billiard room, and dining room that seated 125 people. The second floor was one large room with a "soundless" floor for roller-skating and dancing. The third floor held 50 guest rooms. The hotel was destroyed by fire on December 26, 1929, during a marathon dance contest.

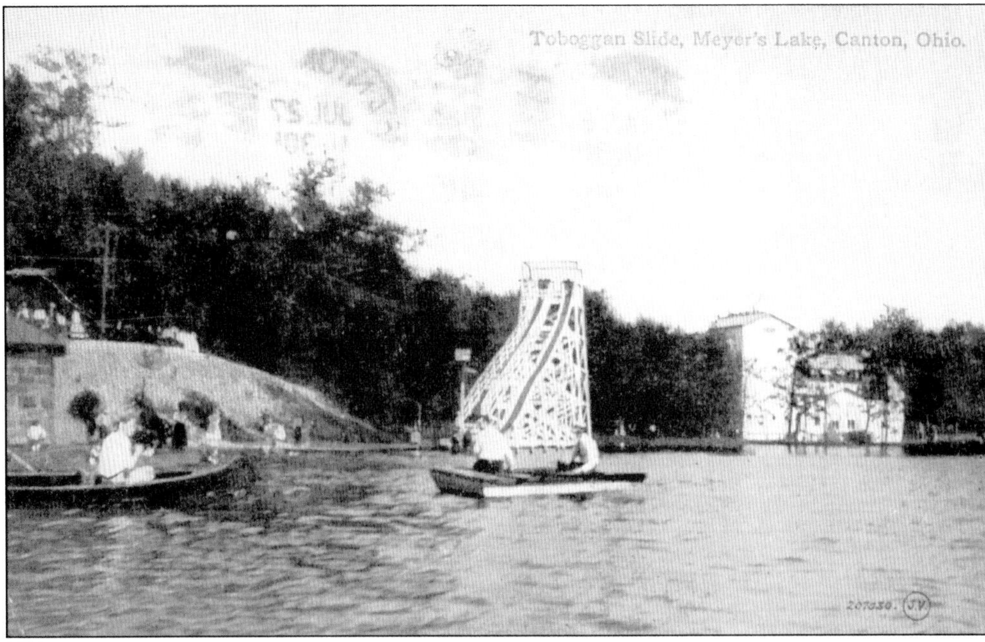

Fishing was a popular activity on Meyers Lake. Many fishermen came from town to try their luck. According to Jeff Brown and Raymond Fete in their book *Meyers Lake Revisited*, Al Schoenber fished the lake for more than 50 years. With a reputation for catching the big ones, Schoenber's secret bait was raw liver. Another fisherman, Dale Shoemaker caught an 18-pound carp that towed him around the lake twice.

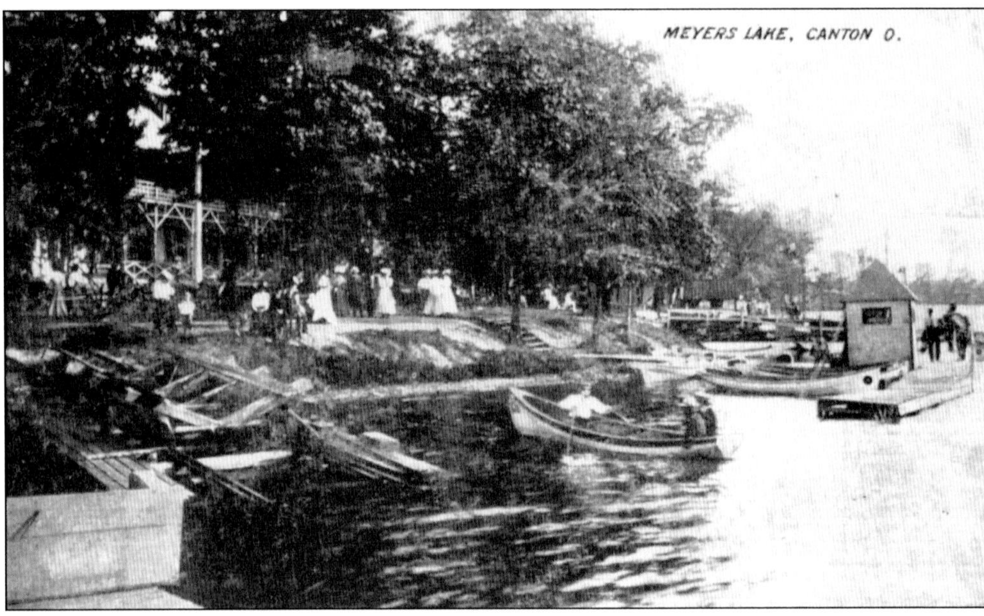

Canoeing was also popular on the lake. This 1908 view shows the Lake Park Theater, the toboggan slide, and a portion of the stone house (far left) that was the intake for the Canton water supply. The Canton Canoe Club was organized in 1910 by a group of young men. They held regattas and decorated their canoes hoping to coax young ladies to join them for a ride. The regattas ended in 1918 due to World War I.

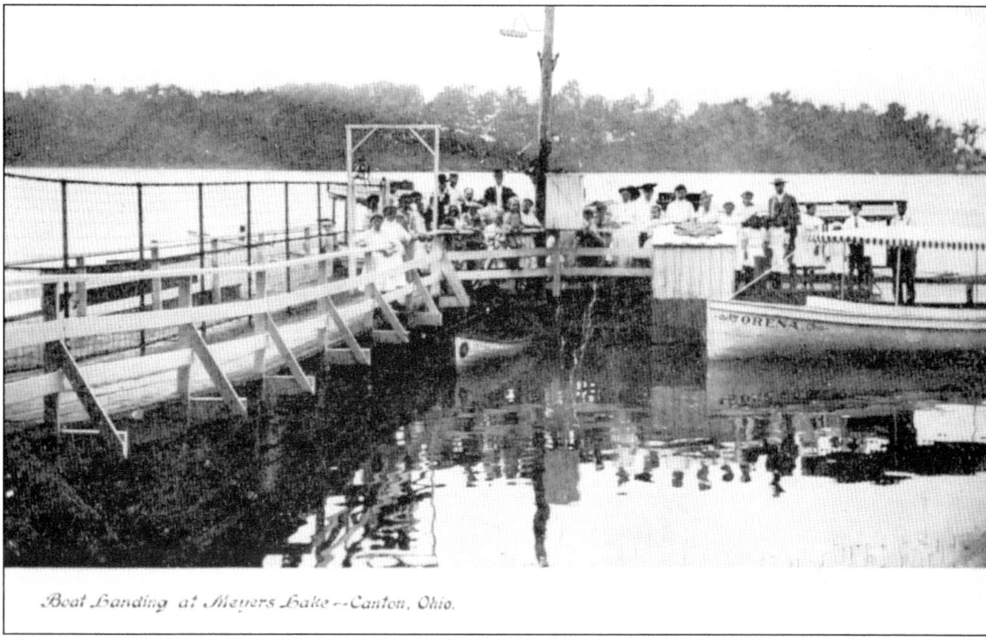

Those who did not wish to rent a canoe could cross the lake via launch. An early boat was named the *Mary Jane* after the daughter of the launch operator John Bast. Later the name was changed to the *June* after the daughter of a park manager. The launch pictured here is the *Orena*.

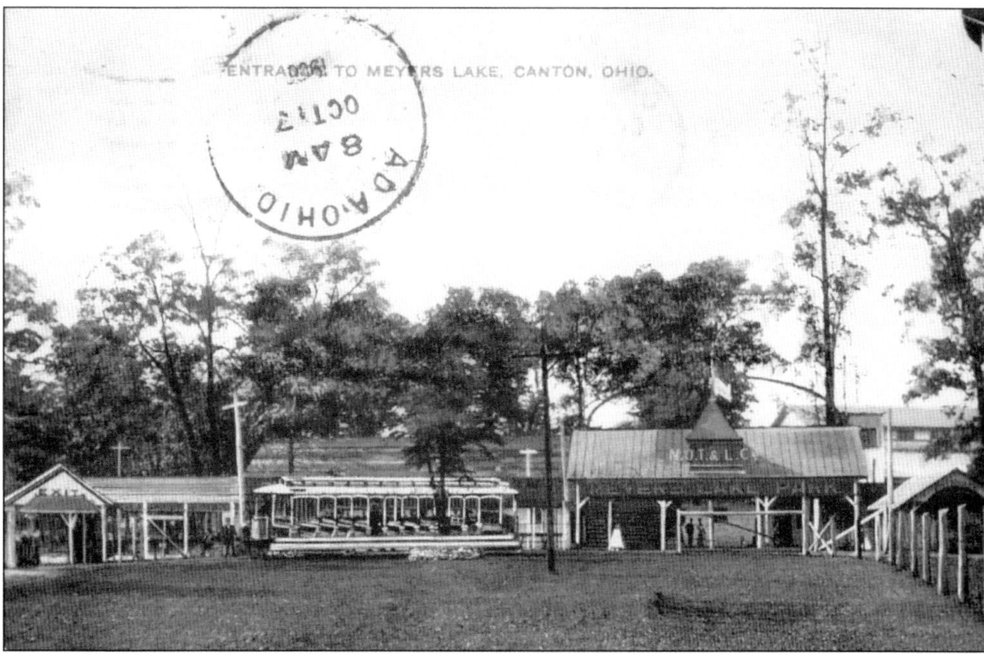

The Northern Ohio Traction and Light Company bought Meyers Lake in 1902. During that time, most park visitors arrived via streetcar from Canton. Originally horse drawn and later steam driven, the streetcars traveled from the downtown square, up Tuscarawas Avenue, to Wertz Avenue, to the park entrance pictured in this 1908 card. During peak hours the Meyers Lake line ran every three minutes from downtown.

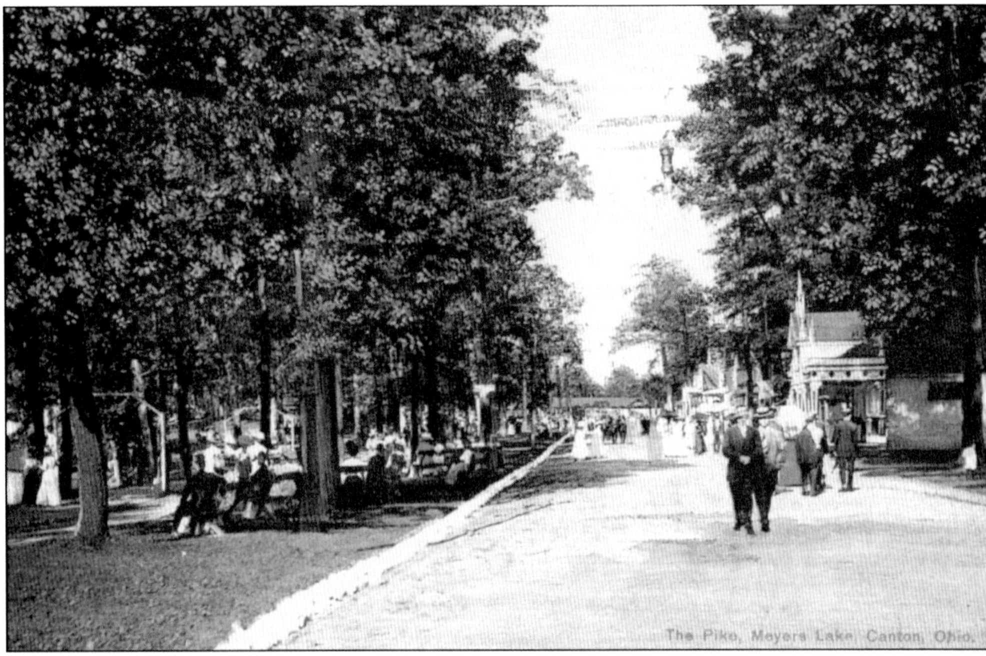

Entering the park from the covered streetcar entrance, one walked down the 1,200-foot gravel paved, "no mud, no dust" pike. In 1910, when this card was mailed, the park included two roller coasters, a merry-go–round, an arcade, and a laughing gallery with distorted mirrors.

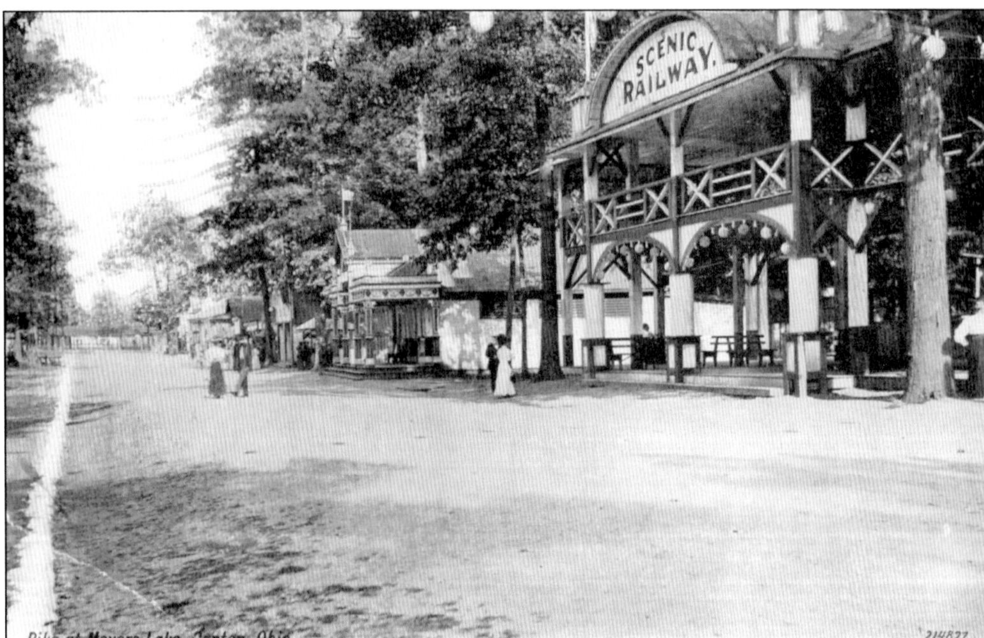

"Harriet" sent this card in 1912 to Edna Snyder of Wooster telling her that she had spent the previous evening at the Meyers Lake Casino. The Scenic Railroad was a roller coaster owned and operated by George Sinclair. Park concessions, games, and rides were owned by individuals, many of whom were associated with the park for many years.

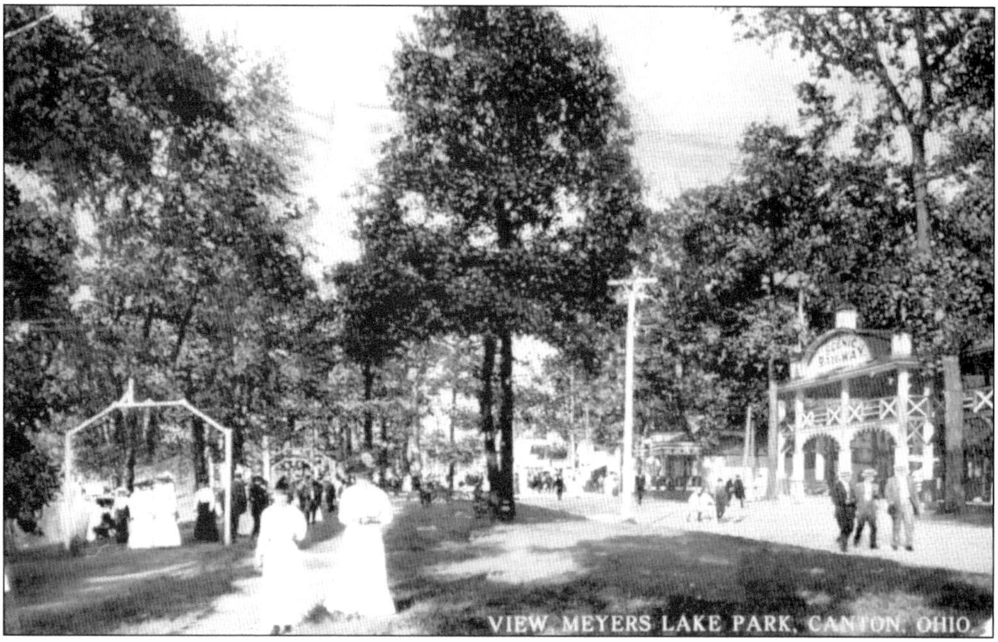

This 1913 view of the pike shows many well-dressed parkgoers. Apparently, gentlemen wore suits, ties, and straw hats, while ladies wore white dresses, hats, and gloves even in the summer heat.

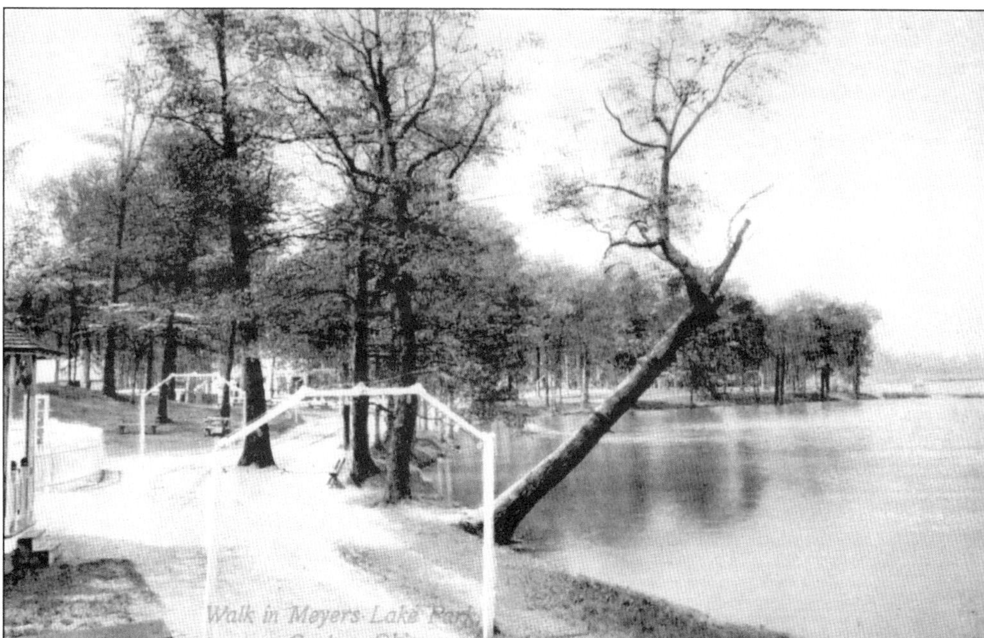

Meyers Lake Park was a good place to take a quiet stroll. The white arches held lights. Evenings were special in the park with lights on the rides and the arches creating a romantic glow. Fireworks were often part of the evening's entertainment, especially on the Fourth of July and Labor Day.

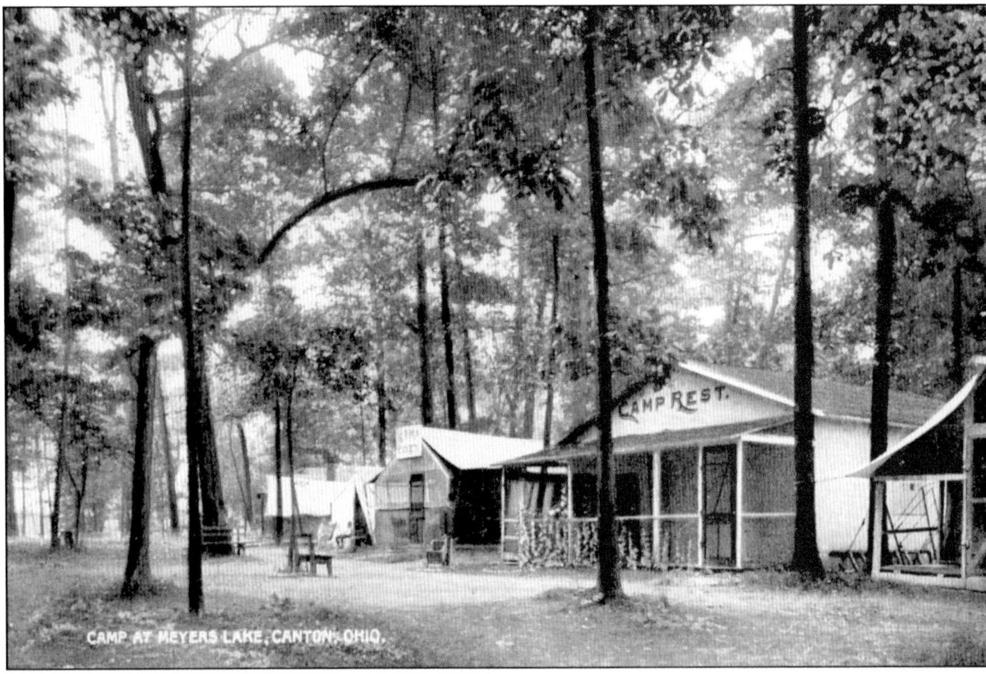

From the 1890s until the 1930s, families would move to the park to escape the summer heat. Living in these makeshift cabins, mothers and children enjoyed the lake while fathers took the streetcar to work. The children were free to wander the park, even riding for free if there were few customers. From 1922 until 1926, the Lakes, a team of camp high school boys, played baseball, football, and basketball against local teams.

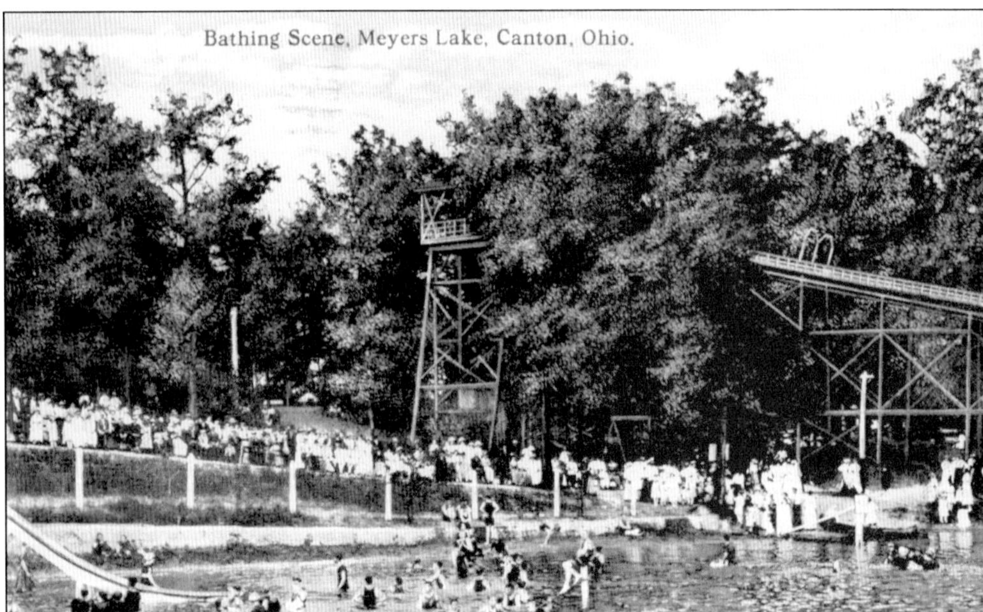

The Shoot-the-Chutes water slide had replaced the toboggan slide by 1918 when this card was sent. The picture also shows the slide from the bathhouse. Apparently, watching people swim was as popular as swimming itself.

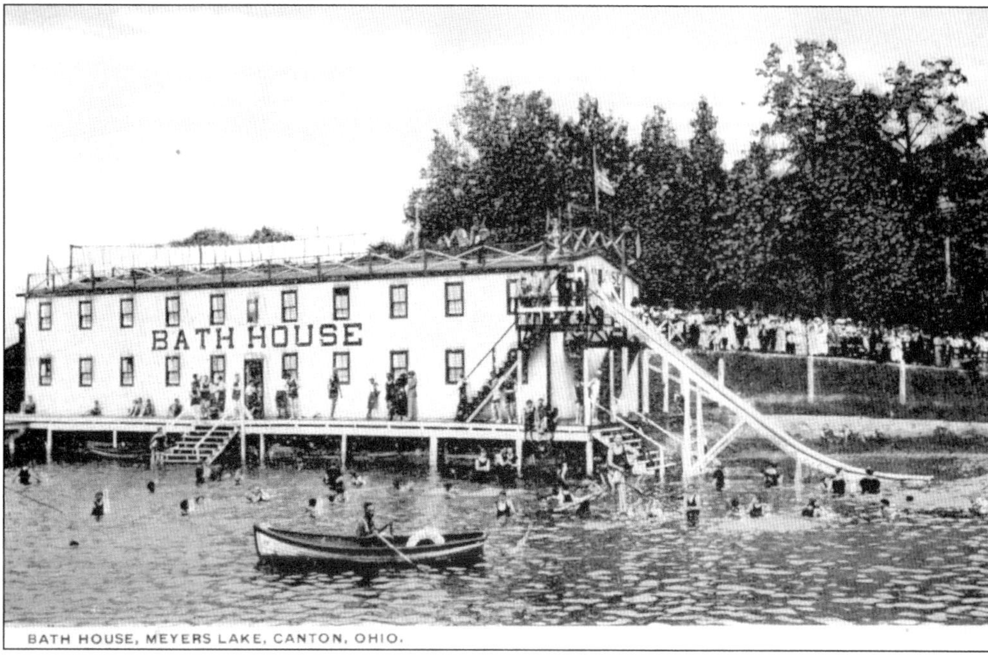

This view of the bathhouse shows towels drying on the roof. Bathing suits and towels could be rented from the attendants.

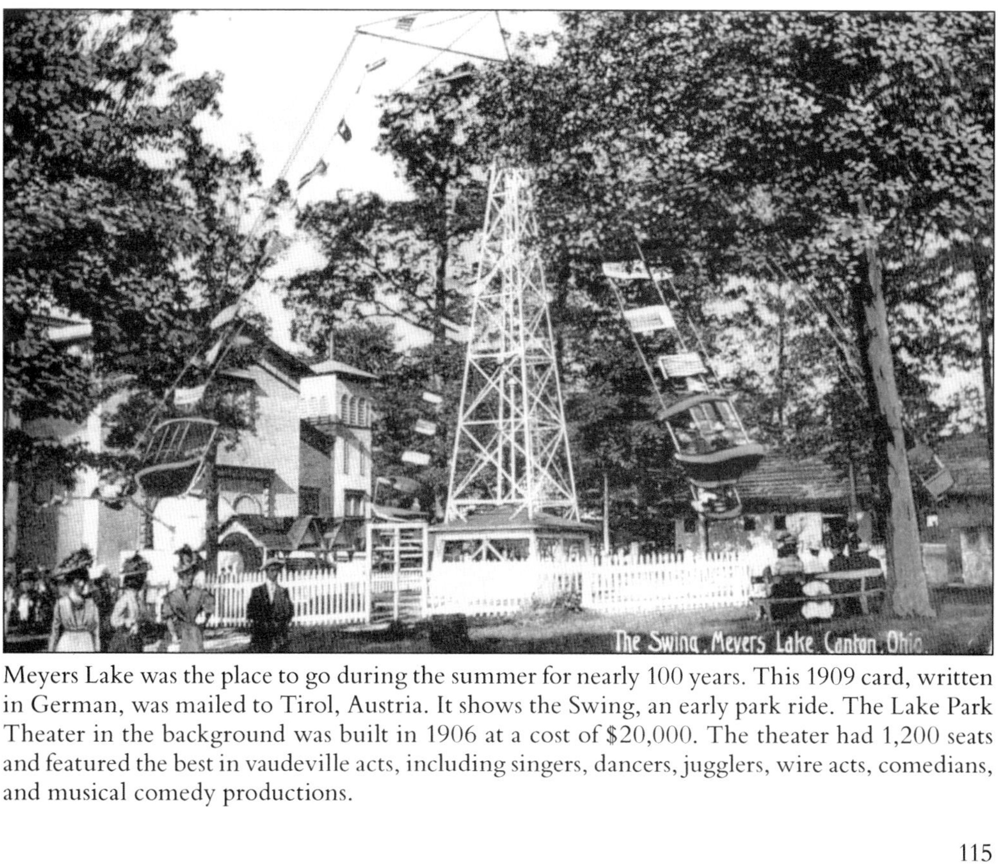

Meyers Lake was the place to go during the summer for nearly 100 years. This 1909 card, written in German, was mailed to Tirol, Austria. It shows the Swing, an early park ride. The Lake Park Theater in the background was built in 1906 at a cost of $20,000. The theater had 1,200 seats and featured the best in vaudeville acts, including singers, dancers, jugglers, wire acts, comedians, and musical comedy productions.

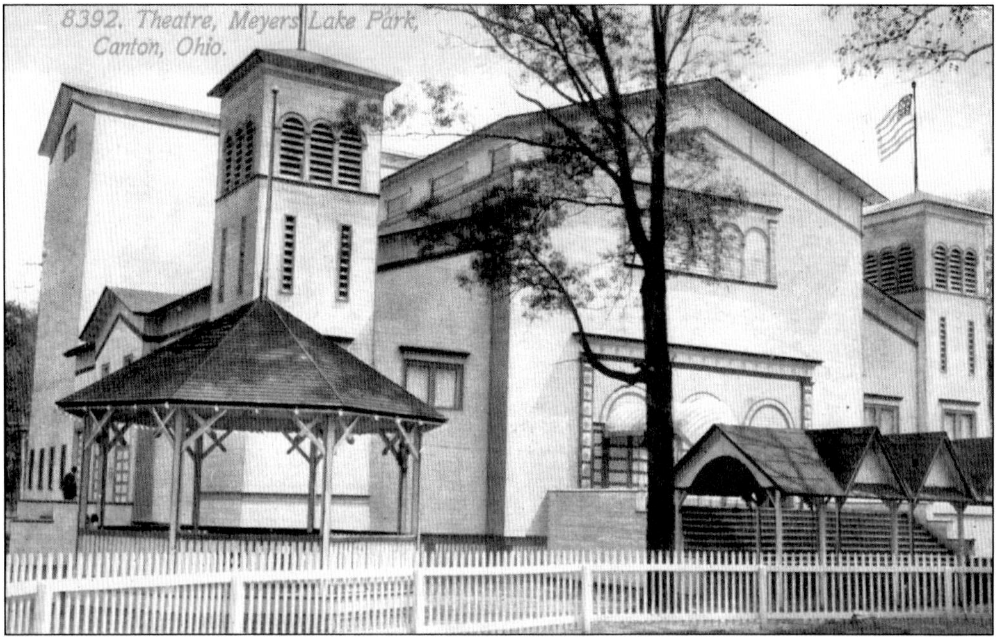

The Lake Park Theater was knocked off its foundation in the 1920s by a windstorm. The Marx Brothers, who were performing at the time, escaped through a window. By 1926, vaudeville was giving way to motion pictures and the Lake Park Theater closed. A week later the new Palace movie theater opened downtown.

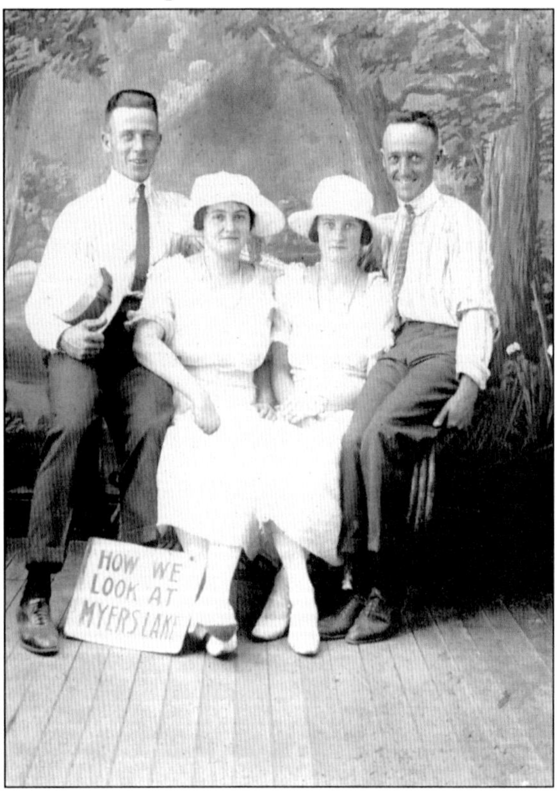

Like the image of these two unidentified couples, a souvenir photograph taken at Oliver Edgell's Meyers Lake studio was a way to remember a happy day spent at the park.

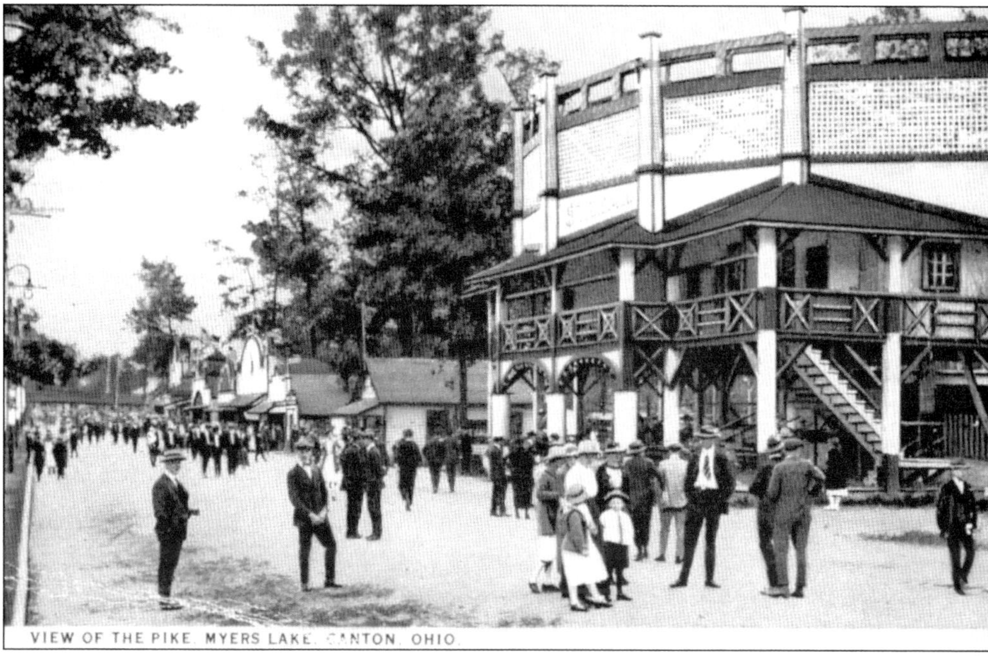

The Blue Streak Roller Coaster, shown in this 1926 card, replaced the Scenic Railway. Owner George Sinclair and his family lived for a time on the second floor of this ride.

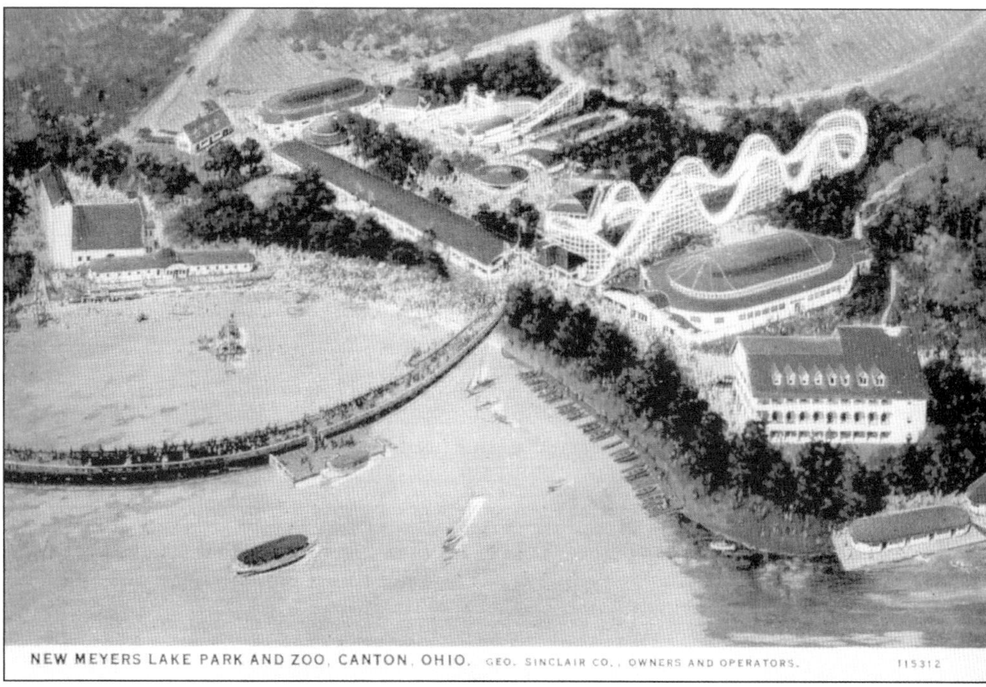

In 1926, George Sinclair took over the management of Meyers Lake Park. Under his management, the park was completely remodeled, swampy areas were drained, and new attractions were added. The Monkey Island, with 50 rhesus monkeys, and the toadstool bandstand were located in the center of the park. This boardwalk, however, never existed. The artist placed it where he thought it should be.

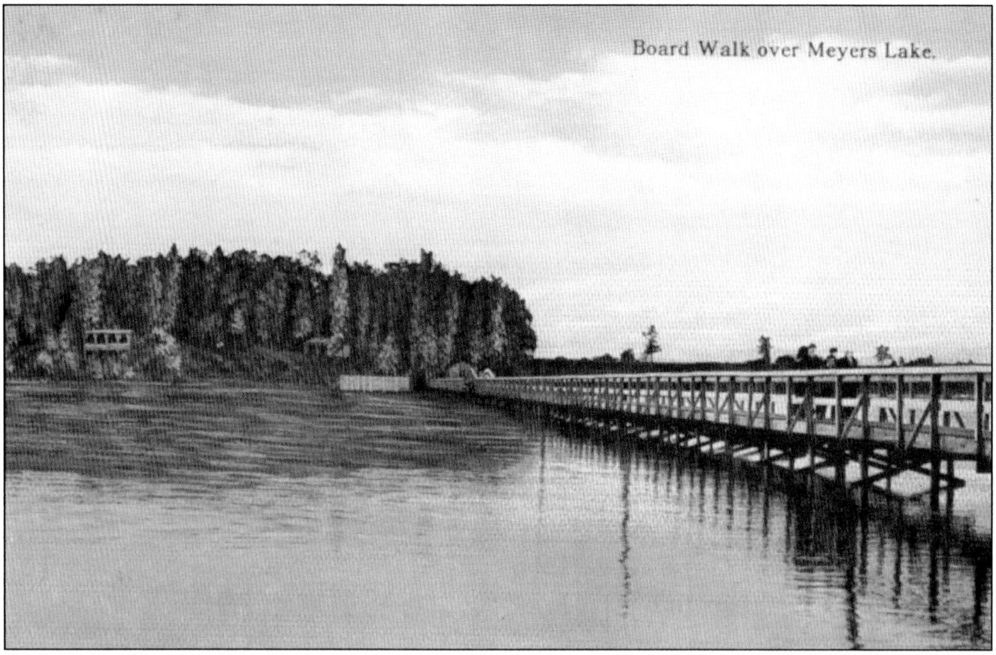

The actual boardwalk over Meyers Lake went from Dead Man's Point to the Lakeside Country Club. It was built with a hump in the middle to allow boats to pass to and from the northeast corner of the lake.

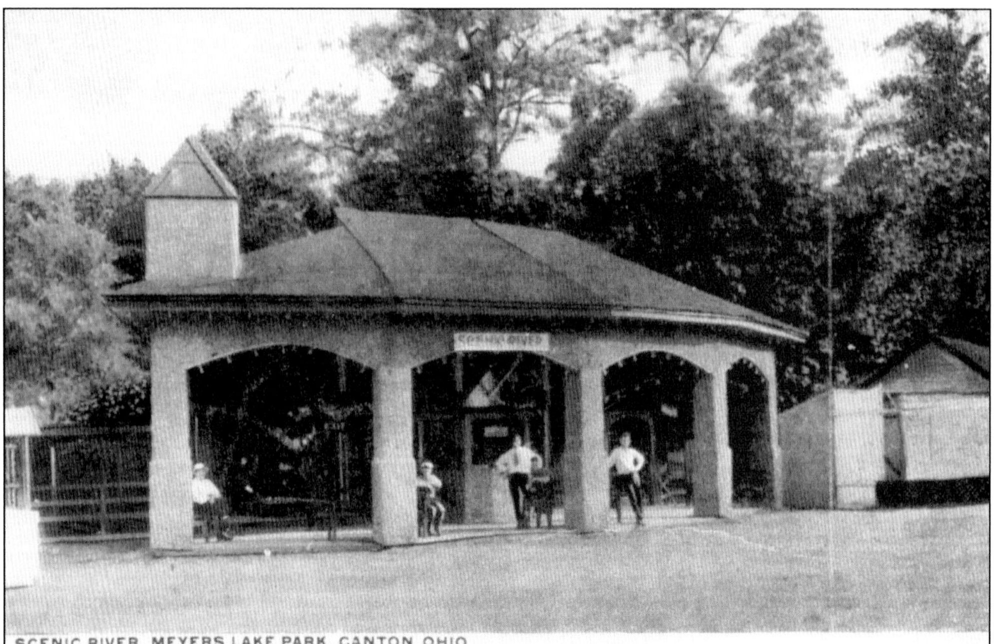

Water rides were popular in the park. The Mystic Chutes, Shoot-the-Chutes, and Scenic River, pictured in this 1926 card, were later joined by the Rocket that went out over the lake. On May 21, 1927, George Sinclair opened the newly remodeled Meyers Lake Park and 20,000 people paid 10¢—5¢ for children—to experience the new rides and zoo.

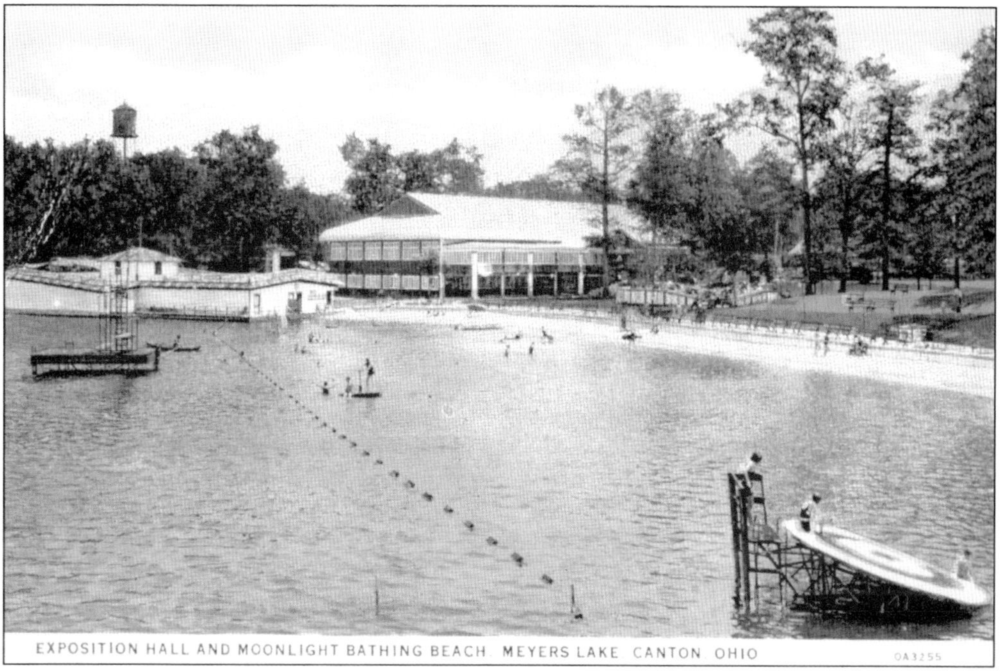

George Sinclair also built a new bathing beach. This scene shows the improved bathing beach, the Park Lake Theater, and the Hofbrau House, a German beer hall.

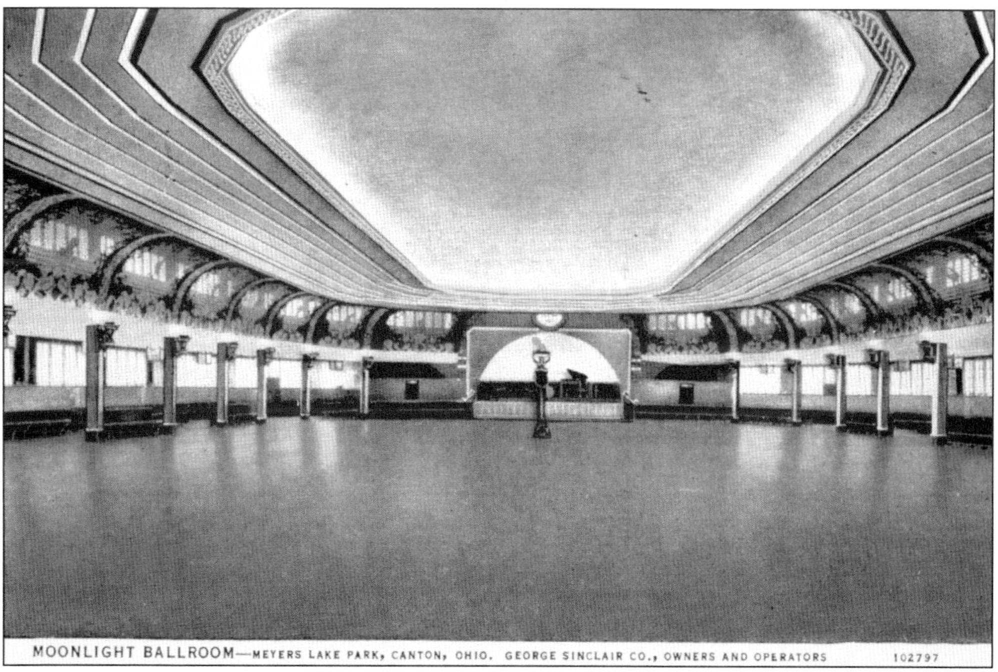

Opened in 1926, the Moonlight Ballroom featured nationally known performers and bands, including Glenn Miller, Benny Goodman, Gene Krupa, Cab Calloway, Duke Ellington, Perry Como, and Tony Bennett. Ella Fitzgerald performed on December 6, 1941, the evening before the attack on Pearl Harbor. The ballroom burned in 1979 following a performance by the Glenn Miller Orchestra.

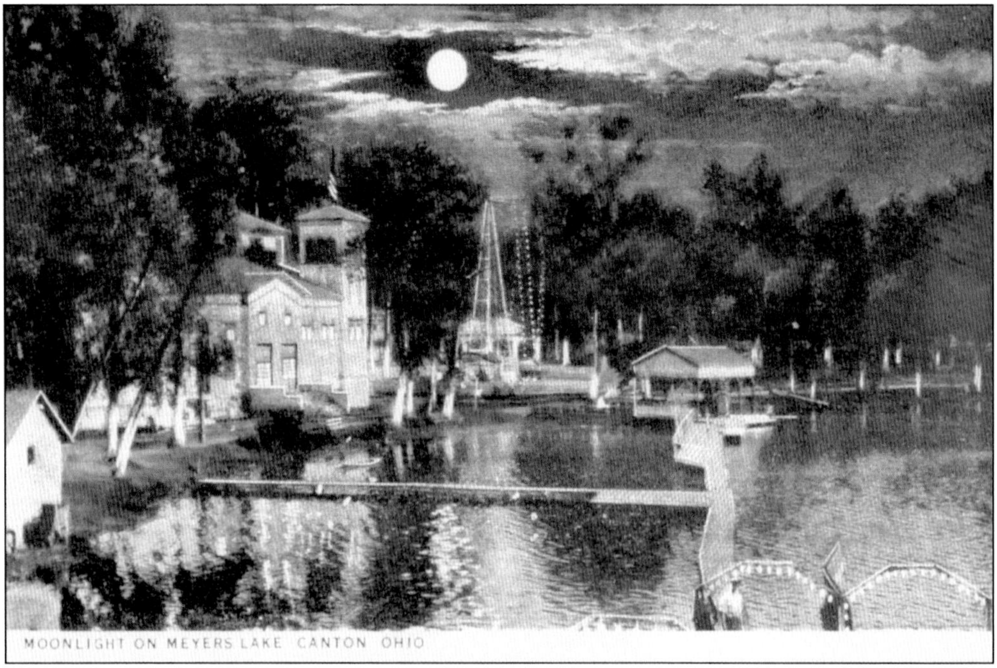

The Moonlight Ballroom and the outdoor Moonlight Gardens held dances nearly every night in the 1930s and 1940s. In addition to big name bands, there were also several house bands, including Harry Woodfield's Orchestra, the Charlie Pickens Band, Dom Clivi and His Orchestra, and the Jack Halkide's Band.

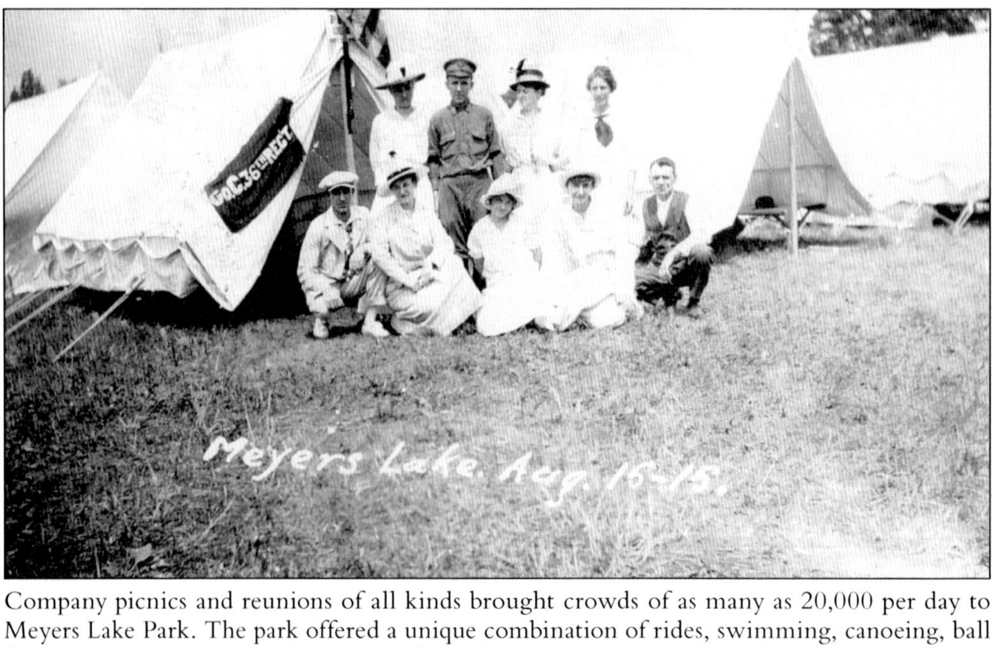

Company picnics and reunions of all kinds brought crowds of as many as 20,000 per day to Meyers Lake Park. The park offered a unique combination of rides, swimming, canoeing, ball fields, live entertainment, dancing, and arcade games. Concessions included such goodies as baked waffles, caramel corn, and legendary soft custard with 12 percent butterfat. This military reunion group probably enjoyed all these attractions.

Ten

Along the Lincoln Highway

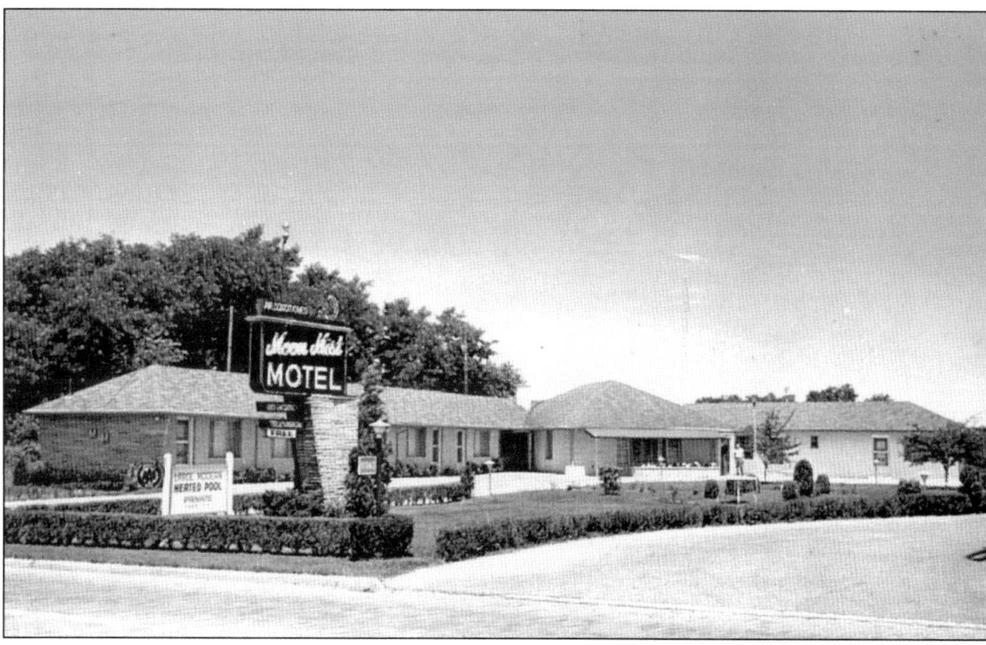

The Lincoln Highway, U.S. Route 30, extends from Times Square in New York City some 3,389 miles to Lincoln Park in San Francisco. Begun in 1913, as cars were beginning to be mass-produced and better roads were needed, the highway passes through Stark County. The Moon Mist Motel on East Tuscarawas Street was one of the many motels, restaurants, and other businesses serving travelers along the route.

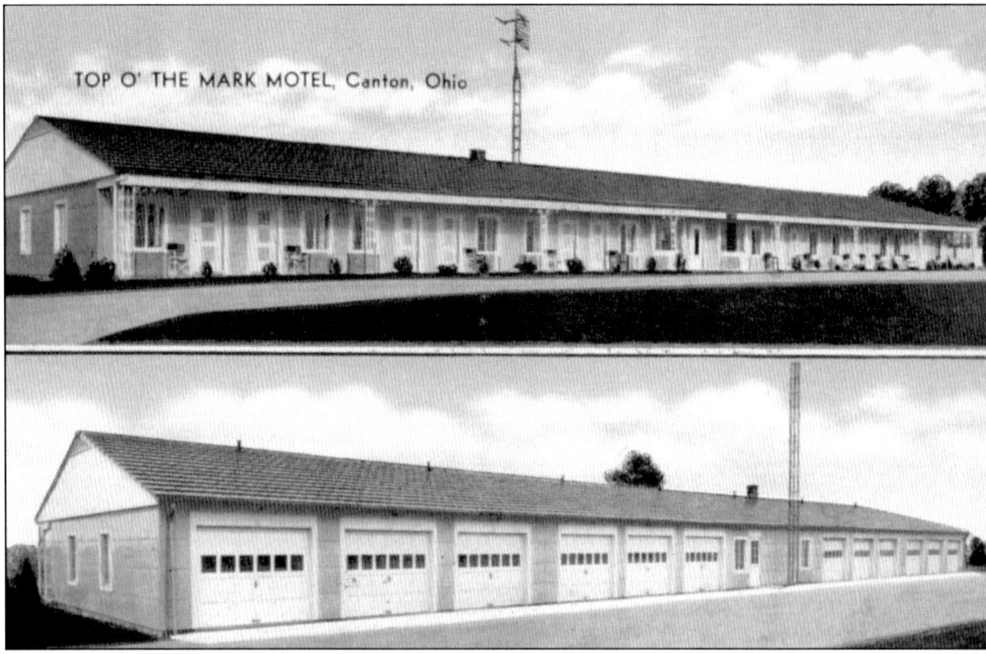

Located on East Tuscarawas Street, two miles east of Canton, the Top O' the Mark Motel was built in 1953. Each of the 32 rooms had a tile shower, wall-to-wall carpeting, and television. The motel also featured private garages interconnected with each room. Built before the construction of interstate highways, most such small motels were locally owned.

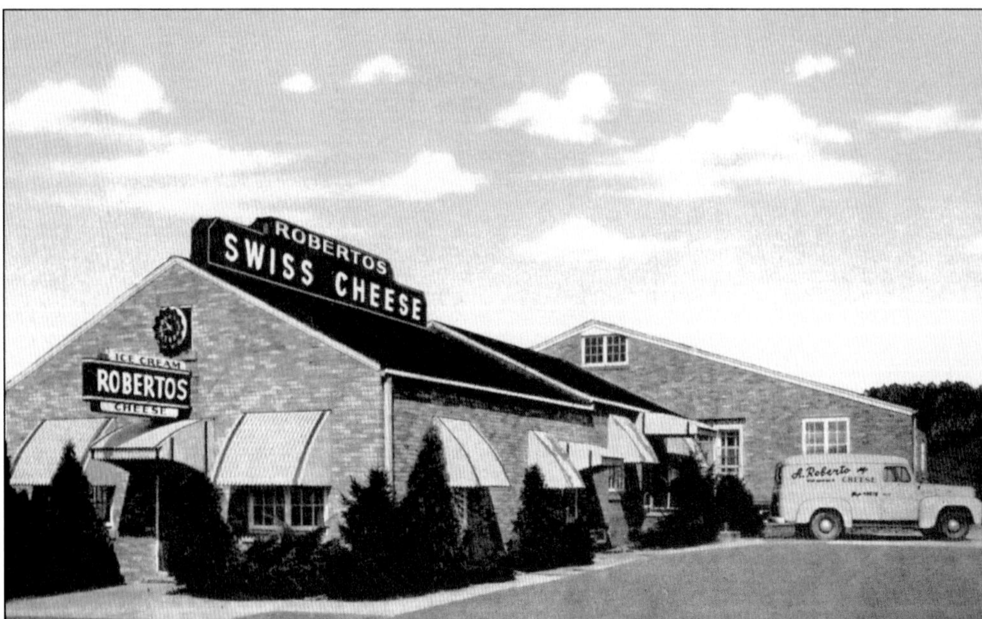

Located on Route 30 in East Canton, Angelo Roberto claimed that his was "Ohio's most beautiful cheese factory." He made swiss cheese, scamorze, provoloni, ricotta, beer cheese, limburger, longhorn, and gorgonzola, among others. Apparently, one could also buy ice cream.

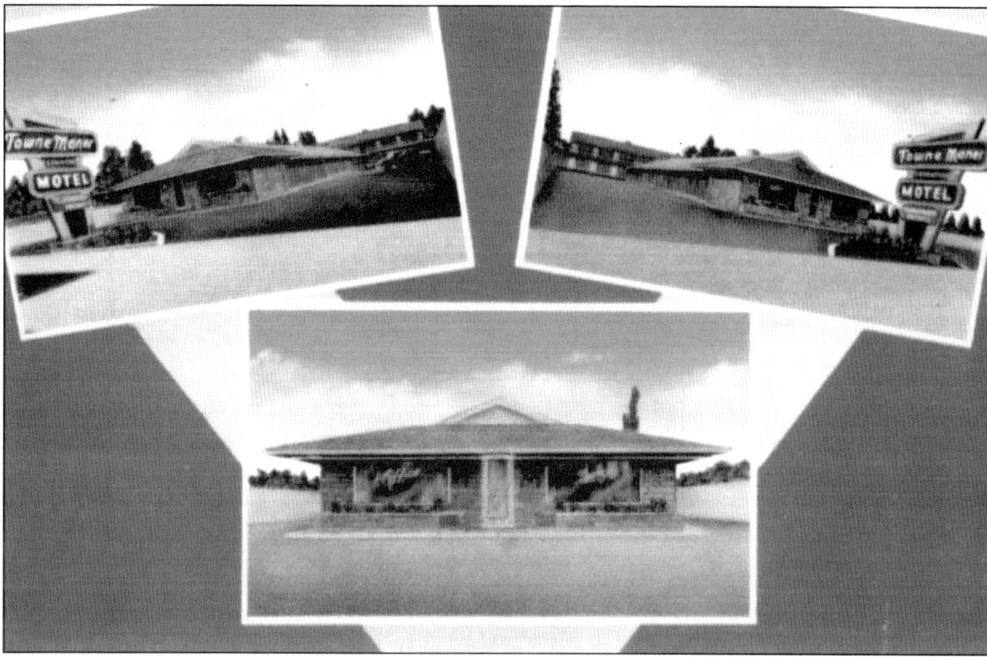

Located on West Tuscarawas Street four blocks from the public square, the Towne Manor Motel was part of the move spurred by the development of highways like the Lincoln from large downtown hotels to small motels. In 1928, Boy Scouts from communities along the highway began placing 2,500 concrete marker posts.

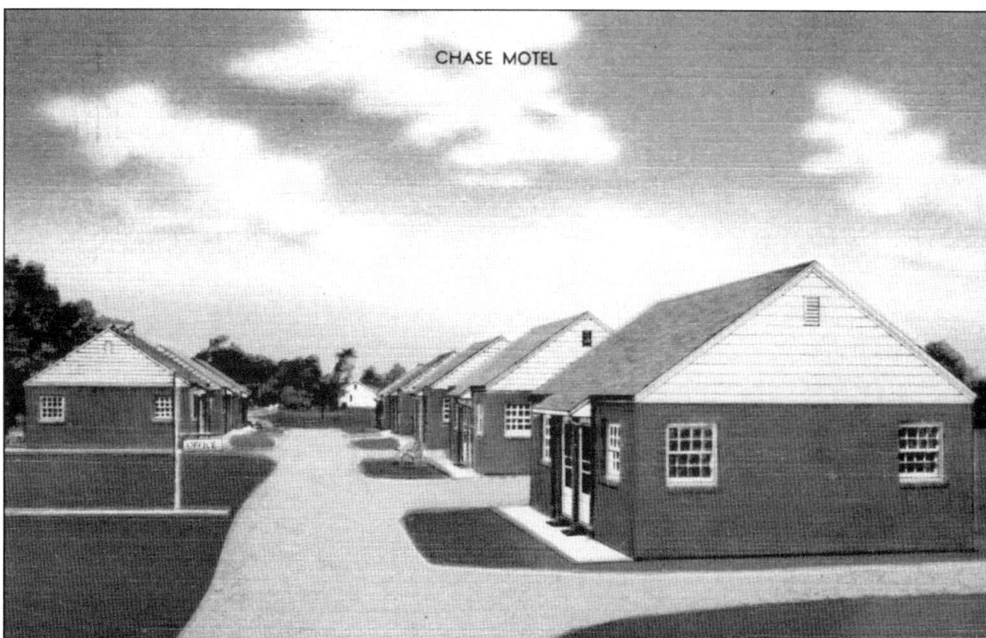

Some of the markers placed by the Boy Scouts along the Lincoln Highway can still be found in Stark County. These posts have a medallion of the Lincoln Highway logo featuring a bust of Abraham Lincoln and the inscription "This highway dedicated to Abraham Lincoln." The Chase Motel was located on Route 30 between Canton and Massillon.

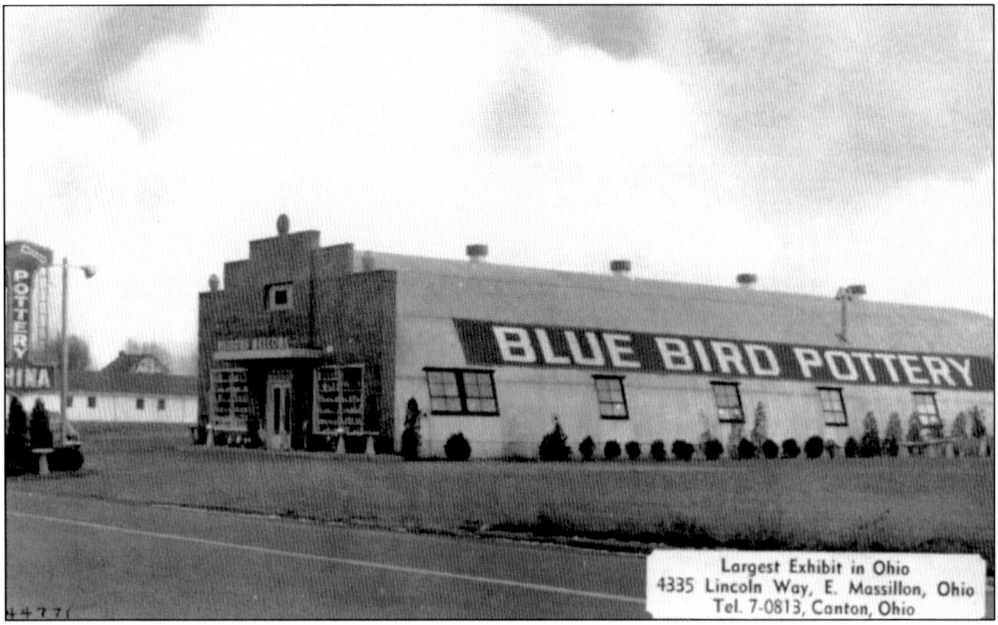

Due to its favorable clay deposits, Ohio has long been a center of pottery manufacture. The Blue Bird Pottery, located on Route 30 between Canton and Massillon, sold "dinnerware, Roseville pottery, Fiesta Ware, and Lu-Ray." It shipped to "all parts of the world." The business closed in 1954.

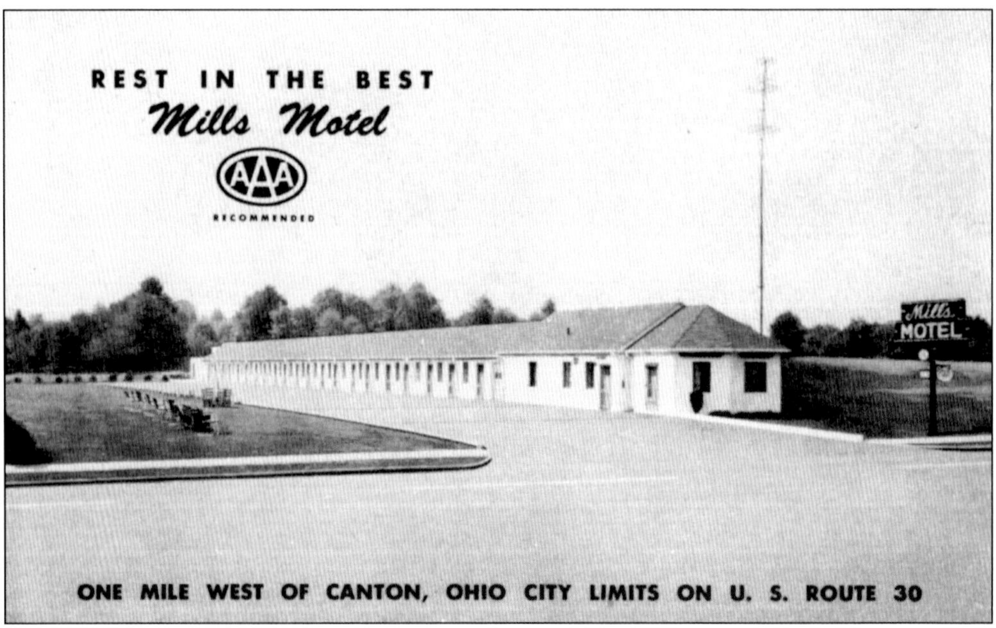

The Mills Motel advertised "20 rooms with radios in each room, private shower baths, city water, and radiant heat." The men who helped create the Lincoln Highway included Frank Seiberling of Goodyear Tire, Henry Joy of Packard Motor Company, and Carl Fisher of the Prest-O-Lite Company and founder of the Indianapolis Speedway.

The Chanticleer, located on the corner of West Tuscarawas Street and Post Road, was one of the many restaurants located along the Lincoln Highway.

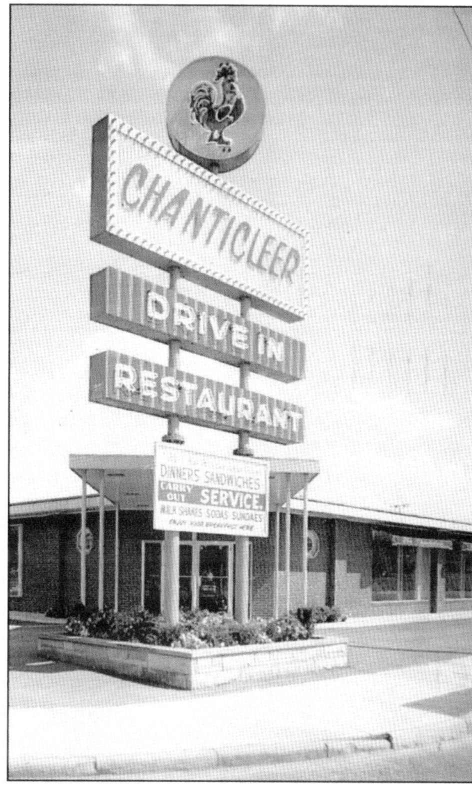

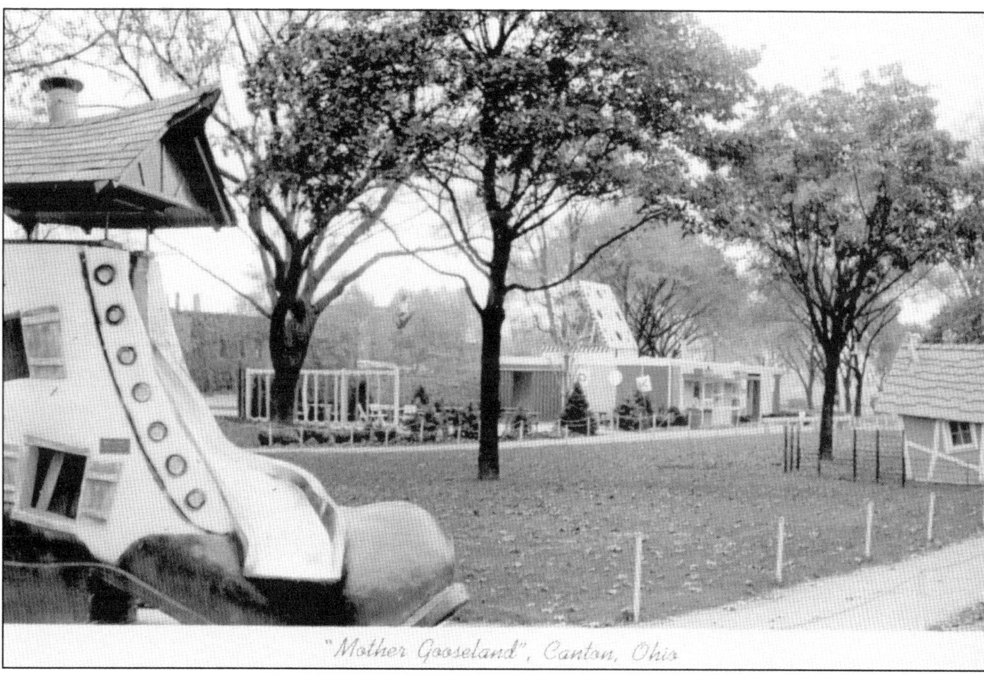

Mother Gooseland, located on West Tuscarawas Street, was one of the small tourist attractions along Route 30. "Mother Goose Land was presented to the children of Canton by the Canton Junior Chamber of Commerce."

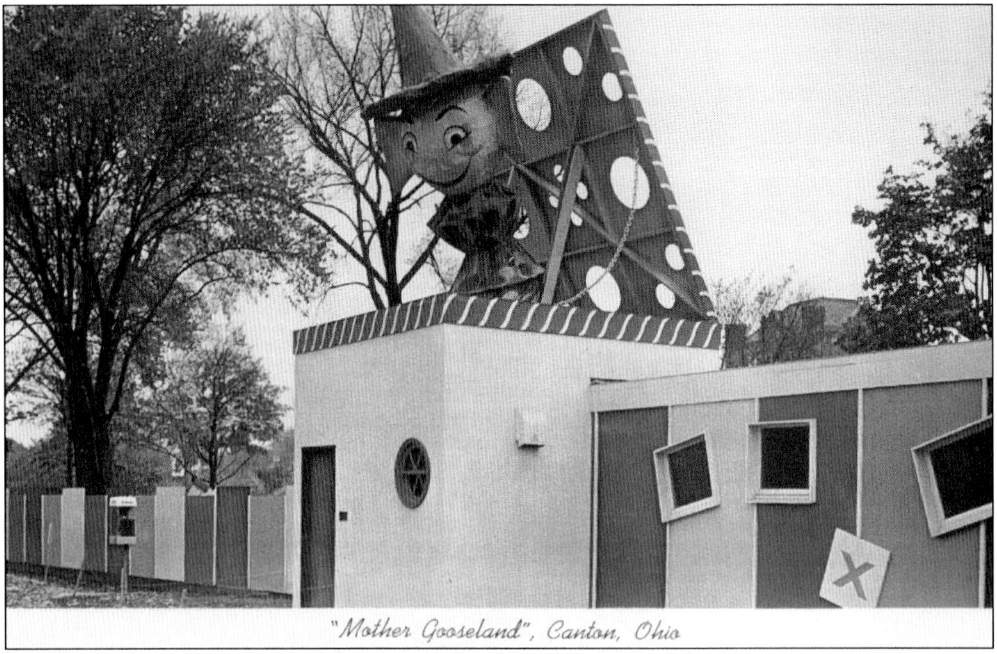

The back of this postcard of the administration building reads, "Through this building pass the young-at-heart into Mother Gooseland."

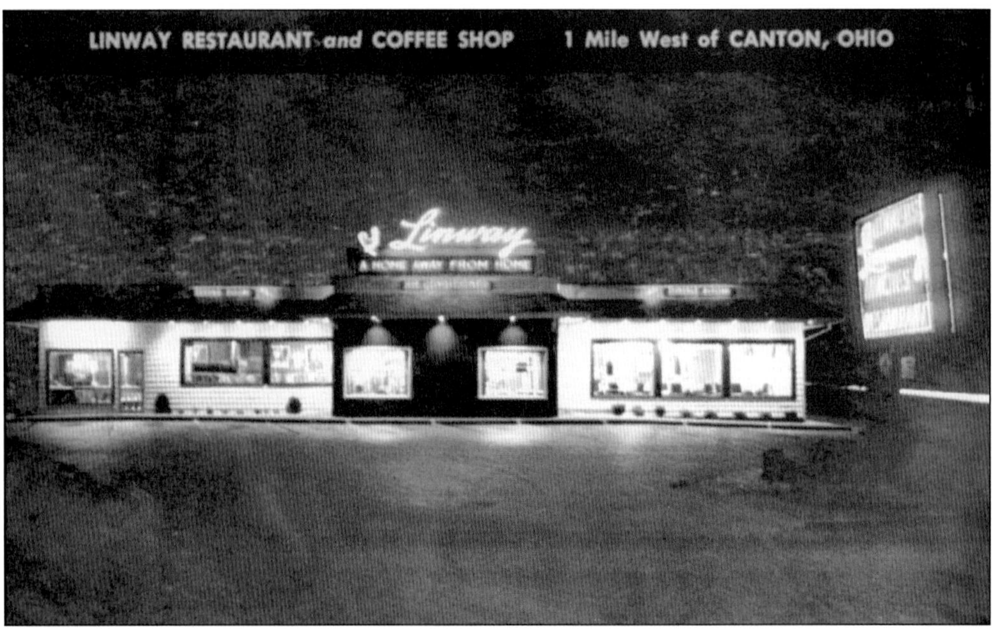

The Linway Restaurant and Coffee Shop was located on the Lincoln Highway west of Canton. In business for over 20 years, it specialized in delicious fresh baked pastries.

Bibliography

Brown, Jeffery and Raymond Fete. *Meyers Lake Revisited.* Canton: Daring Books, 1985.

———. *Meyers Lake A Second Look.* Canton: Daring Books, 1988.

———. *Meyers Lake Park Remembered.* Canton: J&K Printing, 1993.

Canton Preservation Society. *Canton: One of the Greatest Industrial Cities of the State of Ohio from the 1907 Edition.* Canton: Canton Preservation Society.

Heald, Edward. *The Stark County Story, Volume III: Industry Comes of Age.* Canton: Stark County Historical Society, 1952.

———. *The Stark County Story, Volume IV, Part I: Free People at Work.* Canton: Stark County Historical Society, 1955.

———. *The Stark County Story, Volume IV, Part II: The Suburban Era.* Canton: Stark County Historical Society, 1958.

Lincoln Highway Heritage Corridor. "Lincoln Highway Historic Byway Visit the Longest Place in America." Canton: Lincoln Highway Heritage Corridor, 2004.

Kenney, Kimberly. *Canton: A Journey Through Time.* Charleston, SC: Arcadia Publishing, 2003.

"The McKinley National Memorial Celebrating 100 Years." *The Repository.* September 30, 2007.

Stark County Regional Planning Commission. *An Inventory of Historical Sites and Structures.* Stark County: Stark County Regional Planning Commission, 1976.

Stark County Historical Society. *Stark County Bicentennial Story 1776-1976.* Canton: Stark County Historical Society, 1976.

"The Birth of Canton." *The Repository.* January 3, 2005.

Thomas, Harold. *Then and Now of Stark County.* Canton: J&R Photographic Services, 2005.

"Two Centuries of Memories." *The Repository.* November 21, 2005.

Discover Thousands of Local History Books Featuring Millions of Vintage Images

Arcadia Publishing, the leading local history publisher in the United States, is committed to making history accessible and meaningful through publishing books that celebrate and preserve the heritage of America's people and places.

Find more books like this at

www.arcadiapublishing.com

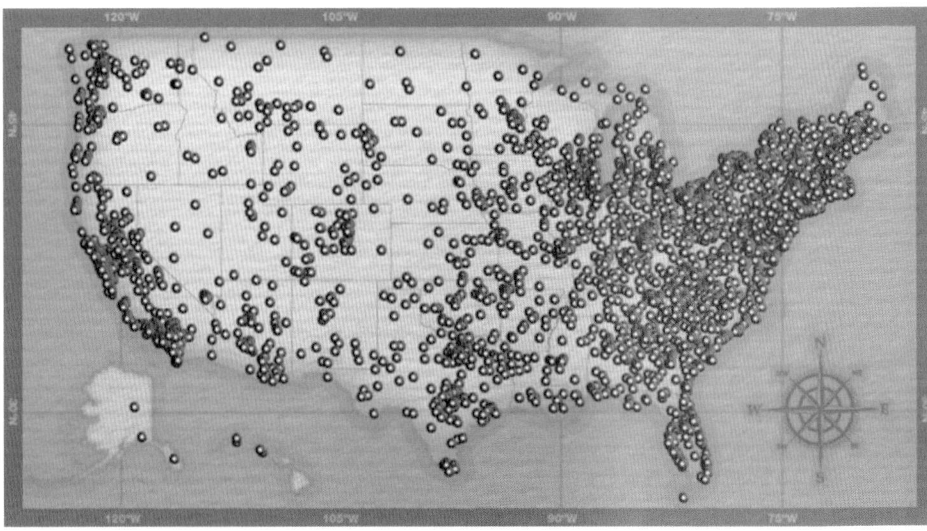

Search for your hometown history, your old stomping grounds, and even your favorite sports team.

Consistent with our mission to preserve history on a local level, this book was printed in South Carolina on American-made paper and manufactured entirely in the United States. Products carrying the accredited Forest Stewardship Council (FSC) label are printed on 100 percent FSC-certified paper.

MADE IN THE USA